Zero Tolerance

China's mistreatment of its Uyghur minority has drawn international condemnation and sanctions. The repression gripping Xinjiang is also hugely costly to China in Renminbi, personnel, and stifled economic productivity. Despite this, the Chinese Communist Party persists in its policies. Why? Drawing on extensive original data, Potter and Wang demonstrate insecurities about the stability of the regime and its claim to legitimacy motivate Chinese policies. These perceived threats to core interests drive the ferocity of the official response to Uyghur nationalism. The result is harsh repression, sophisticated media control, and selective international military cooperation. China's growing economic and military power means that the country's policies in Xinjiang and Central Asia have global implications. *Zero Tolerance* sheds light on this problem, informing policymakers, scholars, and students about an emerging global hotspot destined to play a central role in international politics in years to come.

PHILIP B. K. POTTER is Associate Professor of Politics and Founding Director of the National Security Policy Center in the Frank Batten School of Leadership and Public Policy at the University of Virginia.

CHEN WANG is Assistant Professor in the Department of Politics and Philosophy at the University of Idaho. Prior to UoI, he was an America in the World Consortium (AWC) Postdoctoral Fellow at Duke University, a visiting scholar in the Institute for Security and Conflict Studies at George Washington University, and a research fellow affiliated with the National Security Policy Center in the Frank Batten School of Leadership and Public Policy at the University of Virginia. He studies international security and foreign policy.

T0349202

Zero Tolerance

Repression and Political Violence on China's New Silk Road

PHILIP B. K. POTTER
University of Virginia

CHEN WANG
University of Idaho

CAMBRIDGE
UNIVERSITY PRESS

CAMBRIDGE
UNIVERSITY PRESS

University Printing House, Cambridge CB2 8BS, United Kingdom

One Liberty Plaza, 20th Floor, New York, NY 10006, USA

477 Williamstown Road, Port Melbourne, VIC 3207, Australia

314–321, 3rd Floor, Plot 3, Splendor Forum, Jasola District Centre, New Delhi – 110025, India

103 Penang Road, #05–06/07, Visioncrest Commercial, Singapore 238467

Cambridge University Press is part of the University of Cambridge.

It furthers the University's mission by disseminating knowledge in the pursuit of education, learning, and research at the highest international levels of excellence.

www.cambridge.org
Information on this title: www.cambridge.org/9781009100380
DOI: 10.1017/9781009115247

First published 2023

A catalogue record for this publication is available from the British Library.

Library of Congress Cataloging-in-Publication Data
Names: Potter, Philip B. K., author. | Wang, Chen, 1989– author.
Title: Zero tolerance : repression and political violence on China's new Silk Road / Philip B. K. Potter, University of Virginia, Chen Wang, University of Virginia.
Description: Cambridge ; New York, NY : Cambridge University Press, 2023. | Includes bibliographical references and index.
Identifiers: LCCN 2022023462 | ISBN 9781009100380 (hardback) | ISBN 9781009115247 (ebook)
Subjects: LCSH: Uighur (Turkic people) – Violence against – China – Xinjiang Uygur Zizhiqu. | Uighur (Turkic people) – Government policy – China – Xinjiang Uygur Zizhiqu. | Political violence – China – Xinjiang Uygur Zizhiqu. | Muslims – Persecutions – China – Xinjiang Uygur Zizhiqu. | China – Ethnic relations. | China – Politics and government – 2002–
Classification: LCC DS731.U4 P68 2023 | DDC 305.894/32309516–dc23/eng/20220810
LC record available at https://lccn.loc.gov/2022023462

ISBN 978-1-009-10038-0 Hardback
ISBN 978-1-009-11490-5 Paperback

To my girls – PBKP
To my wife – CW

Contents

Figures

Maps

Tables

Acknowledgments

This book has endured a longer journey than most, but it is one for which we are extremely grateful. The seeds were sown fifteen years ago with a seminar question. Phil was giving a lecture at Tsinghua University on cooperation among militant organizations and was asked something to the effect of "What does this tell us about Uyghur terrorists?" It was a question that he should have anticipated but hadn't.

Pulling on this thread led to years of trying to understand the evolving situation in Xinjiang. It wasn't, however, an easy thread to unravel and real progress came only when Chen came on board. The two of us first met in person in 2015 when Chen joined the University of Virginia (UVA) as a graduate student. Our collaboration, however, preceded that as we began data collection and exchange of thoughts following a series of deadly attacks in China in 2013 and 2014. This was one of those rare partnerships that brought together complementary expertise in militancy, international relations, Chinese politics, and domestic politics in a way that (we hope) produced something greater than the sum of the parts.

The result, however, was somewhat unexpected. Our inquiry revealed as much about China and autocratic politics as it did about political violence, Xinjiang, or the Uyghur people. It turns out that the Uyghur minority, and the small number of militants among them, are just players in a much larger story about the Chinese Communist Party (CCP) political insecurity. The brutal efficiency of Chinese repression in Xinjiang seems exceptional, but in our view the distinction is a matter of degree rather than kind. Repression and political violence in China are also revealing of much larger global trends, particularly among autocracies.

This insight came to deeply influence our thinking on US–China relations. When we presented this work, someone inevitably asked what the United States can do to stop the mistreatment of the Uyghur minority. In our view, the answer, regrettably, is "very little." China has changed policies and personnel in Xinjiang many times but almost always in response to domestic rather than foreign imperatives. This is not to say that sanctions, boycotts, and political snubs that raise costs for the CCP aren't the right thing to do both morally and practically. But there is very little reason to think that that they are going to "work" in the sense that they will forcibly reshape Chinese policies. The drivers of these politics are too intertwined in the regime's perception of its core interests and, ultimately, its survival. And the resources that China has at its disposal mean that it can weather the costs that even powerful states like the United States are willing and able to impose. Once one sees this dynamic, it seems to pop up again and again across the irritants to the bilateral relationships, be it in the South China Sea, Hong Kong, or Taiwan.

We racked up a great many debts in the pursuit of this education in autocratic politics, political violence, and US–China relations – so many that any thanks will inevitably be incomplete. Still, one must try.

Foremost, thanks to our families. From Phil: My wife, Rachel, provided endless support throughout this project. She's the sounding board for all my ideas – sometimes it pays to have two political scientists in the family. Her willingness to help think through thorny issues of politics and presentation – even when she was embroiled in her own academic research – improved this book dramatically. And thanks to my girls, Hazel and Dorothy, who tolerate no pretentiousness and suffer no fools. They keep me on the right track. From Chen: The love and support of my wife and best friend, Ruozao, formed the backbone of this journey. She not only helped keep our home tidy and warm but saved my sanity during the ups and downs. After all, not everyone could enjoy the luxury of having a board-certified music therapist at home who can always offer the right dose of happiness. Her willingness to read our early manuscripts and ask questions as someone with zero interest in the subject also helped improve the readability of this book. And thanks to my parents for always supporting me along the way.

Many researchers assisted with this work and made it what it is. The team at the National Security Policy Center played a pivotal role. David Bartha, Anna Spakovsky, Claire Oto, and Kevin George got deeply engaged with the project and did work that was way beyond the call of duty. Seminar participants at American University in Washington, DC, ENS Lyon, Renmin University, the East Asia Center at UVA, Pennsylvania State University, RAND, the University of Pennsylvania, and American Political Science Association 2019 and 2021 asked the hard questions that refined our thinking. The Quandt fund at UVA provided invaluable financial support for fieldwork. Brantly Womack, Shirley Lin, Harry Harding, Avery Goldstein, Jim Piazza, Charles Gerard, and many others provided generous feedback and critiques along the way. Jamie Douglas did wonderful creative work on the cover and Melissa Castro and Eric Levy proved to be invaluable editors. Finally, thanks to John Haslan and the team at Cambridge for shepherding the work through the progression from manuscript to polished book.

1 | Introduction

In April 2014, two militants attacked the railway station in Urumqi, the capital of the Xinjiang Uyghur Autonomous Region (XUAR) in the far west of China. Little is known about the perpetrators beyond that they were ethnic Uyghur separatists who, according to official reports, had come under the influence of "extremist religious thought."[1] Their tactics and weapons were primitive, consisting of knives and rudimentary suicide bombs. In the immediate aftermath, the Turkestan Islamic Party (TIP) – a small militant organization operating outside China – claimed the attack as a response to Beijing's repression of the Uyghur minority.

This was a minor attack when measured against the increasingly bloody standards of global terrorism. Three were killed, including the two suicide bombers. The consequences, however, were significant. The timing appeared designed to coincide with the last day of President Xi Jinping's visit to the region, during which he had repeatedly touted the regime's successes against terrorism and extremism. The violence was a clear rebuttal to that message, and there is every indication that President Xi took the challenge personally. Just days later, Xi responded in a closed-door speech to Chinese Communist Party (CCP or the Party) leaders, the transcript of which was leaked to the *New York Times*. "We must," he declared, "show absolutely no mercy."[2]

The first delivery on this threat came in the form of a "strike hard" campaign, which heightened the already draconian surveillance and policing tactics in Xinjiang. The mounting repression that followed over the next few years went largely unnoticed in the West, as had prior "strike hard" campaigns. But ignorance turned to outrage when members of the United Nations Committee on the Elimination of Racial Discrimination announced in 2018 that the Chinese government was

---

[1] Wang and Ng (2014).   [2] Ramzy and Buckley (2019).

1

holding as many as one million ethnic Uyghurs in "massive internment camps ... shrouded in secrecy."[3]

Articles, opinion pieces, and editorials called for an international response – the *Washington Post* editorial board led the charge with the headline "We Can't Ignore This Brutal Cleansing in China."[4] The United States subsequently placed sanctions on individuals and businesses implicated in these policies. The United States, Canada, and several European countries went so far as to label the treatment of Chinese Uyghurs a genocide.

A "Core Interest"

While voices in the West felt they could not ignore the dark turn in the situation in Xinjiang, China clearly calculated that it could safely ignore the pressure campaign. There is little evidence that the critiques or sanctions had any meaningful impact on China's policies toward its Uyghur minority. While the most overt signs of repression – barbed wire, cameras, and temporary detention centers – have ebbed from their high-water mark, a subtler but no less pervasive or capable form of subjugation has set in. The doggedness of the Chinese authorities in the pursuit of the cultural suppression and assimilation of Xinjiang represents something of a puzzle given the meaningful cost of both the international condemnation and the repressive policies themselves (more on this in Chapters 4 and 5). The question is, why does the Chinese state persist so unequivocally in these policies in the face of these costs?

The answer lies in the extent to which the CCP perceives a link between its policies in Xinjiang and its core interests, including regime survival. On first inspection, this is surprising given the minimal size and scope of Uyghur unrest and the massive and growing economic and political power of China. However, the Party leadership has articulated a vision of legitimacy in which any crack in the façade represents a threat to the entire edifice.

China has defined stability in Xinjiang as among its "core interests" since 2006.[5] This position has only hardened since that time; Xi Jinping drove the point home in an April 2014 speech:

---

[3] Nebehay (2018).   [4] Editorial Board (2018a).
[5] Foreign Ministry of PRC, 2006.

Countering terrorism has a direct bearing on national security, the people's immediate interests, and reform, development and stability. The battle against terrorism safeguards national unity, social stability and the people's well-being. We must take decisive measures in deterring terrorism and keep up the pressure to thwart terrorism. We should work out a sound anti-terrorism work pattern, improve our anti-terrorism work system and build up our anti-terrorism strength. We should enlist both professional forces and the public in the fight against terrorism, get the general public to carry out different forms of activities against terrorism, build an impregnable anti-terrorism network, and ensure that terrorists are hunted down like rats.[6]

In short, the brutality of the repression in Xinjiang is a feature of the policy, not a bug.

These perceived interests explain Beijing's seemingly disproportionate response to relatively modest critiques, protests, and political violence from Uyghurs in Xinjiang and abroad. These policies arise from deeply held priorities that cut to the very heart of the Party's claim to uncontested authority.

The stylized facts behind CCP claims to legitimacy can be told in three stages, each with implications for the treatment of the country's minorities. Throughout the Maoist era, communism provided a ready-made rationale for single-party rule. As we will detail, while this period was far from idyllic for the Uyghur minority in Xinjiang, the remoteness of the region and notions of the proper treatment of minorities in a communist state (largely borrowed from the Soviet Union) provided some insulation from the worst excesses of the period.

The "opening up" ushered in by Deng Xiaoping – and more fully realized by Jiang Zemin and Hu Jintao – largely dismantled Maoist economic institutions and ideologies and therefore required a new social contract. In lieu of communist ideals, the implicit bargain became a promise of economic growth in exchange for the right to rule uncontested and unquestioned. While China prospered in this period, it did so unevenly, and expectations for autonomy mounted among Uyghurs; when those expectations went unmet, grievances mounted in turn.

Basing legitimacy on economic performance was arguably never a completely stable arrangement, as even the remarkably steep and steady growth the Party delivered over the ensuing decades was bound

---

[6] Xi (2014).

to level off. The rise of Xi Jinping and the increasing personalization of the Chinese regime pushed the Party more rapidly toward nationalism.

This nationalist turn positioned the CCP as the ultimate guarantor of Chinese sovereignty. Much has been written on the narrative of national humiliation in Chinese politics, with the period from the start of the first Opium War in 1839 through the communist victory and the founding of the People's Republic of China (PRC) in 1949 characterized as a "century of humiliation" at the hands of foreign powers – an indignity that can never be allowed to repeat itself.[7]

As Metcalf describes it, "the century of humiliation continues to be used by the CCP to validate its own political legitimacy … the CCP has refined a highly nationalistic historical narrative that emphasizes past injustices inflicted by foreign powers."[8] Threats to China's territorial integrity are therefore particularly unacceptable to the Party. Uyghur grievances are commonly viewed and painted in this light. For example, Uyghur militants are often described in official narratives as "splittists," and frequent references to foreign ties and support are designed to invoke this longstanding concern.[9]

This nationalist turn in the regime's legitimation strategy has been developing in earnest for nearly a decade, though it has roots that go back much further. Shortly after taking office in 2012, Xi Jinping took the members of the Politburo standing committee to an exhibition titled "Road to Revival," which traced the path of China's century of humiliation. During the tour, he encouraged the Politburo to "unite people of all ethnic groups in developing the nation."[10] This seeming non sequitur was no accident and hinted at the nationalism (increasingly tinged with elements of Han ethnonationalism) that was to come. Any difference – be it religion, language, or culture – is painted as out of step with a strong, unified China capable of holding outside threats at bay. Along the same lines, foreign complaints about the treatment of minorities are typically not viewed as sincere concerns over human rights but as insidious attempts to return China to a subjugated status.

---

[7] See, for example, Kaufman (2010, 2011); Metcalf (2020); Callahan (2004); Wang (2008, 2014); Schiavenza (2013).
[8] Metcalf (2020).   [9] People's Daily (2000: 1).
[10] www.china.org.cn/video/2012-11/30/content_27272086.htm.

The reality is that, while the level of repression in Xinjiang may rise and fall at the margins, the underlying posture of the state toward the Uyghur minority is unlikely to shift as long as the CCP perceives its core interests this way. At the same time, the government's intense social controls in Xinjiang and its increasingly heavy foreign policy footprint in Central Asia ratchet up Uyghur grievances and international tensions. The resulting spiral of grievance, political violence, and repression is the subject of this book, along with its implications for China, Central Asia, and the globe. We seek to advance the understanding of the increasingly complex interaction between political violence and government response within modern autocracies and to prepare policymakers for events in China and Central Asia that could occupy their time and attention in the coming years.

Political Violence in China

By the numbers, China does not have a serious problem with domestic political violence. This is in keeping with a broader pattern that is well known to scholars – party-based institutionalized autocracies are generally less plagued by political violence than most of their other autocratic counterparts (Figure 1.1).[11]

Figure 1.1 demonstrates the extent to which political violence has historically been concentrated in autocracies under military rule, though personalistic dictatorships have moved to the front of the pack in the last decade. Wilson and Piazza attribute the resilience of party-based autocracies to their heightened capacity for both effective coercion and co-optation.[12]

China – arguably the most prominent party-based autocracy in the international system – fits that mold. With a population of nearly 1.4 billion people, China averaged fewer than six serious attacks (and about twenty-one citizens killed) per year between 1990 and 2014. Since 2014, the pace of violence has dramatically decreased, due in large part to the extreme levels of repression in Xinjiang. These numbers are dwarfed by those in Russia, Algeria, Egypt, and many other

---

[11] Terrorist attack data are drawn from the Global Terrorism Database. Our coding for regime type is based on Geddes, Wright, and Frantz (2014).

[12] Wilson and Piazza (2013).

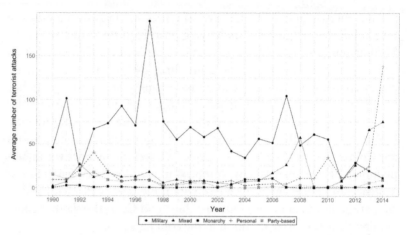

Figure 1.1 Political violence trends by autocratic regime type: 1990–2014

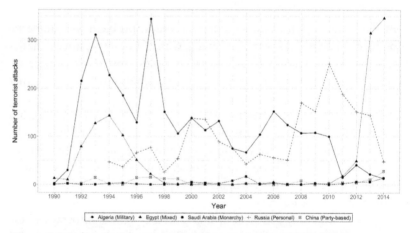

Figure 1.2 Political violence trends in five autocracies: 1990–2014

autocracies ostensibly at peace (Figure 1.2).[13] Thus, despite the country's position as the leading institutionalized autocracy in the international system, it is typically neglected in the burgeoning literature on political violence in autocracies.

---

[13] Data on China are original and will be introduced in Chapter 2. Political violence data on all other countries are drawn from the Global Terrorism Database.

The body of academic work on the relationship between political violence and regime type is vast, but it can be boiled down to two key takeaways: (1) Autocracies excel at repression but (2) struggle to accommodate the underlying grievances that drive violence.[14] In other words, they have short-term advantages but long-term disadvantages when compared to their democratic counterparts. This is, in many ways, the short version of China's experience with political violence in Xinjiang. However, the country's size, system, and development make China stand out.

The CCP has, at this point, fully transitioned from a revolutionary party to the institutionalized ruling authority.[15] As such, many of the blunt (but effective) tools of repression that autocracies have traditionally drawn on to combat domestic political violence require more finesse.

One such tool, which we explore in detail in Chapter 3, is information control. In modern institutionalized autocracies like China, public opinion matters, information control is not absolute, and media can be partially independent and market-driven. Consequently, such governments must deploy more nuanced strategies when disseminating information about militancy and ethnic dissent. Thus, while some autocracies may be capable of limiting the reach of terrorists through tight censorship of traditional media and information, in a partially open society like China obvious censorship can cost the Party popular support and limit opportunities to frame the information strategically.[16] In this environment, strategies of information control become deeply entwined with issues of regime legitimacy.

Chinese authorities calibrate information control to avoid alienating an increasingly connected public while achieving international objectives. Domestically, this means providing acceptable levels of transparency. Internationally, scholars such as Sean Roberts have noted the

---

[14] See, for example, Crenshaw (1981); Li (2005); Wilson and Piazza (2013); Gaibulloev, Piazza, and Sandler (2017).

[15] Gandhi and Przeworski (2007).

[16] Most studies find a positive relationship between press freedom and terrorism. Ross (1993) shows that wealthy countries are more likely to experience terrorist attacks because they have well-developed mass media that allow terrorists to publicize their activities. Li (2005) finds a significant and positive relationship between press freedom and terrorist attacks. See also Hoffman, Shelton, and Cleven (2013).

strategic value the CCP derives from exaggerating Uyghur violence and linking it to the Global War on Terror.[17] Both of these objectives must be coordinated with the ingrained imperative to preserve stability and project an image of strength and control. Thus, leaders in China face a balancing act between starving militants of the "oxygen of publicity," meeting the public's desire for information, framing policies in Xinjiang for an international audience, and maintaining an aura of invincibility.

The literature also consistently finds that the far-reaching repressive capacity that most autocracies have at their disposal enables them to suppress political violence.[18] On this count, China is unsurpassed. However, there are lessons to be learned from the ways in which China's repression is targeted (and the ways in which it is indiscriminate). While much of the literature on repression implicitly envisions an indiscriminately heavy hand, this is out of step with the requirements of a sophisticated, centralized, and increasingly wealthy single-party state. China's vibrant economy could not be sustained in a police state, but that is not the experience of the average Han Chinese citizen. Even in the context of tightening that has occurred since Xi Jinping came to power and the social controls associated with the COVID pandemic, most Chinese citizens are largely free to go about their day-to-day lives.

In contrast, the level of repression faced by the average Uyghur has consistently been labeled as "Orwellian."[19] Notably, however, the level of repression employed in Xinjiang is increasingly stressing given China's formidable capacities. And the attempt to focus repression inevitably creates a stark contrast not only between the economically vibrant coastal cities and Xinjiang, but also between Han and Uyghur within Xinjiang. This creates an incentive to project violence into the less strictly policed and repressed areas of Chinese life. As we discuss in Chapters 2 and 4, restrictions are increasingly impacting economic life across Xinjiang and raising the ire of Han Chinese in the region. A better understanding of these dimensions of targeted repression in autocracies will be required as China seeks to export its brand of digital authoritarianism around the globe.

[17] Roberts (2020).
[18] Gartner and Regan (1996); Davenport (2007); Svolik (2012); Escribà-Folch (2013).
[19] Editorial Board (2018b).

Finally, as is generally the case in autocracies, China finds it difficult to accommodate grievances without risking the regime's grip on power. To compensate, Beijing has turned to high levels of internal security spending. China's treatment of Uyghurs in Xinjiang has long been characterized by a "carrot and stick" approach – one that relies on postattack "strike-hard" campaigns combined with economic and policy carrots. But even the carrots are limited to attempts to buy acquiescence rather than address the actual grievances. In recent years, Beijing has attempted to extract itself from the continuous push and pull by escalating beyond security and repression to attempt a complete social transformation of the region. This has culminated in the establishment of the reeducation camps, forced migration, interference with reproductive rights, and other measures that veer increasingly toward cultural genocide.[20]

Understanding repression and political violence in Xinjiang in the broader context of autocratic politics writ large sheds light on what is going on in China (and why), while integrating a crucially important but understudied case into that literature.

Policy Implications

Repression and political violence in Xinjiang have broader political implications than are commonly recognized. This is a global problem, or at least could become one. Terrorism is generally the last resort of the weak – it is a tool of asymmetric conflict. As such, it is effective only when it provokes an overreaction from the target, and these reactions can have profound consequences. When a ragtag group of Serbian nationalists assassinated Archduke Ferdinand and his wife in Sarajevo in 1914, they set in motion a chain of events that culminated in World War I and the deaths of over sixteen million people. The 9/11 attacks killed nearly 3,000, but the resulting wars deposed regimes, killed approximately 600,000, and cost the United States more than $3 trillion.[21] As an emerging superpower, China's counterterrorism policies have similar potential to reshape global politics.

Many of the factors that led prior serious, but ultimately manageable, incidents to escalate into World War I or a "Global War on

---

[20] Doyon (2019).   [21] Stimson Center (2018).

Terror" are present in the ongoing confrontation in Xinjiang. The implication is that while China's domination of its Uyghur population appears nearly absolute at the present time, the long-term situation may not be as stable.

Domestically, government repression continuously evolves but shows little sign of abating, even as it has given rise to serious grievances among the ethnic Uyghur minority and radicalized a small subset of them. Repression has also pushed Uyghurs out of Xinjiang and into the broader region where some of the more radicalized have developed ties to highly capable regional militant organizations such as al-Qaeda and the Taliban, have demonstrated a capacity for coordinated violence, and have recognized the strategic value of projecting violence into eastern China's population and economic centers. Others have joined conflicts in places such as Afghanistan, Iraq, and Syria, raising the potential that they could return to China as hardened fighters or attack Chinese nationals and assets abroad.

The Chinese authorities and the general public tend to react strongly to militant violence, even when it is small-scale and largely unsuccessful – as violence from weak organizations or radicalized individuals tends to be. This is not, however, particularly unusual. Powerful states frequently overreact to substate violence – even when that violence is ultimately manageable. However, because Western observers tend to view the situation in Xinjiang primarily through the lens of the ongoing human rights violations occurring there, they are often blind to the public-opinion dynamics driving official actions – dynamics that are uncomfortably similar to those in the United States, Europe, and elsewhere.

Among Chinese officials and the general public, there is tremendous intolerance for Uyghur grievances and unrest and a willingness to spend extraordinary sums – and disrupt millions of lives – to drive the resulting threat of violence to zero. The mix of perceived threat and vulnerability creates a political atmosphere that produces an exaggerated state response to even small-scale minority unrest. As Xi Jinping put it in a speech at the Conference on Interaction and Confidence Building Measures in Asia, "We should have *Zero Tolerance* for terrorism, separatism, and extremism."

Adding to this volatility, this conflict is unfolding in the complex neighborhood that is Central Asia, where the Uyghurs are the ethnic and religious brethren of the Turkic peoples across the border – the Tajiks, the Kazaks, and so on – rather than of the Han Chinese majority. As a consequence, China's repressive policies in Xinjiang have the potential to evoke broader grievances in the region that become linked to the specific grievances of the oppressed Uyghur minority – just as China's footprint is rapidly expanding through its "Belt and Road Initiative" (BRI), the country's signature global development strategy. The presence of these Chinese investments and personnel abroad can become irritants in their own right (as well as inviting targets).

Since the end of the Cold War, China has quietly asserted itself as the dominant power in Central Asia, particularly as Russia confronts demographic decline and remains fixated on the West in its foreign policy. Russia's invasion of Ukraine only accelerates this transition. While China's behavior on its naval periphery (be it the South China Sea, the Senkaku/Diaoyu Islands, or further afield in Sri Lanka or Djibouti) might draw more attention because it is in more direct conflict with US priorities, China's grand strategy is equally contingent on the "Belt" portion of its BRI.[22] Chinese economic growth and military power hinge on regional stability in Central Asia, and Uyghur aspirations and grievances threaten that.

Central Asia is now the testing ground for Beijing's vision of a state-centric economic development model, leading to an inevitable rise in local discontent over China's escalating economic and military presence in neighboring countries. The November 2018 attack on the Chinese consulate in the Pakistani city of Karachi by the Balochistan Liberation Army (BLA), a militant organization seeking self-determination for the Baloch people and the separation of Balochistan from Pakistan, is just one of many manifestations of such blowback. Both the Chinese and the Pakistani governments described this attack as an attempt to sabotage the China–Pakistan friendship, but the BLA declared that it was a warning to China to stop exploiting Balochistan's natural resources in the name of the China–Pakistan Economic Corridor, one of China's flagship BRI projects. The threat is not receding – in April of 2022, this same organization killed three Chinese staff and their driver outside the Confucius Institute at Karachi University.

---

[22] Xinjiang and Central Asia are on the "Belt" of the BRI (Silk Road Economic Belt), while "Road" refers to the maritime portion of the strategy (21st Century Maritime Silk Road).

As these external complaints mount, China gives fodder to opponents who can link their opposition to the domestic situation in Xinjiang, just as militant groups throughout the Middle East historically connected their causes and activities to the Israeli treatment of Palestinians. This has already started to happen in the public rhetoric of organizations such as the Islamic State.[23] In 2017, for example, the Islamic State released a video featuring Uyghur militants saying "We will come to you [China] to clarify to you with the tongues of our weapons, to shed blood like rivers and avenging the oppressed."[24] Further escalation in the cycle of state repression and political violence has the potential to draw the country into broader regional conflicts with unpredictable consequences – just as the 9/11 attacks drew the United States into Afghanistan.

We have seen a similar process unfold before. China's growing footprint on the African continent has led to resentment regarding its use of land, resources, and Chinese labor – all factors at play in Central Asia as well. Moreover, as China has expanded its economic presence on the African continent, Chinese nationals have been attacked by domestic militants. For example, in the spring of 2007, militants attacked a Chinese-run oil facility in Ethiopia, killing seventy workers – including nine Chinese nationals. The Ogaden National Liberation Front, a group fighting for independence in eastern Ethiopia, took responsibility for the attack, stating that they refused to "allow the mineral resources of [their] people to be exploited by this regime" or any firms contracting with the regime.[25]

Chinese nationals abroad have also come under threat due to China's support of unpopular or repressive national governments. In 2008, local militants in the South Kordofan state of Sudan kidnapped nine (and killed five) Chinese nationals working for the China National Petroleum Corporation. The group stated that they had kidnapped the workers because "China supports the Khartoum government militarily and helps it marginalize our region."[26] As long as Chinese firms are willing to work in areas with militant groups that have grievances with their own national governments or with China, they are likely to become targets of violence. These conditions are doubly present in Central Asia where the populace's ethnic ties to the

[23] Chaziza (2018).   [24] Gramer (2017).
[25] Gettleman and Knowlton (2007).   [26] Gettleman and Knowlton (2007).

Uyghurs encourage militants to link their grievances to the Chinese government's ongoing brutality in Xinjiang. And as long as nationalism and the robust defense of Chinese interests and prestige are central to the Party's legitimacy, there is potential for disproportionate reactions to any incidents that occur.

China's substantial capabilities may enable it to suppress discontent in Xinjiang indefinitely, much as it has in Tibet. Ongoing cultural genocide could, in theory, make those changes permanent. Geographic and demographic realities, however, make it more challenging to fully pacify the roughly thirteen million Uyghurs with ethnic brethren just across the border than to suppress a population of approximately six million Tibetans hemmed in by the Himalayas. While global attention has diminished from its heights at the apex of the detention centers in 2019–2020, nothing about the underlying situation in Xinjiang has been durably resolved. The resulting potential for instability (and China's potential response) warrants immediate attention and preparation from policymakers across the globe. This is particularly the case with the US withdrawal from Afghanistan, which has left a potential hotbed of militancy, including some Uyghur militancy, on China's doorstep. Even if the focus of US security continues its shift from managing terrorism and insurgency to peer competition, understanding political violence in China (and the state response to it) will be crucial if policymakers are to effectively understand and deal with China's behavior. The Xinjiang issue has already become a key topic of rhetorical competition as the United States and China maneuver for international reputation, legitimacy, and status.

Perspective

We approach these questions as specialists in political violence, foreign policy, and international relations rather than as historians or ethnographers of China or the Uyghur people. And we write this book for a Western, and primarily American, audience. It is our firm belief that to understand foreign policy and political violence, one must first grapple with the domestic political forces and institutions that shape them, and our attention to those issues in this volume is in service of that goal.

This approach is distinct from much of the existing work in this area, which has primarily been conducted by Uyghur specialists and (with substantial justification) focuses on the plight of the Uyghur people and culture in the face of extraordinary levels of government repression.[27]

While we are convinced that our approach to the questions that arise from repression and political violence in China is necessary and overdue, it is fraught with potential pitfalls. Chief among these is that a serious analysis of Uyghur-initiated violence might be used as propaganda to justify and whitewash the Chinese government's repressive policies in Xinjiang. For this reason, some Western scholars have been reluctant to grapple with Uyghur militancy for fear of feeding into a narrative that seeks to justify human rights violations as necessary to fight religious extremism.

Much of this debate has centered on the use of the word "terrorism."[28] The cliché that one person's terrorist is another's freedom fighter is a poor shorthand for the complexity of the moral, ethical, and empirical perspectives involved in identifying acts of "terrorism" or designating individuals or organizations as "terrorists." This debate has spilled into the charged question of when it is right and accurate to label Uyghur-initiated violence in Xinjiang and beyond as "terrorism." The designation of the East Turkistan Islamic Movement as a terrorist group by the State Department in 2002 – and the later removal of the organization from the list in late 2020 – illustrates just how politicized the issue can be.

Among scholars, there is more consensus on some of the potentially defining elements of terrorism – such as premeditation, political motivations, and nonstate perpetrators – than on others – such as the type of target. Writing on political violence in Xinjiang, Roberts adopts a more stringent interpretation of "civilian targets" than the State Department's definition, which covers all "noncombatant targets." He thus concludes that "very few acts of violence perpetrated by Uyghurs can be clearly determined to be acts of 'terrorism'."[29] Mumford, on the other hand, appears to be less bothered by the technical details of definition but casts Uyghur militancy against existing typologies

---

[27] See, for example, Bovingdon (2010); Starr (2004); Dillon (2004); Roberts (2020); Millward (2021).

[28] For a more thorough discussion of the conceptualization of terrorism, see Weinberg, Pedahzur, and Hirsch-Hoefler (2004); Tilly (2004); Schmid (2004).

[29] Roberts (2020: 14).

of terrorism, arguing that "Uyghur terrorism actually constitutes a hybrid model of modern terrorist groups in which religious discourse is used to underline the push for a separatist agenda."[30]

There are real consequences at stake in the rhetorical debate over the labeling of Uyghur political violence, but that contest is outside our scope. Instead, following trends in the broader literature on political violence, we focus on the empirical rather than moral components of Uyghur-initiated violence and government repression. Throughout the book, we shy away from the value-laden and controversial terminology around "terrorism" and "terrorists" in favor of the broader categories of "political violence," "militancy," and "violent nonstate actors." We are in no way justifying the treatment of the Uyghur minority.

As we will detail in Chapter 4, Xinjiang has become a laboratory for authoritarian repression. Mass detention, cultural assimilation, and reeducation are only the beginning. Uyghurs must endure constant security checks, download mandatory software on their cell phones to track and report their behavior and contacts, and submit to bioregistration of DNA, fingerprints, and facial scans under the guise of health checks. Such repression can only be condemned.

At the same time, while perpetrated by a tiny minority and largely in response to this repression, the militant violence in and around China has been real. Moreover, official rhetoric is more in line with the Chinese public's perception of the threat than one might assume. And it is these perceptions, rather than objective facts, that drive political events.[31] Thus, while Chinese policies in Xinjiang are reprehensible, it would be an error to view them as entirely disingenuous or cynical. Mistakenly viewing them in this way risks concluding that these policies can be easily influenced or deterred. We need to understand the facts on the ground and how the CCP perceives its own interests. To do otherwise risks miscalculation.

Much of the scholarly conversation on repression and political violence in Xinjiang boils down to whether the CCP's stated motivations and policies are cynical or authentic. Chinese authorities have clearly cynically leveraged limited Uyghur violence and a global obsession

---

[30] Mumford (2018: 18).
[31] For a more in-depth discussion of this point see Greitens, Lee, and Yazici (2020).

with counterterrorism to achieve policy objectives, just as Roberts and others have noted. However, it is equally true that Uyghur violence, and even the underlying grievances and unmet aspirations that motivate it, is an authentically felt affront to a Party and population increasingly organized around a resurgent sense of nationalism. It can be both.

These realities require that we take seriously the entire feedback loop of perception, repression, and political violence. This approach is essential if we are to grapple with this situation as China understands it – as opposed to how we would like it to be. While it may pain policymakers in Washington to acknowledge it, China's growth and mounting strength render its human rights policies immune to forceful shaping, particularly in regions that the Party perceives as core to its interests, such as Xinjiang. As Greitens and her coauthors put it, "critics of China's policies in Xinjiang are more likely to succeed in changing those policies if their arguments are based on a full understanding of the policies' causes."[32]

Xinjiang

Understanding the story of repression and political violence in China requires some conception of the geographical, political, and historical contexts in which it is unfolding. Western China is, however, unfamiliar terrain for most Western readers.

Media coverage tends to portray Xinjiang as a dusty outpost at the edge of the world, but this misses the region's strategic significance. Located in the far northwest corner of the country, Xinjiang shares borders with many states that people don't think of as bordering China. India, Pakistan, Afghanistan, Tajikistan, Kyrgyzstan, Kazakhstan, Russia, and Mongolia spread around the region like a fan (see Map 1.1). This is the heart of Central Asia and all of its political complexities.

In the Chinese political system, Xinjiang is a so-called "autonomous region." Its full name is the Xinjiang Uyghur Autonomous Region, or XUAR (we use all three labels interchangeably). China's autonomous regions – Tibet, Inner Mongolia, Guangxi, Ningxia, and Xinjiang –

[32] Greitens, Lee, and Yazici (2020: 12).

Map 1.1 Xinjiang and Central Asia

are a legacy of the early years of the PRC in the mid-twentieth century. In many ways, their very existence is in tension with present-day Chinese priorities.

Minority policies of the PRC were originally modeled on those of the Soviet Union and implemented under the guidance and supervision of Soviet advisors.[33] The Soviet blueprint for a multinational state drew on Marxist–Leninist and Stalinist theories as well as the particulars of the experience of the USSR, not all of which translated cleanly to the Chinese context. Leninist doctrine held that while all nations were progressing in the same direction, some were more advanced than others, requiring the accommodation of political differences through regional autonomy. The Chinese Provisional Constitution of 1949, and ultimately the 1954 Constitution, enshrined this philosophy.[34]

---

[33] Dreyer (1999); Jankowiak (2008); Hong and He (2015).
[34] Zhou (2010). As Zhou describes it, "The process of copying and implementing the Soviet model involved two interwoven key issues – models of the state and the scope of minority rights. The first issue was whether the CCP should strive

As is so often the case in China, the facts on the ground almost immediately diverged from the law as written. But at least on paper, the autonomous regions had some discretion: local authority and legislative powers; the right to independent economic development, including budgetary authority; and the right to self-directed cultural and educational development.[35]

These policies were, however, in tension with the long history of China's aggressive assimilation of minorities. The unification of ethnic groups was central to Chinese imperial policy as far back as the Qin dynasty (221 BCE).[36] China's "century of humiliation" at foreign hands and the country's searing revolutionary experience reinforced this tendency to prioritize unity over self-determination, particularly in light of Japan's attempts to set up minority-led puppet governments as a means of weakening the country. Uyghur cultural distinctiveness was preserved primarily by distance, not policy.

The appeal of the Soviet model faded further after the Sino-Soviet split in 1956, and there was a notable reversion to the prior practices of forced unification and assimilation.

Thus, the limited self-rule that existed when the autonomous regions were established has steadily eroded over time. The consistent prioritization of societal "harmony" over any commitment to self-determination amplified this trend.[37] While in principle the autonomous regions should function like provinces with additional independent legislative rights, in practice they receive greater scrutiny and oversight than the rest of the country, particularly when restive. This is doubly true in Xinjiang, where all local authorities (down to the level of religious, cultural, and educational leaders) are hand-selected

to build a multinational state based on Soviet-style federalism, within which minority communities joined as republics or built a unified, multinational state, in which minority communities gained regional autonomy. The second issue boiled down to the choice of two principles: self-determination or regional autonomy for minorities."

[35] In March 1951, the central government issued the first document regarding policies toward ethnic autonomy – "Trial Regulations of Ethnic Regional Autonomy (draft)." Later, the State Ethnic Affairs Commission of the CCP Northwestern Bureau released a survey outline that aimed to consult with local people and collect opinions on the "Trial Regulations."

[36] Of course, the realities of enforcing authority over vast distances led to substantial autonomy in practice, particularly in periods of dynastic decline.

[37] Trédaniel and Lee (2017).

by Beijing, social interaction is tightly controlled, and any semblance of independent civil society is immediately snuffed out.

As the name implies, the XUAR was established as an autonomous region for ethnic Uyghurs, and at its inception, Uyghurs were the predominant majority, perhaps as high as 75 percent of the population. They are a Turkic people whose language, culture, and religion are far closer to – and in some cases nearly indistinguishable from – those of their Central Asian neighbors than to those of the Han Chinese majority.

Xinjiang has long been the Chinese frontier, and the extent of China's control over the region has varied considerably over the course of Chinese history. Uyghur nationalists point to proud periods of independence, while Chinese nationalists roll out documentation of centuries of imperial control. Similarly, the timing and nature of the emergence of a cohesive Uyghur identity among the Turkic people in the area are matters of fierce debate. This is a contested history, but the contestation itself demonstrates the place of this region at the tenuous edge of historic Chinese power.[38]

The modern history of Xinjiang parallels the evolving policies toward the autonomous regions. The Kuomintang finally surrendered the area to the advancing People's Liberation Army in 1949. From the start, there were tensions over the nature and extent of Uyghur autonomy, with some pushing for the comparatively expansive rights of the Soviet model and others favoring more centralized control. For example, in 1951 a small but important conference referred to as "the Forum of 51 Scholars" was held in Ghulja to discuss the future of Xinjiang.[39] This group favored the establishment of a quasi-independent "Republic of Uyghurstan," with autonomous control of public security through an "ethnic army" and observer status in the United Nations under the auspices of the PRC ambassador. However, the conference and all its suggestions were summarily rejected by Wang Zhen, then the general secretary of the Xinjiang Bureau of the CCP Central Committee (the military government). The Uyghur autonomy issue was temporarily put aside.

---

[38] Millward (2009).   [39] Wang (2012).

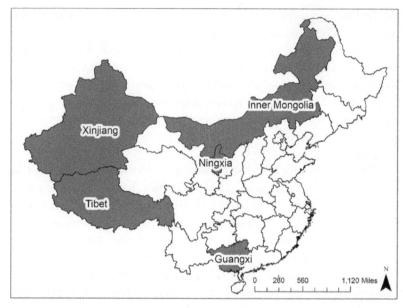

Map 1.2 China's autonomous regions

A year later, upon returning from meetings in Beijing with CCP Chairman Mao Zedong, Wang Zhen asked Saifuddin Azizi (a prominent ethnic Uyghur Party member who eventually became the first chairman of the XUAR) to develop specific plans for the governance and regional autonomy of Xinjiang. Azizi's report to Mao made no mention of either a federation or a republic in the Soviet style but suggested that the name of the Xinjiang government should be "Xinjiang Uyghur Autonomous Government." Later that year, Mao issued the "Program for the Implementation of Ethnic Regional Autonomy of the People's Republic of China," which closely reflected Azizi's proposals.[40]

One of the key tensions then and now was the extent to which policy toward the autonomous regions would acknowledge ethnic divisions. For example, in 1954, three years after Mao issued the

---

[40] People's Daily (1995). Notably, while in 1995 Azizi's recollections of these events were published in the *People's Daily* (the official Party mouthpiece) without controversy, by 2007 his writings were banned in Xinjiang. This shifting treatment of the historical record is just one small indication of the extent of change in policy and sensitivity toward the region over the past two decades.

initial program for implementation, Azizi was called to a meeting with Xi Zhongxun (Xi Jinping's father), who wished to know opinions on the name "Xinjiang Autonomous Region."[41] Many years later, Azizi recalled that he told Xi that "autonomy is not granted to mountains and rivers, but to a nation or an ethnic group. That's why it is called 'ethnic regional autonomy.'" He insisted that the name of the region should be "Xinjiang Uyghur Autonomous Region."[42]

That name endures to this day, but it represents an awkward middle ground that seeks to acknowledge minority rights without providing room for separatism. When the chips are down, however, there is no ambiguity in how China ranks these objectives. Chinese policy has consistently prioritized unity and control over minority rights. Zhou Enlai clearly articulated this balancing act, stating that

[b]efore liberation, there were some people conducting separatist activities in Xinjiang in the name of Eastern Turkestan. Given that, we decided that Uyghurstan is not an appropriate name for Xinjiang. Xinjiang has not only one Uyghur ethnic group but also 12 other ethnic groups. We cannot then establish 13 -stans.[43]

Uyghur Separatism and Militancy

The debates about the naming and governance of Xinjiang were dominated by Beijing and regional Party leadership, with little meaningful input from or impact on the actual residents of the area. As the Chinese saying goes, "The mountains are high and the emperor is far away," and in the middle of the twentieth century, Beijing was very far away from the lives of ordinary Uyghurs in the XUAR. Xinjiang was poor and strategically insignificant, but its isolation and economic underdevelopment also shielded it from the worst of the political convulsions of the Maoist era.

---

[41] Burhan Shehidi was the province chairman of Xinjiang under the Kuomintang regime but joined the CCP and rose to become a member of the Xinjiang Bureau Standing Committee.

[42] Xi passed this opinion on to Mao. Later in the same year, the Standing Committee of the National People's Congress passed "The Decision on Establishing the Xinjiang Uyghur Autonomous Region to Replace the Former Xinjiang Province." People's Daily (1995).

[43] Zhou (1957).

As a consequence, the XUAR was not particularly restive for the first several decades after its establishment in 1955. Nonetheless, there is evidence that international influences played an early and long-standing role in breeding Uyghur resistance, even during this period of relative peace. During the early years of the PRC, the expelled nationalist government (and the United States, to a lesser extent) provided "foreign support" to boost the combat capability of Uyghur militants. As the likelihood of the nationalists' return to mainland China diminished, and after the Sino-Soviet split, Soviet forces filled the vacuum with propaganda, a modest weapons supply, and training.[44] Nevertheless, militancy and violence remained low throughout this period.

This relative quiet stood in contrast to the situation in Tibet, where there was sporadic violence throughout the middle of the twentieth century. That conflict became a Western cause célèbre, owing in large part to the leadership and charisma of the Dalai Lama. The influence the Dalai Lama exerts from beyond Beijing's control has sustained the Tibetan cause, aided by Western (and particularly American) treatment of the issue. Hollywood films have chronicled the plight of Tibet and the exiled Dalai Lama, and nearly every US president since George H. W. Bush has met with the Dalai Lama while in office, with the exception of Donald Trump.

To date, the Uyghur minority has no such charismatic figure. Chinese authorities and academics frequently raise the concern that elements of the global Salafist jihadist movement could fill this role, but this is far from a foregone conclusion. While linkages exist among militant elements of the Uyghur diaspora and Salafist organizations, there is no evidence of broader support among Uyghurs. And major jihadist organizations have only haphazardly and inconsistently attempted to claim the Uyghur cause in their rhetoric and publications.

The contemporary history of repression and political violence in the XUAR begins with the centrifugal forces unleashed by the collapse of the Soviet Union. The cascade of new states in Central Asia led to a push for self-determination among Uyghurs who saw

---

[44] Bovingdon (2010); McMillen (1984); Dillon (2018); Wang (1998). This Soviet support declined as the USSR became embroiled in their war in Afghanistan and China's capacity increased under Deng Xiaoping.

their ethnic brethren gaining independence. The Chinese authorities, however, reflecting many of the same tendencies presaged in the debates surrounding the early history of the autonomous regions, were unreceptive. The response was heavy policing, harshly assimilationist policies, information control, and state-supported Han migration into the region. These policies suppressed political organization among Uyghurs but have led to mounting grievances and periods of both peaceful protest and violent unrest among the Uyghur population. The result has been escalating waves of repression and violence.

In our analyses, we identify four phases in the ebb and flow of violence and repression in the region. The first begins with the rebellions of the late 1940s and 1950s, which should be viewed in the context of the broader national unrest surrounding the consolidation of CCP power and the end of the Chinese Civil War. The second is a period of civil resistance and unrest that accompanied Deng Xiaoping's "reform and opening up." The third – a period of heightened violence – began with the uptick in expectations, repression, and violence that accompanied the collapse of the Soviet Union, continued through the lead-up to the 2008 Beijing Olympics, and culminated in the surge in attacks in 2013–2014. The fourth is ongoing and is characterized by extraordinary levels of repression within Xinjiang that has suppressed violence but internationalized the struggle by pushing its remnants largely outside China's borders.

Each time violence has erupted within China, authorities have been able to regain control and end the campaign by increasing repression, only to have violence emerge again worse than before. We are currently in one such lull, but because nothing has been done to address the underlying sources of tension – and repressive tactics have grown even harsher – there is substantial reason to worry that this is once again a calm before the storm.

We will detail these waves of political violence in Chapter 2, but two incidents that occurred in the span of just over six months in 2013 are useful examples of the dangerous cycle of repression and violence that has characterized the struggle. In both cases, repression and mounting grievances fueled Uyghur violence, which in turn galvanized a harsh response from both the government and the broader Chinese population.

In October 2013, Usman Hasan, his wife Gulkiz Gini, and his mother, Kuwanhan Reyim, drove off the thoroughfare on the north side of Tiananmen Square, mowing down pedestrians before crashing into the ornate Jinshui Bridge and bursting into flames under the iconic Mao portrait at the entrance to the Forbidden City in Beijing. One Chinese and one Filipino tourist were killed, along with all three attackers. Dozens were injured. Police and Chinese media reported that the license plate of the burned vehicle was from Xinjiang and that it contained canisters of gasoline, knives, and an extremist flag. Abdullah Mansour, a leader of the Turkestan Islamic Party (TIP) (the preeminent Uyghur terrorist organization at the time), claimed responsibility in a Uyghur-language audio recording, saying that the attack was a "jihadist operation" by holy warriors, though there is no independent evidence of direct TIP involvement.[45] Police called it a "premeditated, violent, terrorist attack" and arrested five purported accomplices in Xinjiang, three of whom were executed in 2014 for masterminding the attack.[46] This incident was significant for two reasons. First, its location at the symbolic center of the Chinese state was an unambiguous political challenge. Second, the attackers demonstrated their capacity to project violent power into the east and far from its usual Xinjiang locus, thereby countering the strategy of keeping Uyghur grievances bottled up far from the consciousness of the broader Chinese public.

Less than six months later, a group of eight militants attacked the railway station in Kunming, Yunnan Province. Though the perpetrators were armed only with knives, the operation was organized, and security personnel were slow to respond. The result was 31 dead and 141 wounded. Four of the attackers were eventually shot and killed at the scene. Four more were apprehended and eventually tried for terrorism and homicide. Three were sentenced to death while the fourth, Patigul Tohti, was reportedly sentenced to life in prison because she was pregnant.[47]

The Kunming attack was a turning point. By choosing a soft target, the attackers emphasized the vulnerability of civilians to violence and the inability of authorities to protect them. Though the Tiananmen attack was in a more prominent location, casualties were more limited

---

[45] SITE Intelligence Group (2013).   [46] Wan (2013).   [47] Blanchard (2014).

and the security response was nearly instantaneous. This allowed Chinese authorities to rely on traditional mechanisms of information control, a point that we will explore in detail in Chapter 3. Kunming was different because its scope involved so many families, each looking for answers and sharing stories. The resulting public fear, hostility, and recriminations presented an immediate challenge to authorities in Beijing and their legitimacy.

These incidents were embedded in a broader campaign of Uyghur-initiated violence in 2014, following on the heels of the attack in Urumqi. This unprecedented spike in the frequency, sophistication, and reach of violence spooked authorities and led to the extraordinarily harsh, repressive policies that have characterized the years since (phase 4). The ability of militants to project violence outside Xinjiang – and into the core of CCP symbolic power and Chinese daily life – upset the equilibrium and spurred the official response.

Chinese policy has long been to isolate its Xinjiang problem in the region and keep it out of sight of the broader population, thereby minimizing its perceived impact. As we will discuss in Chapter 4, this strategy is predicated on maintaining "two Chinas" – a police state in Xinjiang and a comparatively open east. In response, militants recognized the strategic value of projecting violence outside the XUAR where it would be observed and felt by the broader population, threatening the core interests of the CCP. Chinese authorities then further tightened their grip in Xinjiang, undercutting militant capability at its base and pushing grievances back out of sight but increasing them overall. As security in Xinjiang has tightened, the militants have also moved into the broader Central Asian regions where Chinese nationals and assets remain vulnerable.

The result is the escalating cycle of repression and violence summarized in Figure 1.3. Repression and unmet expectations in Xinjiang give rise to political violence, which leads to the increasing securitization of the region (discussed in detail in Chapter 4). This, in turn, increases grievances while making it nearly impossible for militants to operate within the XUAR. The securitized environment in Xinjiang incentivizes militants to project violence into other parts of China or for displaced militants to strike Chinese assets in neighboring countries. That violence then leads authorities to crack down and increase repression in Xinjiang – and the whole cycle begins again.

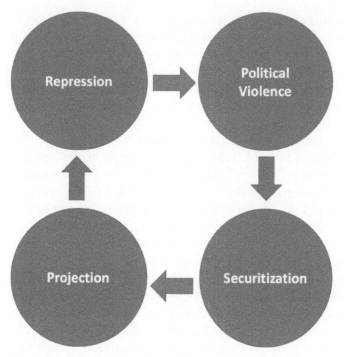

Figure 1.3 The cycle of violence and repression

The question is, what comes next? This spiral of action and reaction suggests that Uyghur militants are highly incentivized to impose costs by perpetrating violence outside Xinjiang. However, the tightened security environment now makes it much harder to strike symbolic or soft targets elsewhere in China. Moreover, Chinese actions abroad have severely impaired the capabilities of Uyghur militants, even when they operate outside Chinese borders. As a result, the militant Uyghur elements that exist are relatively weak, disorganized, and located outside of China.

Given the state of militancy and the level of security and repression within China, the most obvious points of vulnerability are Chinese nationals and investment along the "Belt" of the Belt and Road Initiative. These comparatively vulnerable targets are located in unstable regions with considerable militant activity of their own and substantial Uyghur populations displaced by the crackdown in Xinjiang. If Chinese assets abroad suffer violence, and particularly if that violence is visible enough to challenge CCP prestige, then we are potentially off to the races with an escalating cycle of actions and reactions throughout Central Asia. Relatedly, increased militancy outside China, particularly if it produces successful and prominent attacks, has the potential to inspire violence by disaffected individuals within Xinjiang, even if Uyghur militant organizations relegated to elsewhere in Central Asia lack actual assets within China. This too could escalate the level of repression experienced by ordinary Uyghurs still further.

Plan for the Book

While the mounting repression and violence in Xinjiang have drawn increased attention from scholars, there are important unanswered questions that motivate the chapters that follow. What is the scale of political violence in Xinjiang and how has it changed over time? What political sensitivities underlie and animate the government's response? What explains the recent escalation in repression? And how are responses to militancy and counterterrorism shaping China's foreign policy?

Chapter 2 examines the militant violence emanating from Xinjiang. We provide the most comprehensive data on Uyghur initiated attacks assembled to date, which we draw upon to investigate the causes and consequences of militancy. We detail trends in that violence and assess the tenuous linkages that exist (or have existed) between Uyghur militants and militant organizations active in Central Asia.

Chapter 3 explores the government's sensitivities to domestic political violence. If the situation in Xinjiang and along the BRI escalates into something with broad international implications, we argue that it will be in large part because Chinese domestic politics push it in that direction. Consequently, it is vital to understand where official sensitivities lie and how authorities choose to talk about and engage with political violence. To develop this insight, we turn to the state media's coverage of attacks to illustrate how Chinese authorities weigh domestic and international priorities when addressing Uyghur-initiated violence. We show that while transparency can promote the Party's long-term objectives (such as painting the mistreatment of Uyghurs as a necessary byproduct of counterterrorism efforts) officials nearly always put domestic political stability first. This reveals the extent to which Chinese policy is, and will likely remain, deeply conservative and risk-averse on these issues.

Chapter 4 documents and analyzes China's domestic security policies in Xinjiang. We identify the evolving mix of forces involved in China's security efforts in Xinjiang and analyze the historical trends in Xinjiang's security-related expenditures. By juxtaposing the data on expenditures against data regarding levels of violence in the region, we provide a systematic assessment of the feedback loop of violence and repression in Xinjiang. We demonstrate that increased security expenditures are highly inefficient, especially in the long run. Chapter 4 also traces the recent strategic shift in China's policies, away from post-attack securitization and toward the active and forcible promotion of ethnic mingling and "de-extremification" measures. This has escalated into mass internment and cultural genocide. While some attribute this policy reorientation to Beijing's desire for stability, our analysis suggests that it results from competing priorities and deeper institutional changes within the Chinese government.

Chapter 5 focuses on the role of "counterterrorism" in China's foreign policy. China is increasingly militarizing its engagements with regional partners and reframing these engagements as counter-terrorism efforts. We offer the first systemic examination of the strategic considerations that underpin this trend, which has drawn little attention in either academic or policy circles. China leverages joint military counterterrorism exercises to enhance its security forces' capabilities, protect the growing number of Chinese nationals and assets abroad, and build an image as a responsible and constructive stakeholder in the international system. However, these goals tend to be at odds with its desire to avoid being identified as a US-style hegemonic power, to minimize grievances associated with its economic expansion and pursuit of resources abroad, and to thereby avoid becoming the target of international terrorist groups. Empirical analyses of original data on the counterterrorism joint military exercises further establish a theme of cautiousness. China is highly selective in promoting military cooperation in counterterrorism, limiting it to partners with whom there is both substantial investment and a significant domestic terrorism risk.

Chapter 6 concludes the book with a discussion of the long-term implications of China's handling of its Uyghur minority. Just as the

9/11 attacks drove US foreign policy in unexpected directions, so too could political violence within China and the region. Given the US withdrawal from Afghanistan, the complexities of Chinese and American relations with Pakistan, and the increasing presence of Chinese nationals around the globe, it is easy to imagine a seemingly manageable precipitating event leading to outsized effects.

2 | Political Violence in Xinjiang

The deep distrust that prevails between the CCP and the Uyghur population in Xinjiang did not arise spontaneously or suddenly. Rather, it is the culmination of events and policies that can be traced to the very founding of the People's Republic of China (PRC). In this chapter we lay out these policies and the trajectory of the political unrest and violence that followed.

We delineate this cycle of repression and political violence into four phases: rebellion (1949–1958); civil resistance (1977–1989); political violence (1990–2014); and internationalization (2015–).[1] This is an academic artifice, of course, and elements of these phases overlap, but dividing the history in this way clarifies what has changed over time and what remains constant. In the process of tracing the evolution of the region, we introduce the most complete data available on Uyghur-initiated political violence in Xinjiang and beyond, which we draw on throughout the remainder of the volume.

As we noted in the Introduction, the interests that drive this conflict are deeply rooted and largely nonnegotiable – both for Uyghurs and for the CCP. Uyghurs have authentic and deeply seated grievances against a relentless onslaught of repression and assimilationist policies. At the same time, the Chinese state's own interests and strategies leave it little room to provide Uyghurs the type of meaningful autonomy that might relieve tension. The remainder of this chapter will contextualize the conflict in Xinjiang within the political violence literature before delving into each of the four phases of violence in Xinjiang.

---

[1] The period 1959 to 1976 is marked by the two largest nationwide political movements in the history of PRC – the Great Leap Forward and the Cultural Revolution – which suppressed most separatist resistance in Xinjiang.

Contextualizing Repression and Political Violence in Xinjiang

Scholars have long debated the motivations that drive terrorism and political violence around the globe. While arguments continue to rage on the fine details, there is general consensus that unrest is fueled by (1) a lack of effective political representation, combined with (2) the absence of nonviolent outlets for grievances, such as the opportunity to congregate in protest.[2]

While China's scale always sets it apart from other countries, many of the established elements that drive political violence elsewhere are at play in Xinjiang.

As an oppressed minority living under a strong authoritarian regime, Uyghurs clearly lack political representation. Even within the Uyghurs' so-called autonomous region, in 2017 Han Chinese occupied 64 percent of the senior political positions available, according to a report by Uyghur Human Rights Project.[3] Uyghurs, on the other hand, held just 21 percent of the positions.

The underrepresentation of Uyghurs in the military and Party systems is even more pronounced. In 2016, there were thirty-one leadership positions in the two regional military districts, the PLA Xinjiang Military District and the Southern Xinjiang Military District. Uyghurs occupied just two of those posts. Meanwhile, there was only 1 Uyghur among the 110 Party secretary positions at the prefecture and county levels in Xinjiang.[4] Quality data for recent years are lacking, but these trends have almost certainly worsened.

Uyghurs in China fare little better when it comes to alternative outlets for political discontent. For example, Cao and his coauthors find that within Xinjiang, counties with a higher mosque density have historically experienced significantly fewer violent incidents in a given year.[5] They credit the conflict-dampening effect of local religious institutions and their function as an information bridge that allows local people to channel their grievances.[6]

---

[2] See, for example, Crenshaw (1981); Li (2005); Wilson and Piazza (2013); Gaibulloev, Piazza, and Sandler (2017).
[3] Uyghur Human Rights Project (2017).
[4] Uyghur Human Rights Project (2017).   [5] Cao et al. (2018a).
[6] Eubank and Weinberg (1994, 2001); Cao et al. (2018b).

Mosques, however, are themselves under fire by the Chinese government as part of its effort to destroy the Islamic identity of Uyghur and other Muslim communities in Xinjiang. Sixteen thousand mosques in Xinjiang have been either destroyed or damaged by CCP efforts to erase and redefine the region's cultural traditions, according to satellite imagery of the region. That represents 65 percent of all Xinjiang mosques, with most of the damage occurring since 2017.[7]

Only prominent mosques near major tourist destinations – for example, in Kashgar – have largely avoided destruction, but religious services there are carefully curtailed and the buildings have been largely recast as tourist attractions. Thus, even this modest outlet for expression is now essentially nonexistent in the region.

This notion that unrest and grievance can arise from a lack of political outlet is broadly referred to as the "political access" school.[8] There is also a parallel "strategic school" of thought that emphasizes the extent to which the many tools of authoritarianism effectively suppress violence.[9] Strict restrictions on assembly and movement, seamless surveillance systems, and harsh punishments increase the risk and cost of violence. In addition, media censorship and information control can deprive militants of the "oxygen of publicity" they rely on to deliver their message.[10] China offers a case in point for both schools of thought.

The situation in Xinjiang also closely mirrors the hypothesized relationship between economic prosperity and political violence. While cross-national studies find a mixed relationship between violence and poverty, they consistently find that extremism arises among aggrieved groups that are not impoverished in an absolute sense but rather in comparison to other local populations.[11] This is certainly the situation afflicting the Uyghur minority in Xinjiang.

The overall economic numbers for Xinjiang are in the middle of the pack compared to other Chinese provinces and autonomous regions.[12] Owing primarily to its oil reserves, mineral resources, and agriculture,

---

[7] For a detailed map of the destroyed religious sites, see Ruser et al. (2020).

[8] Schmid (1992); Eyerman (1998); Li (2005).

[9] Eyerman (1998).   [10] Nacos (2007).

[11] See, for example, Drakos and Gofas (2006); Bueno de Mesquita (2008).

[12] For a general review of the relationship between economy and terrorism, see Bueno de Mesquita (2008).

Xinjiang ranked between tenth and fourteenth among thirty-one Chinese provinces in terms of GDP per capita throughout the 1990s and early 2000s. It was consistently the most prosperous of the five autonomous regions.[13]

As we will show in Chapter 4, state security measures imposed after the July 5, 2009, Urumqi riot severely interrupted economic life; even so, Xinjiang's gross domestic product per capita remained higher than one-third of all Chinese provinces. It is, however, the *relative* economic deprivation most Uyghurs suffer that fuels their grievances.

Deng Xiaoping reportedly said that the open and reform policy would "let a part of the population get rich first."[14] For a variety of reasons, in Xinjiang, this part of the population has been almost entirely Han rather than Uyghur.[15]

For one, Han Chinese disproportionately live in more urban areas of the Xinjiang Uyghur Autonomous Region (XUAR). Cao's work reveals that, in the 1990s, Xinjiang experienced even more pronounced increases in rural–urban income disparities than the rest of China.[16] In addition, several studies have shown that job segmentation and discrimination exist between ethnicities in Xinjiang, as both state-owned enterprises and private businesses prefer hiring Han over Uyghurs as regular employees.[17] Finally, minorities are paid lower wages across China – and the gap is even wider in the autonomous regions.[18]

This allocation of wealth and resources reflects the Party's preoccupation with Han, rather than Uyghur, discontent. There is a longstanding, and likely well-founded, worry that the security situation in Xinjiang could lead to a mass exodus of Han migrants, as has occurred during and after past periods of unrest. At the same time, grievances among the Han in Xinjiang are much more likely to reach a receptive audience (and thereby undercut CCP legitimacy) in the rest of China through family, friends, and the inexorable creep of social media. The Party guards against these risks by ensuring that Xinjiang remains a land of opportunity for Han migrants, even if it is not so for its longstanding minority populations. This

---

[13] National Bureau of Statistics of China.   [14] Hilton (2012).
[15] Hasmath (2011).   [16] Cao (2010).
[17] Hannum and Xie (1998); Howell and Fan (2011); Maurer-Fazio (2012).
[18] Wu and He (2018).

strategy, however, is coming under increasing pressure as the economy is increasingly burdened by the expanding securitization of the region. In response, authorities have at times slowed or withheld residency permit (*hukou*) transfers for Han Chinese seeking to leave the XUAR.[19]

This is reflective of a larger issue driving the dynamics in Xinjiang. The CCP believes that its legitimacy relies on public approval – and specifically that of Han citizens located in population and economic centers – and it eagerly promotes all credible indications of such support. For instance, the state was quick to cite a July 2020 Chinese public opinion report by the Ash Center at Harvard University, which showed that between 2003 and 2016 "Chinese citizen satisfaction with government has increased virtually across the board."[20]

It might seem odd for an authoritarian state to give such weight to public opinion, but it is part and parcel of longstanding trends both in China and institutionalized autocracies more generally. Institutionalized autocracies are those in which leaders manage the political process through parties or legislatures – that is, those other than military, personalist, and monarchical autocracies.[21] These democratic trappings are not representative or competitive, but by relying on them, autocratic leaders can build support by regularizing the delivery of political rents.[22] The result, however, is that ordinary citizens in these contexts are better positioned to extract policy concessions – in other words, public opinion matters more.

This is clearly the case in China, though the regime has become increasingly personalized under Xi Xinping. In 2008, following then president Hu Jintao's call to "develop a new pattern of public opinion guidance," *People's Daily* established the People's Public Opinion Office to monitor, analyze, and direct public opinion.[23] Since then, data mining and online discourse analysis have become cornerstones in the state's effort to maintain stability. By 2014, more than 800 businesses, with more than two million employees, were monitoring the Internet and airwaves to gauge and shape Chinese public

---

[19] Yang (2019).   [20] Cunningham, Saich, and Turiel (2020).
[21] Brownlee (2007); Gandhi (2008); Geddes, Wright, and Frantz (2014).
[22] Boix and Svolik (2013); Lust-Okar (2005); Reuter and Robertson (2015).
[23] Jia (2019).

opinion.[24] Echoing this theme, in April 2016, when chairing a symposium on cyber security, President Xi (re)emphasized that officials and cadres "must learn to follow the mass line through the internet ... understand what the masses think and hope, collect good ideas and good suggestions, and actively respond to netizens' concerns."[25]

Cultivating positive opinion requires that the CCP utilize more carrots than sticks with the Han population in the region. This typically means generating money and opportunity – or pumping up nationalist sentiments when those two wells run dry.

This focus on Han opinion has driven investment and resources toward that portion of the population of Xinjiang. As a result, the socio-economic inequality between Uyghurs and Hans has grown and has become the most widely cited source of political grievance in the region.[26]

Ironically, these investments show how effective more carrots could actually be. While mining and oil production typically breed conflict in resource-rich regions,[27] Hong and Yang find that areas of Xinjiang with substantial resource production actually have *lower* rates of violence – and they find this relative peace is driven by improved local economic opportunities for Uyghurs rather than by demographic changes or by the increased public security measures associated with resource extraction.[28]

The literature on global contentious politics teaches us that educational inequality also drives ethnic violence. This too appears to extend to China, where ethnic violence increases in regions where a greater portion of Han have completed lower secondary school compared to the minority citizenry.[29] Also, Liu finds that Xinjiang counties with higher local education expenditures tend to experience significantly fewer violent incidents.[30]

For both scholars and policy makers then, the persistence of Uyghur violence should come as no surprise. Xinjiang is but another case that comports with well-established patterns in civil conflict. The long-standing relative deprivation of Uyghurs sustains their grievances and intensifies interethnic tensions. Assimilation efforts, combined with religious and cultural repression, add fuel to this fire. The lack of

---

[24] Creemers (2017).   [25] Thomas (2019).   [26] Fuller and Lipman (2004).
[27] Collier and Hoeffler (2004); Humphreys (2005); Lei and Michaels (2014); Ross (2006).
[28] Hong and Yang (2018).   [29] Cao et al. (2018a).   [30] Liu (2019).

legitimate outlets for these and other grievances eliminates other viable alternatives, leaving violence as one of the few remaining options,
albeit a costly and unproductive one.

Yet, despite persistent and mounting grievances, the frequency and
lethality of Uyghur violence has been comparatively low, particularly
since 2014. The present equilibrium, however, has only emerged in the
last decade and in the presence of levels of state repressive capability
with few equals around the globe.

Phase 1 – Armed Rebellion (1949–1958)

The first wave of contemporary Uyghur resistance arose in the context
of the revolutionary upheaval that accompanied the establishment of the
PRC and the end of the Chinese Civil War. In keeping with the broad
civil conflict that persisted throughout the country in this period, much
of the violence in Xinjiang took the form of full-scale armed rebellion.

The intensity of these Uyghur revolts was among the highest in
the region's post-1949 history, but they were not outside the norm
in postwar China. The number of participants sometimes numbered
in the thousands and battles lasted for months.[31] However, this owes
as much to the early weakness of the regime as to the strength of the
Uyghur uprisings.

The violence in Xinjiang in the first half of the 1950s was part
of an extended period of national consolidation that occurred after
the nominal end of the Chinese Civil War (see Figure 2.1). Across
China, there were 816 armed uprisings aimed at overthrowing the
newly established regime in just the first ten months of 1950.[32] Most
of these insurgencies were led by local warlords, residual members of
the defeated Republic of China Army, or sympathetic militants.

In Northwest China, the major insurgent force – approximately
14,000 Muslim troops – was comprised of former members of the
Republic of China Army under the command of General Ma Bufang,
an ethnic Hui and a prominent warlord who ruled Qinghai Province
during the Republic of China era that preceded the civil war.[33] Ma

---

[31] Bovingdon (2010).
[32] Party History Research Office of the CCP Central Committee (2010).
[33] Ma Bufang served as the representative of the KMT to Egypt from 1950
through 1957, and he then served as the Republic of China's ambassador to

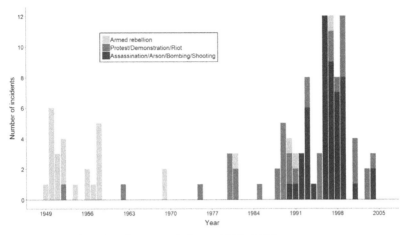

Figure 2.1 Political violence in Xinjiang, 1949–2005
Source: Bovingdon (2010).

announced the start of the Kuomintang Islamic insurgency in 1950 during a visit to Cairo, vowing that "China's 50,000,000 Muslims never will be reconciled to Communist control of the country."[34]

Within Xinjiang, Ma's forces often fought along with militants led by less prominent local leaders on the Kuomintang (KMT) payroll. Two leaders in the Xinjiang insurgency were of particular note. Osman Batur was a Kazak warlord who had fought for regional autonomy with support from a rotating cast of sponsors, including the Soviet Union, Mongolia, and the United States. The other was Yulbars Khan, a Uyghur general affiliated with the KMT.[35] After battles in Changji, Qitai, Hami, and Yiwu, these uprisings were eventually put down by the new Communist government following the arrest and then execution of Osman in 1951.[36] Yulbars, on the other hand, fled to Taiwan and was later appointed by the KMT government as the governor of Xinjiang *in absentia* – a titular position he held until his death in 1971.[37]

By the mid-1950s the Communist Party had largely stabilized northern Xinjiang, but violence did not stop entirely. Another

Saudi Arabia until 1961. He remained in Saudi Arabia until his death in 1975 at age 72 (Hutchings 2001).
[34] The Montreal Gazette (1950).
[35] Forbes and Forbes (1986); Benson (1988); Jacobs (2010).
[36] Jacobs (2010).   [37] Forbes and Forbes (1986).

organization, dubbed the Emin Group, quietly emerged in southern Xinjiang, where the population was (and remains to this day) more densely ethnically Uyghur.[38] The Emin Group formed a provisional government and launched a brief rebellion by raiding a prison camp in Karakash on December 31, 1954. After killing eight people and seizing weapons, the group moved on to nearby towns, including Khotan and Kashgar.[39]

According to Chinese internal documents, in the two years during which the Emin Group was active, there were eight major disturbances in the Khotan area, of which five were successfully thwarted.[40] While the numbers involved in these uprisings in southern Xinjiang were relatively small compared to the KMT-backed battles, their secessionist agenda represented a challenge to Beijing.[41]

This first phase of violence faded as the CCP finally established firm control across the country in the late 1950s. Once the country and regime were stabilized, Uyghurs actually fared somewhat better than many other minorities in the early years of the PRC, owing primarily to their distance from Beijing.[42] Many Uyghurs welcomed some early Party policies – particularly land reforms that helped small local farmers gain more economic control and the placement of Uyghurs in decision-making roles in local government.[43]

There were also clear political efforts to signal to potentially restive Uyghurs that their concerns were heard. Mao Zedong, for example, famously sought to reassure ethnic minorities in his 1956 speech, *On the Ten Major Relationships*, emphasizing his opposition to Han chauvinism. "Local-nationality chauvinism must [also] be opposed, but generally that is not where our emphasis lies," he said.[44]

This relatively benevolent guiding principle – termed "prudent and steady development" (*shenzhong wenjin*) – did not last long. The Great Leap Forward (1958–1962) was slow to spread to Xinjiang, but

---

[38] Dillon (2018).   [39] Dillon (2018: 36).   [40] Zhang (2003).
[41] The KMT-backed uprisings in early 1950s were mostly led by nonsecessionist ethnic leaders who were loyal to the Republic of China. Muhammed Emin Bughra, after whom the Emin Group was named, worked for the Republic of China as well. However, he fled to Turkey after 1949 and became more pro-independence. In 1954, Emin and other exiled Uyghur leaders tried to persuade the KMT government in Taiwan to drop its claims to Xinjiang, but the demand was rejected (Ismail and Ismail 1960).
[42] Zhao (2010: 43).   [43] Thum (2018).   [44] Mao (1956).

when it did it brought with it a much stronger emphasis on assimilation, including attempts to banish religion. This movement, coupled with deteriorating economic conditions, ignited discontent among Uyghurs, culminating in the exodus of over 60,000 to Kazakhstan in 1962.[45] The deepening of the Sino-Soviet split exacerbated tension and mistrust, particularly as Moscow incited minority unrest in Xinjiang in order to weaken China's position.[46]

Herein lie early roots of the CCP's deep and longstanding (but usually mistaken in the present day) suspicion that grievances among Uyghurs in Xinjiang are the product of outside agitators rather than legitimate domestic concerns arising from Party policy. The target of those accusations has shifted over time from the USSR to the United States, the members of the Uyghur diaspora, al-Qaeda, and the Islamic State, but it is a consistent theme in Party rhetoric.[47] By emphasizing the role of outside agitators, the CCP positions itself as the sole legitimate voice within the country while delegitimizing dissent and deflecting attention from human rights abuses.

The political turmoil of the late 1950s and early 1960s proved minor in comparison to the upheavals of the Cultural Revolution (1966–1976), which sought to purge any remnants of capitalist and traditional elements from Chinese society. In Xinjiang, this manifested as repression against the increasingly vibrant Uyghur nationalist movements arising at the time.[48] The anti-rightist and anti-nationalist campaigns within the Cultural Revolution ultimately purged many Uyghur and even some Han cadres who were labeled as retaining pro-Soviet sympathies.[49]

The Xinjiang region was, however, of increasing strategic importance. This led the central authorities to be less tolerant of the resulting chaos than they were in some other regions of the country. As the factional battles between radical Red Guards and Party chief Wang

---

[45] McMillen (1984: 571). According to Bovingdon (2010: 51), the Sino-Soviet split played an important role in this event as the radio propaganda from the Soviet side kept advertising far superior living conditions and Soviet consular officials helped distribute travel papers.

[46] Clarke (2015: 246).   [47] Barbour and Jones (2013).

[48] Burgeoning nationalist sentiment was arising around the globe at the time as intellectuals were denouncing colonialism and promoting states' rights to self-determination.

[49] Thum (2018).

Enmao dragged on, the central authorities feared that the unrest might threaten the nuclear test center at Lop Nur and invite further Soviet meddling. In response, they placed the region under direct military control.[50]

Xinjiang quickly transformed into a heavily securitized zone where publicly recognizable manifestations of Islam – such as Islamic schooling, religious texts, and even mosques – were largely suppressed.[51] As in nearly every other region in China during that period, there was little room for ideologies that even slightly diverged from Maoist thought, let alone appeals for greater ethnic autonomy. However, Xinjiang was unique (with the possible exception of Tibet) in the extent of direct militarization. This legacy carries forward to this day in the form of the security policies that we detail in Chapter 4.

The repression and turbulence of the Maoist years suppressed most separatist violence in Xinjiang, and this is reflected in the data in Figure 2.1. However, the abuses of the Great Leap Forward and Cultural Revolution only exacerbated the underlying grievances of the population, causing pressure to grow. Once the system opened up, even marginally, these grievances bubbled to the surface. Notably, however, this occurred alongside the emergence of outlets for some political expression, which moderated the level of violence.

There are clear parallels to the present moment of high repression and cultural chauvinism in Xinjiang. An equally virulent variant of these policies occurred during the Cultural Revolution but did not stamp out Uyghur identity or aspirations.

Phase 2 – Civil Resistance (1977–1989)

After Mao's death in 1976, Deng Xiaoping's rise to power ushered in the open-and-reform era in China. However, unlike much of the rest of China, the end of the ten-year catastrophe that was the Cultural

---

[50] McMillen (1984: 571). For a more general discussion of how PLA troops were dispatched to guard important military installments during the Cultural Revolution, see Wang (2021).

[51] Thum (2018). To some extent, the radical cultural policies became the only common ground for Hans who belonged to different political factions during this period.

Revolution – and the partial opening of society that followed – did not bring immediate improvement to local conditions in Xinjiang.

The region's weak leadership, heavy military and security presence, remoteness, harsh environmental conditions, and longstanding under-development all conspired against its economic success.[52] The over-all situation in Xinjiang only began to improve in mid-1981 after the return of Wang Enmao, who had served as XUAR Party chief before the Cultural Revolution.[53] Wang reimplemented policies that gradu-ally increased agricultural and industrial production and somewhat ameliorated interethnic tensions.[54] The normalization of relations with the United States added an additional layer of stability, in part because it led to the 1980 establishment of a jointly operated electronic intelligence-gathering station in Xinjiang to monitor Soviet missile tests.[55]

Loosened social controls, however, were not accompanied by any meaningful attempt to address the ethnic grievances that had been festering in the region. This contributed to large-scale protests in 1980 and 1981 and to the start of a second phase of Uyghur resistance characterized by civil disobedience.[56] In this regard, Xinjiang again reflected broader trends in Chinese society, as there was a parallel explosion in the number of public protests nationwide during this period. The sudden end of the Cultural Revolution and the unexpected political opening unleashed pent-up demand for rights and political participation, especially among intellectuals and students. A growing number of Chinese citizens began to adopt what O'Brien refers to as a semi-institutionalized "rightful resistance," including reliance on peti-tions and the legal system to express grievances.[57] When these efforts failed, people turned to more aggressive approaches such as sit-ins, marches, and hunger strikes.[58]

---

[52] McMillen (1984).

[53] Wang Enmao was the first Party chief of the civilian XUAR government. His rule of Xinjiang was branded a "revisionist independent kingdom" by radical leftists during the Cultural Revolution, and he was removed from the position in 1969 (McMillen 1984).

[54] McMillen (1984: 582).   [55] Taubman (1981).

[56] For a detailed documentation of these events, see the appendix in Bovingdon (2010). This period also marked a surge in the number of demonstrations and petitions by resettled Han youths who demanded to return home.

[57] O'Brien (1996).   [58] O'Brien and Li (2006); Pils (2006).

While civil resistance was increasingly widespread across China in this period, Uyghurs in Xinjiang had distinct and specific complaints. Whereas governmental corruption and economic underdevelopment were the main issues elsewhere, Uyghurs disproportionately protested "the system of autonomy, nuclear weapons testing, Han migration, family-planning policies, and discrimination against Uyghurs or Muslims."[59]

But the tools of "rightful resistance" available to Han Chinese in this period, such as petitioning the government, were often less tolerated when employed by Uyghurs, thus forcing the aggrieved in Xinjiang toward more confrontational forms of civil resistance.

Uyghurs' resistance in this period differed from that of the prior phase of open armed rebellion in four significant ways, all of which comport with the broader literature on repression and political violence.

First, the level of violence and its lethality were considerably lower in the second phase. A 1950s government campaign against "bandits" substantially reduced access to lethal weapons and brought an end to the first phase of violence.[60] As a result, even the most violent riots in this second period were mostly limited to sticks, knives, axes, and farm tools.

Second, popular participation increased, as is typical of mass movements.[61] While rebellions in the first phase were mostly fought by former regular forces and paramilitaries, the vast majority of demonstrators in this second wave were ordinary people, ranging from peasants to students. As an internal CCP document described it, "In the [thirty] years between 1949 and 1979, almost no demonstration was held by the Xinjiang minority students in Xinjiang, but after 1980, student demonstrations have broken out one after another."[62]

Third, riots and protests in this period were generally spontaneous responses to official provocations.[63] For example, on April 9, 1980,

---

[59] Bovingdon (2010: 123).
[60] In CCP parlance, "bandits" refers to any counterrevolutionary or anti-regime forces. In the context of Xinjiang, the term was usually used to describe Osman and his followers.
[61] Chenoweth and Stephan (2011).   [62] Zhang (2003).
[63] Bovingdon (2010: 123) argues that these protests were not completely spontaneous and that "there was evidence of coordination of both the content and the timing of demonstrations."

in response to the killing of a Uyghur in custody by a public security officer, Uyghurs stormed the jail and staged a protest that rapidly escalated to about 3,000 people demanding that ethnic Han leave Xinjiang.[64]

Fourth, while most of the early armed rebellions were fought in relatively remote areas of Xinjiang, protests in this period were centered in cities and spread to other provinces in China – much to the alarm of authorities. In December 1985, for example, demonstrations that initially broke out in Urumqi, Khotan, and Aksu spread to major Chinese cities such as Nanjing, Beijing, and Shanghai, where more than 2,000 university students participated and chanted separatist slogans.[65]

These developments suggest that grievances among Uyghur communities and their desire for greater autonomy did not fade over forty years of suppression. If anything, they had become more pervasive.

And again, the legacy of this period carries forward to the present – this mass civil resistance is etched in the memories of CCP decision-makers as a possible consequence of state permissiveness. The idiom "If you give an inch, they will take a mile" comes to English from the Chinese – and it certainly applies to CCP thinking on Xinjiang.

Phase 3 – The Escalation of Violence (1990–2014)

The fall of the Soviet Union and the resulting independence of its Central Asian republics emboldened the nascent Uyghur nationalist movement but also reduced the Chinese authorities' tolerance for open expressions of discontent. The sudden emergence of independent Turkic states on the periphery of Xinjiang raised hopes among the Uyghur minority.[66] In the minds of many, if the mighty Soviet Union could collapse, then it only stood to reason that comparatively weak and poor China was also on the wrong side of history. This supposition was, of course, badly mistaken.

For their part, CCP authorities were categorically unwilling to acquiesce to Uyghur nationalists' escalating demands, even in part. Lessons drawn from both the Soviet breakup and the Tiananmen Square protests of 1989 led to a hard line against any increase in autonomy, not

---

[64] McMillen (1984: 575).   [65] Bovingdon (2010: Appendix 179).
[66] Gladney (2004a: 108–109); Holdstock (2015).

to mention independence.[67] This confluence of heightened expectations and increased state rigidity greatly increased tensions and forced the CCP toward much greater reliance on enforcement, surveillance, and repression to maintain control over the region.

Again, this legacy extends to the present in the overbearing police presence and cultural repression that are now the norm in Xinjiang. The present status quo – simmering tension punctuated by sporadic violence – is the direct consequence of the Uyghurs' dashed hopes and grievances that continue to mount.

Following the Chinese government's brutal repression of the 1989 student protests in Tiananmen and the end of the Cold War, the CCP adopted a more hardline approach to its domestic affairs, particularly in the minority regions. This largely closed the door to the sort of large-scale civil protest that had prevailed in the prior decade. With mass assembly increasingly off the table as an outlet for rising nationalist sentiments, resistance shifted to low-scale violence perpetrated by a much smaller but far more militant subset of the population.

The transition from civil resistance of the second phase to the violence of the third phase was gradual, but a seminal moment came on April 5, 1990, in Baren, a rural township in Akto County, when Zeydin Yusup, the founder and head of the East Turkestan Islamic Movement, purportedly led more than 200 men in a protest. The situation quickly devolved into a riot and an assault on CCP offices. According to official accounts, six policemen were killed, thirteen were wounded, and five were captured. Yusup was reportedly among those killed in the violence.

Some official reports asserted that the attack was supported by Afghan-trained militias.[68] There is, however, little independent evidence outside of government accounts to corroborate any aspect of the incident.

In response to the violence, the CCP leadership quickly dispatched military and paramilitary forces to the area. The conflict ended with a confrontation on April 10 that resulted in the deaths of 23 people and the capture of 232 Uyghur fighters.[69] The level of violence clearly alarmed Chinese authorities, leading the XUAR People's Congress to implement tighter regulations governing protests.[70]

---

[67] Gladney (2004b: 376); Rudelson and Jankowiak (2004: 307–308).
[68] Wayne (2007: 81); Gunaratna (2002).
[69] Guo (2015a: 45).   [70] Bovingdon (2010: 125).

This, however, served only to drive most resistance underground.[71] From that point forward, the resistance came mostly in the form of small-scale attacks.

This shift to small-scale attacks ushered in the contemporary mode of political violence in the region. To properly understand it, we developed comprehensive data on all known incidents of Uyghur-initiated violence in China from 1990 to 2014.[72] Figure 2.2, which graphs these data, indicates two distinct campaigns within this phase of violence. The first arose around the initial push for autonomy after the fall of the USSR and reached its peak in 1997 when 15 attacks resulted in 148 casualties. The lead-up to the 2008 Beijing Olympics marked the beginning of the second campaign, which culminated in 2014 with 28 incidents that killed 164 people and injured 426 others. Figure 2.2 also indicates that, in line with global trends, attacks shifted over time toward increased civilian targeting.[73]

Figure 2.3 shows the average casualties from the Uyghur-initiated attacks in that period. Congruent with global trends and the growing sophistication of Uyghur militant organizations, the lethality of this violence increased through 2014.[74] The difference amounts to an average of three more deaths and eight more injuries per attack. However, while deaths and injuries did increase, they remained relatively low when compared to global averages. This is primarily because weapons and tactics were notably crude; knives and simple bombs account for approximately 39 percent and 42 percent of all these attacks, respectively. Thus, while violence in the period escalated, it never remotely approached the levels seen in global hotspots.

---

[71] It is worth noting, however, that there were also several large-scale riots during this period, including in Ghulja in 1997 and Urumqi in 2009.

[72] We collect our data from four main sources: (1) widely used databases on terrorism, such as the Global Terrorism Database (GTD), the RAND Database of Worldwide Terrorism Incidents, and Minorities at Risk Organizational Behavior; (2) English-language news media, such as the *New York Times*, *Reuters*, and *Radio Free Asia*; (3) widely used and recognized non-state-run Chinese websites, such as *Sina*, *Tencent*, *ifeng*, and *Sohu*; and (4) secondary data from Bovingdon (2010), Reed and Raschke (2010), and Cao et al. (2018a). Details about data collection and coding are available in the appendix of this chapter.

[73] Civilian targets now make up the majority of global attacks (LaFree, Dugan, and Miller 2014). However, government targets remain in the majority in East Asia and Central Asia.

[74] Potter (2013).

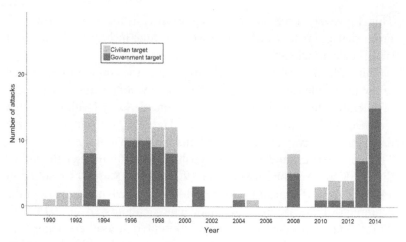

Figure 2.2 Uyghur-initiated violent incidents, 1990–2014

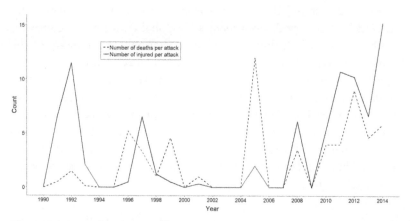

Figure 2.3 Casualties per attack, 1990–2014

Figure 2.4 plots variation in weapons and tactics over time. Counter-intuitively, the first surge of violence in Phase 3 (1990–2001) featured somewhat more advanced weapons. Among the total of seventy-six incidents in the first wave, bombs or explosive devices were used thirty-five times, knives seventeen times, guns eleven times, incendiary devices four times, and poison once.

In the second surge, knives were used thirty-seven times in sixty-one attacks, while bombs or explosive devices were used twenty-three times,

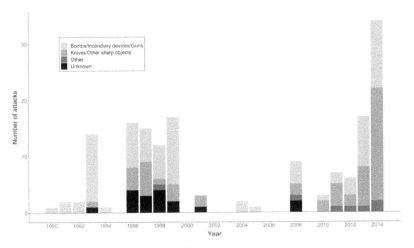

Figure 2.4 Weapons and tactics, 1990–2014

incendiary devices ten times, and guns only once. This change reflects the government's tightened grip on the region – particularly the crackdown on the widespread use of uncontrolled explosives in small-scale mining and demolition – which made access to any lethal weapons or materials more difficult.

As we will detail in Chapter 4, it was the intensity of the violence in the first campaign in the 1990s that led Beijing to elevate Xinjiang's stability to a national-level issue.[75] This likely had a substantial impact on the operational capability of any militant organizations operating in the region, reducing their capacity to plan, support, and coordinate violence.

At the same time, the six vehicle-ramming attacks that emerged in the second campaign, including the high-profile 2013 Tiananmen attack, indicate that perpetrators were also strategically adjusting their tactics in response to the government's countermeasures. Vehicles have become a common weapon in other regions (prominently in Europe around 2016–2017) where state control and policing tactics have limited access to guns and explosives and where militant organizations are under duress.

[75] Li (2018).

Cars can be nearly as deadly as bombs in crowded spaces and their ubiquity and centrality to daily life make it nearly impossible to impose effective countermeasures. Notably, this approach to violence requires little or no preplanning or collaboration. In Europe, it was the tactic of choice for lone wolves *inspired* by Islamic State and an immediate consequence of the *decline* of that organization. Facing setbacks in Syria that degraded its organizational capacity, Islamic State leaders resorted to exhorting the aggrieved to launch individual, low-tech attacks rather than supporting them in more complex and coordinated violence or drawing them into the organization itself. In other words, the fact that vehicular attacks in China escalated in this period is likely an indication that the state's repression was working – as domestic militant organizations falter, it becomes more difficult to carry out coordinated violence.

Although political exclusion and socioeconomic inequality are plausible sources of grievances that could incentivize violence in the first place, these have been consistent features of the Uyghur experience under CCP rule. As such they are incomplete explanations for the ebb and flow of violence over time, revealed in Figures 2.2–2.4. The variation reveals an underappreciated dynamic in this struggle – the extent to which discontented Uyghurs have, at times, timed violence to maximize engagement with international audiences, thereby delegitimizing the CCP.

Beginning in the 1990s, many Uyghur activists both inside Xinjiang and in the diaspora, began to target their appeals more directly toward international audiences to call for outside intervention. There is some evidence to suggest that Uyghur militants have historically initiated attacks at moments when China's international position was weak or vulnerable. For example, as China anticipated the return of Hong Kong in the spring of 1997, there was widespread belief among Uyghurs in Xinjiang that "despite the constant barrage of triumphal messages emanating from Beijing and the gigantic clock ticking down the seconds in Tiananmen Square, Britain would not relinquish its colony without a fight [...] Xinjiang was rife with rumors that Uyghur organizations were preparing to take advantage of the ensuing chaos to stage a military uprising."[76] The North Atlantic Treaty Organization

[76] Bovingdon (2010: 92).

(NATO) intervention in Kosovo offers another such example. Shortly after the 1999 US bombing of the Chinese embassy in Belgrade, a group of Uyghurs attacked a Public Security Bureau in Lop County, Xinjiang, shouting "We'll invite the US and NATO to come, and we'll blow up Xinjiang."[77]

The series of attacks in 2008 as well as efforts by Uyghur and Tibetan activists abroad to disrupt the Olympic torch relay adhere to this same logic of using violence to engage international audiences.[78] As the world's enthusiasm for the Beijing Olympic Games mounted, Uyghur activists sought to make their voices heard and undercut CCP messaging. In a public invitation to the "Freedom Torch Relay" demonstration scheduled for June 25, 2008, in Brussels, the exiled World Uyghur Congress wrote:

Chinese authorities are trying to use this [torch relay] event to conceal the widespread discontentment of Uyghurs with the totalitarian Chinese regime by creating a false atmosphere of [a] 'harmonious society' and to mislead the world community about continued, massive and systematic violations of human rights in East Turkestan.[79]

To systematically examine the relationship between international conditions and Uyghur violence in this period, we used machine-coded events data from the Integrated Crisis Early Warning System (ICEWS) to model the relationship between the timing of militant violence and the international diplomatic environment facing China.[80] We extracted all international events in which China was a target, each of which is assigned an "intensity score" by the ICEWS project. These range from –10 to 10, with lower values indicating more hostile interactions and higher values indicating more cooperative interactions.[81] We then assessed the favorability of China's international diplomatic position (*International Condition*) by taking the monthly average value of the intensity scores of all these events.[82]

---

[77] Bovingdon (2010: 93).   [78] Bennhold and Rosenthal (2008).

[79] World Uyghur Congress (2008).

[80] Boschee et al. (2018). Since the ICEWS data only go back to 1995, our analysis is based on a truncated 1995–2014 sample.

[81] The intensity score, which is similar to the Goldstein Conflict–Cooperation Scale (Goldstein 1992), measures the related intensity of the event type, as defined by the CAMEO (Conflict and Mediation Event Observations) coding scheme. For more detail, see Gerner et al. (2002).

[82] Mattes and Rodriguez (2014) adopt a similar strategy to measure the degree of cooperation between two states using the 10 Million International Dyadic

We controlled for other factors that may affect the probability and intensity of violence, including China's *Domestic Condition* (similarly calculated by assigning intensity scores to domestic events in the ICEWS dataset); a dummy variable indicating whether a given month represented a *Politically Sensitive Month*; the number of *Worldwide Terrorist Attacks* in a given month; and yearly measures of *Xinjiang's Public Security Expenditure, Education Expenditure*, and *GDP*.[83]

Table 2.1 presents the results from a series of models with the number of monthly violent incidents as the dependent variable.[84] The results show a statistically significant negative relationship between the number of attacks in a given month and the tenor of China's international environment in the previous month. This pattern suggests that attacks from Uyghur militants coincided with external pressures on Beijing; in other words, they are more likely to initiate violence when the Chinese government is already facing international headwinds (Figure 2.5).

The results also indicate that violence is more likely to occur when China's domestic conditions improve (Models 3, 5, and 6). This pattern is congruent with evidence from other studies finding that Chinese authorities tend to employ a preemptive repression strategy against domestic unrest. For instance, Truex shows that periods shortly preceding or during politically salient moments in China are usually associated with spikes in dissident detentions.[85] Similarly, Carter and Carter find that anniversaries of failed prodemocracy movements represent a salient focal moment in China that are accompanied by nearly 30 percent more protests than other days, and these protests are also significantly more likely to be repressed by the government.[86]

Chinese officials have consistently taken the possibility that Xinjiang could become an avenue for foreign interference very seriously – arguably too seriously. An internal CCP article circulated during the NATO

Events data. We include one-month and two-month lags in the model to account for temporal correlation.

[83] Details regarding the data sources of these additional variables are available in the appendix of this chapter.

[84] These are negative binomial models, which are most appropriate for dependent variables that are counts – as is the case here. In the appendix of this chapter, we explore alternative model specifications to examine the robustness of the finding. The pattern revealed here still holds when we employ vector autoregression (VAR) models to handle temporal correlation.

[85] Truex (2019).   [86] Carter and Carter (2022).

Table 2.1 *The timing of violence, 1995–2014*

	Negative binomial model					
	(1)	(2)	(3)	(4)	(5)	(6)
International Condition	−0.337*	−0.116	0.115	−0.144	0.070	0.060
	(0.177)	(0.176)	(0.168)	(0.166)	(0.178)	(0.163)
International Condition (one month lag)	−0.716***	−0.453***	−0.263**	−0.391***	−0.243**	−0.261**
	(0.139)	(0.132)	(0.111)	(0.115)	(0.109)	(0.105)
International Condition (two months lag)	−0.302**	−0.249***	−0.090	−0.113	−0.061	−0.069
	(0.131)	(0.074)	(0.078)	(0.111)	(0.086)	(0.074)
Domestic Condition		0.149	0.306**		0.338*	0.361**
		(0.163)	(0.154)		(0.176)	(0.165)
Domestic Condition (one month lag)		0.145	0.236**		0.280***	0.266**
		(0.106)	(0.120)		(0.095)	(0.112)
Domestic Condition (two months lag)		0.020	0.116		0.124	0.136
		(0.094)	(0.088)		(0.093)	(0.096)
Politically Sensitive Month		0.079	0.182		0.173	0.168
		(0.339)	(0.307)		(0.310)	(0.296)
Worldwide Terrorist Attacks		0.001*	0.002***		0.001**	0.001
		(0.0004)	(0.001)		(0.001)	(0.001)
Xinjiang Public Security Expenditure (one-year lag)			−2.124			−2.911
			(2.576)			(2.520)
Xinjiang Education Expenditure (one-year lag)			−0.068			0.210
			(2.132)			(1.898)

Table 2.1 (*cont.*)

	Negative binomial model					
	(1)	(2)	(3)	(4)	(5)	(6)
Xinjiang GDP (one-year lag)			2.025			3.839
			(3.319)			(3.600)
Constant	2.210**	0.415	10.265*	0.832	-0.377	3.645
	(0.937)	(0.723)	(5.331)	(0.685)	(0.604)	(6.233)
Presidency-fixed Effect	No	No	No	Yes	Yes	Yes
Observations	238	238	238	238	238	238
Log Likelihood	-216.613	-205.242	-190.472	-200.762	-188.390	-186.338
Akaike Inf. Crit.	441.226	428.485	404.945	413.523	398.779	400.675

Note: Robust standard errors clustered on years are in parentheses. *p<0.1; **p<0.05; ***p<0.01

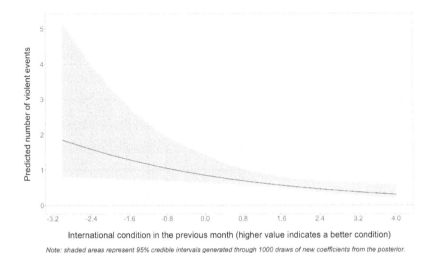

Figure 2.5 The relationship between violence and the international environment

operation in Kosovo put this concern in explicit terms. "We believe that the things that happen today in Kosovo might very possibly occur in Xinjiang," the document reads.[87] The CCP saw, and continues to see, absolute control in Xinjiang as necessary to preserve stability and guarantee its continued future rule of the region, a point we will return to in Chapter 4.

An important outstanding question is the extent to which this third-phase turn to violence was primarily the product of organizations or aggrieved individuals. As a matter of policy, the CCP seeks to muster international support for its Xinjiang policies by playing up the role of organizations, their capacity, and their links to major international terrorist groups such as al-Qaeda. CCP claims regarding the strength of Uyghur militant organizations past and present are cartoonishly overwrought, but organizations have existed and have, at times, played a meaningful role in the struggle. Thus, an important element of this third period of violence was the reemergence of these militant organizations as a feature of the conflict. While these organizations have been relatively weak and subject to extensive state countermeasures, their emergence presented a substantial challenge to the CCP even when their capacity for actual violence was low and their activity was primarily rhetorical.

[87] Bovingdon (2010: 162).

That said, after nearly a decade of ever-tightening repression, there is no credible evidence of continued militant organizational capacity within China. There is, however, evidence that this capacity existed relatively recently and that the remnants of these organizations moved abroad and retained interests in the struggle in China.

Chief among these organizations is the Turkestan Islamic Party (TIP). While there is some disagreement among observers over the origins of TIP, evidence suggests that the group is the current manifestation of the aforementioned East Turkestan Islamic Movement (ETIM).[88] However, this was more about branding than a smooth transition with continuous leadership of a single organization. TIP seemingly took up both the ETIM name and the leading position in the Uyghur militant hierarchy after the prior iteration of ETIM (which was always a relatively weak organization) had been largely disbanded due to extended pressure and loss of leadership.[89] Governments and media outlets use both names to describe the activities of a single organization, but the US State Department reported in 2019 that there is "a lack of independent evidence" that a group calling itself ETIM is still active.

Let's rewind a bit to explain these organizations' backstories, which remain somewhat murky. While ETIM claimed roots in organizations dating to the 1940s, it seems to have been established in its more recent manifestation around 1997 by Hasan Mahsum, who was trained in an Islamic school by Abdul Hakeem during the relative freedom of the Deng reform period. Hakeem had been active in the first wave of violence in the 1950s.[90]

As it was for many of the central figures of the violence in the third phase that gripped Xinjiang beginning in 1990, the Baren rebellion was a formative experience for Mahsum. He was jailed for a year after Baren and the experience seems to have radicalized him further. This is a common story. In this period, students, militants, and innocents were often jailed together in close quarters with little supervision for long periods of time, leading to radicalization and new networks. After a series of false starts, Mahsum was able to connect with both al-Qaeda and the Taliban, which appear to have provided only modest

---

[88] Vagneur-Jones (2017).   [89] Clayton (2020).   [90] Reed and Raschke (2010).

resources and allowed his ragtag group of ETIM militants to operate in Afghanistan.[91]

ETIM's demands centered on an independent, fundamentalist Muslim state for Uyghurs in northwest China. This was, however, a notably small and weak organization with limited capacity for, or engagement in, actual violence.

China blamed ETIM for over 200 attacks between 1990 and 2001, though this number is highly suspect and almost certainly driven by political motivations. The United States, for its part, designated ETIM on its Terrorist Exclusion List (though not on the more significant Foreign Terrorist Organizations List) in 2002 – based ostensibly on its ties with al-Qaeda but more immediately on the United States' desire to curry favor with China in order to gain its acquiescence in the war on terror.[92]

Mahsum was killed by Pakistani troops in 2003 during a raid on a suspected al-Qaeda hideout near the Afghanistan border.[93] While the circumstances of his death imply linkages to al-Qaeda, it also demonstrated the organization's underlying weakness and lack of resiliency. Decapitation led ETIM into a period of dormancy through 2007. At some point in this period (accounts differ as to when), Abdul Haq took the reins of what was left of the organization and its legacy and has been referred to since as the leader of ETIM, which evolved into TIP.[94]

There is some evidence to suggest that ETIM, to the limited extent that it was ever operationally capable, had fully lost that capacity and its organizational structure by 2007 – and thus ceased to exist. In this interpretation, Abdul Haq's resurrection of the organization and rebranding as TIP was more about making a claim to legacy, and the legitimacy that might accompany it, rather than any kind of organizational continuity. There is general agreement, however, that the organization was not functioning in a meaningful way in the period between Mahsum's death and the emergence of TIP in 2007 under Abdul Haq.

In either case, TIP began to make its renewed presence known in the runup to the Beijing Olympics in 2008. Abdul Haq ordered several

---

[91] Reed and Raschke (2010).
[92] The State Department later removed the organization from the list.
[93] Xu, Fletcher, and Bajoria (2014).
[94] Abdul Haq was believed to have been killed in a US drone strike in North Waziristan in 2010, but he reemerged in 2014 (Roggio 2015).

attacks on the games – some of these were successful and disruptive, but police arrested most of the TIP operatives who were sent to China for these missions before they were able to execute attacks.[95] For the most part, however, TIP was active and excelled in communication and propaganda rather than operations.

For example, shortly following the 2009 Urumqi riots Abdul Haq released a widely circulated video exhorting followers to target the Chinese "both at home and abroad." "Their embassies, consulates, centers, and gathering places should be targeted. Their men should be killed and captured to seek the release of our brothers who are jailed in Eastern Turkistan," Haq said in the video.[96]

TIP claimed responsibility for several subsequent attacks, but the veracity of many of these claims is questionable – underlining the limited capability of the organization, even at its prime. As Roberts describes it, TIP's forte was in rhetoric and credit-claiming (particularly in the form of videos), rather than in orchestrating violence.[97]

Rhetoric and credit-claiming should not be dismissed as inconsequential. The former can foment individual violence, which can be particularly important when an actual in-country organizational presence is rendered impossible by state countermeasures, as is the case in Xinjiang. Islamic State and al-Qaeda videos have played an equivalent role in the West. Claiming credit, even when none is due, can add legitimacy and an organizational veneer to the sporadic violence committed by or on behalf of an aggrieved population. In either case, these actions represented a meaningful challenge to the CCP.

TIP claimed responsibility for two bus bombings in Kunming and another bombing in Shanghai, but Chinese authorities asserted that non-Uyghur citizens were responsible for the attacks. There are a number of high-profile attacks for which Chinese authorities have concurred with TIP's claims of responsibility, including the 2011 mass stabbing in Kashgar that left eighteen people dead;[98] the 2013 suicide car-bombing in Tiananmen Square that killed five people;[99] and the 2014 suitcase bombing at the Urumqi train station that killed

[95] United Nations Security Council (2011).
[96] Reuters (2009): https://ctc.usma.edu/the-seventh-stage-of-terrorism-in-china/ - reference33.
[97] Roberts (2020).   [98] Wines (2011).   [99] Kaiman (2013).

one and injured seventy-nine people.[100] It is worth noting, however, that an odd confluence of mutual interests between these adversaries could lead both TIP and the CCP to claim or attribute an attack even if TIP had no meaningful operational control.

Nevertheless, TIP claimed neither the 2014 bombing of the Urumqi street market nor the 2014 mass stabbing at Kunming train station. While Chinese authorities blamed Uyghur separatists for both attacks, they did not specifically cite TIP. Notably, Kyrgyz authorities blamed a 2016 suicide car bombing of the Chinese embassy in Kyrgyzstan on TIP, but the organization has not publicly claimed responsibility for the attack. Chinese authorities also refrained from making any attribution.[101] The violence attributed to TIP/ETIM faded with the end of the third phase.

As we've noted, China's strong repressive response to organized militant violence quickly killed, captured, or pushed most militants outside of China's borders. This process of displacement helped create a web of relationships linking TIP to organizations throughout the region (see Figure 2.6).[102]

On first inspection, Figure 2.6 seems to present a worrying web of relationships, particularly because it includes highly capable organizations such as al-Qaeda. Strong international alliances with capable organizations are known to contribute to the ability to mount attacks.[103] Relationships lead to the diffusion of tactics and capabilities that can increase the sophistication and lethality of violence.[104]

However, the depth of the ties between Uyghur organizations and better-known militant organizations in the region has been the subject of fierce debate. Chinese authorities have gone to great lengths to link organizations active in Xinjiang – particularly ETIM/TIP – to al-Qaeda.[105] Independent information, however, indicates that prior to 2001, ETIM's relationship with al-Qaeda involved some training and funding but relatively little operational cooperation.[106] Nonetheless,

---

[100] Martina and Rajagopalan (2014).   [101] Dzyubenko (2016).
[102] Data from the Terrorism Knowledge Base, supplemented with open-source academic and media publications.
[103] Horowitz and Potter (2014).   [104] Horowitz, Perkoski, and Potter (2018).
[105] The United States and United Nations also assert that a link exists.
[106] Reed and Raschke (2010).

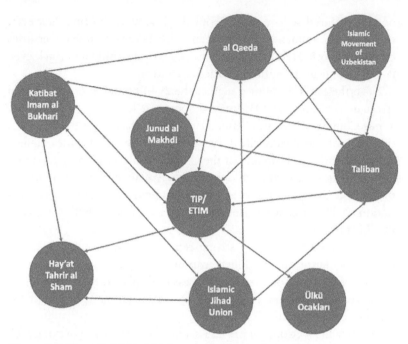

Figure 2.6 Phase 3 (2009–2014) organizational relationships

evidence shows that displaced Uyghurs have joined militant organizations in Central Asia and the Uyghur cause has, at times, become a
rhetorical touchpoint in the global jihadist movement.

There is substantial evidence to indicate that more meaningful
global jihadist relationships, or at least attention to the issue, developed as the situation within Xinjiang deteriorated for Uyghurs. For
example, in October 2009, al-Qaeda's media production unit released
a video of Abu Yahya al-Libi, a high-ranking al-Qaeda leader, giving a
speech entitled "East Turkestan: The Forgotten Wound." In the video,
al-Libi denounces "China's attempts to separate the Muslims from
their faith and obliterate their identity" and claims that it is the "duty
of Muslims today to stand by the side of their wounded and wronged
brothers in East Turkistan."[107]

In the October 2014 edition of al-Qaeda's English-language maga-
zine, *Resurgence*, an article titled "10 Facts about East Turkistan"

[107] Gunaratna et al. (2010).

described Xinjiang as "a longtime independent state that has only recently been brutally colonized by Han Chinese, who are determined to obliterate its Islamic heritage." Another article in the same edition labels China as one of the enemies of the global jihadist movement, stating that "the victory of the Ummah" will be a "deathblow" and a "bitter defeat ... for America, Iran, Russia, China and all those who have fought this war by proxy against Muslims."[108]

While the jihadist community has, for the most part, failed to go beyond rhetoric to actively support the Uyghur "cause against China," Uyghur militants have benefited, at least to a limited degree, from their relationships with established organizations such as al-Qaeda and the Taliban.[109] Uyghurs in Afghanistan were at the periphery of the international jihadist cause prior to 2001, but there is evidence that Uyghur militants subsequently took leadership roles in global jihadist organizations. For example, according to *Karachi Islam*, a jihadist newspaper, Abdul Shakoor Turkistani, a leader within ETIM/TIP, also commanded al-Qaeda forces and training camps in the tribal regions of Pakistan. He was killed in 2012 by a CIA drone.[110]

The fact that the head of ETIM/TIP was also head of al-Qaeda forces in the most volatile region of Pakistan indicates that considerable cross-fertilization among militant organizations had already occurred. Indeed, the 2012 airstrike that killed Shakoor also killed two Tehrik-e-Taliban Pakistani commanders and fifteen other militants of unknown organizational affiliation while they were engaged in a joint training exercise.[111]

Another Uyghur militant, Abdul Haq al-Turkistani, had also been central to al-Qaeda activities and a member of al-Qaeda's *shura majlis* (executive council).[112] The al-Qaeda leadership regarded Abdul Haq so highly that he served as a mediator between rival Taliban factions

[108] Keck (2014).   [109] Azman (2020).
[110] After his death, Shakoor was replaced as the head of ETIM/TIP by Abdullah Mansour, another Chinese national from Xinjiang. Chinese authorities accused Mansour of planning attacks on Chinese nationals in Pakistan and orchestrating the ETIM/TIP campaign prior to the 2008 Olympics. He also claimed prominent attacks in the 2014 campaign on behalf of TIP.
[111] Roggio (2012).
[112] Shakoor is also thought to have been appointed to this body when he was given command of al-Qaeda forces in the region.

and played an integral role in military planning. He attended meetings in Waziristan with Baitullah Mehsud, the primary Taliban official in Pakistan at the time, and participated in discussions among senior Taliban, Haqqani Network, and al-Qaeda leaders regarding the Pakistani military's operation in South Waziristan.[113] Importantly, however, the presence of these leading Uyghur militants within al-Qaeda and other organizations indicates the extent to which, in this period, Uyghur militancy was largely co-opted and subsumed by other causes (rather than the other way around as CCP authorities have asserted).

By cooperating with international jihadist organizations, Uyghur militants gained limited access to training and resources. However, prior to 2011, there was little evidence to suggest that foreign fighters had substantially infiltrated Xinjiang or that those perpetrating attacks in China had been trained abroad. This changed with the July 2011 attacks in Kashgar, a far western city close to the borders with Afghanistan and Pakistan. These attacks were complex and coordinated, involving bombings, hijacking, stabbings, and shootings over the course of two days. Chinese authorities asserted that the captured perpetrators confessed to jihadist motives and membership in ETIM/TIP, which subsequently claimed responsibility. The degree of operational sophistication suggested collaboration with international terrorist organizations. This was confirmed a month later when ETIM/TIP released a video showing one of the attackers training in a Pakistani camp. Subsequently, China issued a list of six ETIM/TIP members accused of engaging in collaborative terrorist activities throughout Asia, including in "a certain South Asian country," a veiled reference to Pakistan.[114]

By 2014, ongoing massive government repression put an end to the third phase of violence, but it again failed to resolve any of the underlying issues that gave rise to the unrest in the first place. Instead, the accelerating cycle of violence and repression that occurred from 2008 to 2014 led to overreliance among CCP officials on harsh securitization as a response to unrest, taught militants the value of

---

[113] Abu Yahya al-Libi, the aforementioned Libyan al-Qaeda leader who called for attacks on China, was also in attendance. Roggio (2011).

[114] The Ministry of Public Security of the PRC (2012). Subsequently, relations between China and Pakistan improved dramatically, particularly in the realm of counterterrorism.

projecting violence onto softer and more visible targets outside Xinjiang, and pushed radicalized militants out of China and into the broader region.

As a consequence, Beijing now finds itself in a position where it takes ever more repression to maintain the appearance of peace in the face of mounting grievances.

Phase 4 – Repression and Internationalization (2014–)

The fourth phase, the one in which China is currently embroiled, is characterized by mass repression and cultural genocide within Xinjiang, accompanied by a growing threat of violence outside China.

During this phase, Uyghur militancy has become more inflected with jihadist and Salafist ideologies, and the resistance is burrowing deeper into global webs of grievances and the organizational linkages they offer. We use the term "internationalization" to characterize this phase, because both sides have sought to frame their efforts as part of a broader struggle for or against Islamic jihad. This internationalization of the conflict threatens Chinese investments and personnel along its Belt and Road Initiative – a pillar of China's development and foreign policy goals in Central Asia.

The internationalization of Uyghur grievances is reflected in the ideological identification of the militant organizations involved. In many regards, this parallels earlier CCP attempts to frame its repression in Xinjiang in the context of the Global War on Terror (GWOT). In much the same way, the remnants of the Uyghur militant movement have attempted to recast their separatist Muslim state agenda in light of the most attractive and powerful militant ideology of the day – Salafist jihadism.

This sort of ideological framing is typical of organizations and movements with intrinsically nationalist motivations. Separatism is almost definitionally a local concern, but organizations commonly seek partnership and support from a wide network of militants in order to bolster their capability and chances of success.[115] Reframing separatist struggles in the ideological zeitgeist of the day facilitates this cooperation because it is these pan-national ideologies that lubricate the

---

[115] Horowitz and Potter (2014); Blair et al. (2022).

friction inherent in international networks. While this remains jihadism in much of the world, in a prior generation it was leftist extremism
that animated alliances on each side of the proxy competition between
the United States and the Soviet Union.

While the internationalization of the religious component of the
struggle is new, religion itself has long played a role. This is, in part,
because shared religious identity precedes the emergence of a shared
Uyghur ethnic identity. Xinjiang's geographical location and history
have made Islam a consistent component of Uyghur resistance, but
religion's role has grown and morphed over time with the rise first of
political Islam and then of Salafi jihadism.

The seeds of this evolution can be found in the rebellions of
Phase 1. As the ultimate CCP victory over KMT forces became
more assured, the motivation for resistance shifted to religion and
particularly the notion that Islam was incompatible with communism. For example, in 1952 Osman explicitly established a "religious army."[116] Similarly, fighters and followers of the Emin Group
were also recruited from mosques and religious foundations in
Khotan, Karakash, and Lop, where they took an oath on the Koran
and pledged their support for Islamic rule.[117] The language of Islam
also played a key role in motivating and sustaining the anti-PRC
rebels during the second half of the 1950s. Slogans like "Allah
orders us to fight for religion" and "Communists robbed Muslims'
land, food, minerals, and other property" offered a loosely worn
mantle to help forge common identity.[118] But actual religiosity and
religious practice varied considerably among Xinjiang's Muslim
Uyghur population at that time.

Islam's potential as a political tool increased as the liberal policies
of the Deng reform period allowed increasing numbers of Muslims
across China to go to Mecca for the annual Hajj pilgrimage. This
set the stage for the eventual internationalization of the Uyghur
struggle on a religious dimension.[119] As a consequence of this
travel, more Uyghurs encountered Islam as practiced in the Middle East, particularly Salafism, and brought these more orthodox
strains home with them. Correspondingly, while anti-government

---

[116] Bovingdon (2010: 175).   [117] Dillon (2018: 35).   [118] Zhang (2003).
[119] Fuller and Lipman (2004: 330).

protests in the 1980s often had some religious element, this became ubiquitous in the 1990s.[120] Attempts to internationalize the conflict along this religious dimension only gained more significance as resistance evolved into violence – and this was quickly reflected in the insurgents' rhetoric.

For example, shortly before the 2008 Olympics were held in Beijing, TIP claimed responsibility for a chain of bus bombings in Xinjiang, Yunnan, and Shanghai, characterizing it as "our blessed jihad in Yunnan."[121] Language of this variety quickly became the norm, indicating growing linkages between some Uyghur militants and global Islamist/Salafist discourse.

Despite the growing salience of religious components in Uyghur resistance, it would be misleading to put Uyghur political violence firmly into the category of the "religious wave" of modern terrorism.[122] Although Uyghurs have migrated to Pakistan and Afghanistan in large numbers since the 1990s, most of them fled Xinjiang in hopes of gaining political asylum and avoiding repression in China. Further, only a fraction of Uyghur *militants* opted to join radical Islamist militant groups operating in Central and South Asia. This owes in part to a distinction in their motivations. Rather than being driven by ideology, religious orthodoxy, and deep commitment to Salafism, Uyghur grievances and militancy arise from governmental restrictions on ordinary religious practice and suppression and erasure of Uyghur identity and culture in Xinjiang. This overlaps with religion but is not entirely defined by it.

Perhaps the best description of the current state of Uyghur violence is what Mumford calls "a hybrid model of modern terrorist groups in which religious discourse is used to underline the push for a separatist agenda."[123] Chinese officials implicitly acknowledge this complex

---

[120] Bovingdon (2010: 121).   [121] Charles (2008).

[122] The most widely used explanation of the evolution of modern terrorism is the "four waves" typology introduced by Rapoport (2004): the Anarchist wave (1880–1920), the Anticolonial wave (1920–1960), the New Left wave (1960s–1979), and the Religious wave (1979–). More recently, Kaplan (2010: 1) has argued that a "fifth wave" of modern terrorism has emerged, one that is "particularistic, localistic, and centered on the purification of the nation through perfection of a race or tribal group."

[123] Mumford (2018: 17).

hybridization in references to the desire to stamp out the "three evils" of Uyghur terrorism, separatism, and religious extremism.

For their part, the TIP and other Uyghur militant groups have also internationalized their political concerns. While TIP is not known to have directly carried out any attacks against China between 2015 and 2020, the organization maintained a steady propaganda campaign, producing online letters and videos in Arabic, Uyghur, Mandarin, and Urdu praising the accomplishments of its fighters and criticizing the Chinese, Russian, and Syrian governments.[124]

While several videos involve Abdul Haq encouraging Uyghurs to launch attacks on Chinese targets, others encourage Uyghurs to go abroad to serve as foreign fighters. Other videos celebrate attacks and setbacks in China in terms designed to appeal to the global jihadist movement.[125] For example, in a video released in February 2020, TIP asserted that the outbreak of the coronavirus in China was "punishment from God" for its oppression of Uyghurs. The TIP spokesman claimed the outbreak occurred in China because the government "destroyed their mosques, burned the Qur'an, and raped [their] women." The video closes with a prayer that the virus "be a reason for the destruction of the atheist Chinese state."[126]

At the same time, the Uyghur cause has continued to receive attention from the global jihadist movement. In a 2016 video, al-Qaeda's leader Ayman al-Zawahiri praised TIP fighters for their commitment to global jihad and celebrated the "historical role" of Hasan Mahsum, the founder of ETIM. The "warriors of Islam should be ready to conduct holy war against the atheistic Chinese regime, to liberate [the] west province of Xinjiang from Communist occupants," al-Zawahiri said.[127]

However, despite this support and praise, the TIP leadership has been dissatisfied with the jihadist community's level of attention to the plight of Uyghurs in Xinjiang. In the spring of 2019, Abdul Haq sent a public message that "indicated that he did not think the Uyghurs' cause has received enough attention from jihadists."[128] Haq appealed to the leadership of the Taliban and al-Qaeda, imploring them to offer additional support for the Uyghur cause.

---

[124] Vagneur-Jones (2017).   [125] United Nations Security Council (2011).
[126] Weiss (2020).   [127] Botobekov (2016).   [128] Joscelyn (2019a).

Al-Qaeda quickly responded with a public statement of its own that emphasized its unity with TIP and the Uyghur people, assuring Abdul Haq that "our issue is your issue."[129] However, the message did not contain any promises of future actions against China, and experts have noted that conducting attacks in China would create risks that al-Qaeda would rather avoid.[130] Along similar lines, Stewart has identified a decline in Islamic State references to the plight of Uyghurs in its propaganda.[131] One can only infer the intent behind this decline, but it is plausible that these organizations are judging the risk of provoking an assertive China to be more than they are willing to take on.

As of 2022, most Uyghur militant capability is scattered outside China's borders in Syria, Afghanistan, Pakistan, Kazakhstan, Tajikistan, and Uzbekistan. Evidence suggests that in 2020 most TIP leadership, and approximately 300 fighters, were based in Afghanistan's Badakhshan Province, including Abdul Haq, Abdullah Mansour, Haji Furkan (head of training), and Abu Salam (head of ideology).[132]

While the TIP leadership remains in Afghanistan and Pakistan, the majority of fighters serving under the TIP banner were, as of 2020, in Syria. After the outbreak of the Syrian civil war in 2011, TIP began sending recruits to Syria to fight alongside al-Qaeda and its affiliates against the Syrian regime. The exact number of TIP fighters who fought in Syria is uncertain,[133] but some observers estimate that at the height of the conflict there were approximately 2,000 TIP-aligned Uyghurs operating in Syria under the umbrella of the former al-Qaeda affiliate Hay'at Tahrir al-Sham.[134] This presence has become an increasingly important motivation for Chinese engagement with the Taliban since the US withdrawal from Afghanistan.

These forces fought the Syrian regime primarily around Idlib province, where TIP declared an Islamic emirate in November 2018 – a Uyghur separatist organization helped found an Islamic emirate 2,000 miles and 6 countries from Xinjiang.[135]

The TIP leadership in Afghanistan appears to have been in communication with its forces in Syria, but the level of actual control over TIP

[129] Joscelyn (2019a).   [130] Noonan et al. (2019).   [131] Stewart (2021).
[132] United Nations Security Council (2020).
[133] Blanchard (2017).   [134] Clarke and Kan (2017).
[135] Jedinia and Kajjo (2018).

fighters there was likely low. In 2018, two TIP members in Afghanistan were sent to Syria to take on the roles of "general emir" and "military commander" of TIP forces presumably to strengthen those ties and improve communication.[136]

The majority of Uyghur fighters in Syria appear to have aligned with militant groups affiliated with al-Qaeda, but a minority joined the Islamic State.[137] Responding to the rise of Islamic State in 2016, Abdul Haq told TIP forces in Syria to shun Islamic State and instead aid forces affiliated with al-Qaeda in waging jihad against the Syrian regime. Abdul Haq also emphasized that they "must be willing to return to China to emancipate the Western province of Xinjiang from the communist invaders."[138]

Abdul Haq's statement underlines the extent to which the organization's leadership remains motivated by the struggle in China – engagement in Afghanistan and Syria are framed as a means to an end. The priorities of their foot soldiers, however, appear to be more mixed. The fear among Chinese counterterrorism experts is that if TIP can return its attention to China, it will do so with fighters – domestic and foreign – hardened by years of war abroad. But present levels of repression in Xinjiang, as well as Chinese efforts to put additional pressure on Uyghurs abroad (primarily through pressures on the governments that host them), make a reorientation toward China unlikely in the short term.

At present, TIP is at an uncertain point in its organizational evolution. The majority of its fighters have been engaged in the Afghan and Syrian conflicts for years. TIP forces continue to fight against the Syrian regime, but that conflict has wound down and their efforts appear unsustainable. While the extent of the organization's casualties in that conflict are unknown, nearly all organizations involved lost substantial numbers of fighters. If the organization is to return to its pursuit of an Islamic caliphate in Xinjiang, it will need to recall its members and rebuild its ranks. A key component of the Chinese strategy will be limiting the safe havens in which that could happen – particularly in Afghanistan and Pakistan. Taking on that role on the international stage, however, comes with its own risks. This is an issue that we will return to in Chapter 5.

---

[136] Joscelyn (2019b).   [137] Duchâtel (2019).   [138] Clarke and Kan (2017).

It is unknown, however, whether TIP maintains the allegiance of the Uyghurs fighting in far-flung jihadist hotspots to an extent that would be operationally useful. Even if they do, it is unlikely that these fighters would be able to penetrate into China in sufficient numbers to produce strategic shifts in a battle against the Chinese state, at least in the immediate term. Even a few, however, could have a psychological and political impact that could spur unpredictable responses from the CCP.

Regardless of their capabilities, many of the TIP fighters in Syria may be unwilling to return to China. Some, particularly those who brought their families, may view their efforts as part of a "religiously-based refugee resettlement program" rather than an independence movement bound to the liberation of their home country.[139]

Any who desire to return to Xinjiang will face serious impediments. China has placed strict controls on the border it shares with its neighbors in Central Asia, forcing militants to travel primarily through Southeast Asia and Turkey. While China has faced some challenges in extradition cases with Southeast Asian countries, and Turkey has historically been accommodating to Uyghurs, the prospects of returning to Xinjiang are increasingly difficult. The future of TIP fighters in Syria will be highly dependent on Turkey's wishes, namely whether it will encourage fighters to stay in Idlib, provide them safe haven in Turkey, or allow them to pass through Turkey to other countries. If China is able to exert enough pressure and Turkey continues its shift away from the West toward China, Turkey may simply abandon the TIP fighters in Syria to their fates.[140]

If the TIP fighters do not remain in Syria and Turkey allows them to travel through the country, their likely destinations will be in Southeast and Central Asia. Southeast Asia, particularly Indonesia, has already become an alternative battleground for some fighters, so Uyghur militants could follow their counterparts who have joined regional organizations linked to al-Qaeda or Islamic State. Others who are still committed to the fight against China may make their way to Central Asia.

Chinese intelligence agencies are hardly naïve to these possibilities. In December 2020, Afghani security arrested at least ten Chinese nationals on espionage charges but later released them under pressure

---

[139] Clarke and Kan (2017).   [140] Duchâtel (2019).

from Beijing. The Chinese spies were reportedly attempting to create a fake ETIM cell to entrap real ETIM operatives in the region.[141]

That said, even if China's substantial domestic security capabilities allow it to close its doors to trained Uyghur militants, Uyghur grievances may still motivate attacks on Chinese nationals, facilities, and assets abroad. This process is already underway as China expands its economic and security footprints in Central Asia, Southeast Asia, and the Middle East. For example, Pakistani Taliban militants claimed responsibility for a deadly suicide attack that killed nine Chinese workers in northern Pakistan on July 14, 2021.[142]

The Evolution of China's Internationalization of the Xinjiang Struggle

Despite the long history of the Uyghurs' political struggle, the conflict did not draw much attention from the outside world until the beginning of the twenty-first century. This owes generally to the opaque nature of Chinese politics but particularly to CCP insistence that the unrest in Xinjiang was a domestic concern shielded by sovereignty.

The 9/11 attacks on the United States led China to fundamentally reassess its longstanding insistence that its treatment of minorities was an internal matter cloaked by sovereignty. This attitude shift allowed China to begin equating Uyghur resistance (particularly as it turned more violent in the third phase) with the international terrorism the West abhorred.

The US-led "global war on terror" provided the Chinese government with an opportunity to reframe its policies in Xinjiang while smoothing over a particularly rough patch in the US–China bilateral relationship. By placing separatist violence in Xinjiang in the same context as the 9/11 attacks, Chinese policymakers leveraged US anti-terrorism policy to pitch its own handling of violence in western China as being congruent with the standards of the international community, rather than subject to international criticism of human rights infringements.[143]

---

[141] Shakil (2021)
[142] We discuss attacks on Chinese overseas assets and personnel in Chapter 5, but for a useful reference, see Duchâtel (2016).
[143] Potter (2013); Roberts (2020).

We detail the strategic thinking that governs the official media coverage of Uyghur violence in Chapter 3, but even a cursory comparison of the official rhetoric surrounding Uyghur violence in the periods shortly before and after the 9/11 attacks reveals a clear change in framing.

Before 2001, any public discussion of Uyghur violence was extremely rare. When government officials did mention it, they emphasized a separatist agenda. For example, in 1999, during a press conference, Li Peng, then chairman of the National People's Congress, described ETIM as an "anti-China separatist force."[144] Similarly, in 2000, when the then premier Zhu Rongji met with the minister of interior of Turkey, Sadettin Tantan, he referred to Uyghur dissidents operating in Turkey as "anti-China splitters," a pejorative for separatists.[145]

This framing almost immediately transitioned after 9/11. On January 21, 2002, the *People's Daily* published an article that officially acknowledged and detailed many violent incidents and attributed them to ETIM forces for the first time. Although the article asserted underlying separatist motivations, the title emphasized that East Turkestan militants were "Terrorist Forces."[146] This article also marks the starting point of CCP attempts to establish and emphasize connections between Uyghur militants and Osama bin Laden and al-Qaeda. In general, the period was marked by increasing rhetorical (and policy) attention to religious extremism, rather than separatism, as the underlying source of violence – the former being far less internationally legitimate than the latter as the United States rallied support for its "global war on terror."

The United States, eager to build an international coalition (or at least acquiescence) for its objectives in Afghanistan and then Iraq, reciprocated by officially identifying ETIM as a terrorist organization. Thus, by internationalizing the conflict, China was able to improve bilateral relations with the United States while clearing space to enact its preferred policies in Xinjiang.

However, while the US fixation on terrorism during the George W. Bush administration was useful to China in this regard, the "global" part of the GWOT made the Chinese foreign policy establishment deeply

---

[144] *People's Daily* (1999a: 6).   [145] *People's Daily* (2000: 1).
[146] *People's Daily* (2002a: 3).

uncomfortable. Most notably, Chinese decision-makers have tended to object to the degree that the war on terror has served as the basis for American unilateralism, though they have done so strategically.[147]

This tension in China's strategy persists to this day and China's efforts to internationalize have consequently remained largely rhetorical. Duchâtel notes that, when it comes to the UN's counterterrorism agenda, "China makes tactical use of the UN in practice, and strategic use only rhetorically."[148] Similarly, a 2009 report to the US Congress on US–China counterterrorism cooperation pointed out that China was not included among the fifty countries in the Pentagon's June 2002 report on foreign contributions to counterterrorism and that "the Obama Administration has proposed that China increase contributions and coordination in investments and assistance to help stabilize Pakistan and Afghanistan."[149] As we will see in Chapter 5, China has engaged in counterterrorism cooperation but has preferred to do so strategically and on its own terms.

China's transition to a more engaged role against international terrorism only emerged after the rise of Islamic State and the mounting threats posed to China's growing overseas interests and assets. In an influential opinion piece published in *People's Daily* in 2016, Fudan University professor Zhang Jiadong called for an "external therapy for an internal disease," reflecting the broader official view that counterterrorism efforts abroad should be the next phase in China's approach to potential unrest in Xinjiang.[150] This willingness to engage in multilateral counterterrorism efforts, however, has mostly been limited to regional partners in Central, South, and Southeast Asia, where China feels both vulnerable to potential Uyghur foreign fighters and capable of dominating the agenda.

Not only has China gradually increased the frequency and depth of counterterrorism joint military exercises within the framework of the Shanghai Cooperation Organization and with other regional counterparts (detailed in Chapter 5), but Beijing has also sought to build, expand, and institutionalize regional intelligence sharing, joint border

---

[147] See Shen (2007: 10–17). We provide detail on China's international cooperation and the process of internationalizing the Uyghur problem in Chapter 5.
[148] Duchâtel (2016).   [149] Kan (2010).   [150] Zhang (2014)

control and management, and judicial assistance.[151] This includes the extradition of alleged Uyghur militants to China by Thailand and Indonesia in 2015; the establishment of the "Quadrilateral Cooperation and Coordination Mechanism" between China, Afghanistan, Pakistan, and Tajikistan in 2016; and a reported patrol by Chinese forces inside Afghan territory in 2017.[152]

As the GWOT has lost its sheen and relations with the United States have soured, China has gradually changed its international legitimization strategy. Instead of allying itself with US counterterrorism efforts, it now seeks to win support from a select group of Muslim countries. For instance, when Western countries in 2019 condemned China's Xinjiang policies in a letter sent to the UN Human Rights Council, Beijing quickly secured countersupport from forty-five countries including Egypt, Iran, Iraq, Pakistan, Palestine, Saudi Arabia, Syria, and the United Arab Emirates.[153]

Beijing is also reverting to its original rhetorical insistence that the Xinjiang issue is an internal affair shielded by sovereignty. The government's efforts to broadly internationalize the Uyghur conflict are rapidly fading and being replaced by more focused regional engagement and periodic objections to Western interference in "internal matters." In the official white paper on Xinjiang released by the government in 2019, the title of the very first section of the report is "Xinjiang Has Long Been an Inseparable Part of Chinese Territory," and when it comes to the origin of violence, the report firmly argues "separatism is the hotbed in which terrorism and extremism take root in Xinjiang."[154]

These developments (both the violence and the countermeasures) present a complex strategic situation for Beijing – one that is characterized by mounting external threats met by regionalized cooperation but also intensified criticism from the West.

Conclusion

Contentious politics in Xinjiang has evolved substantially over time. There has been a steady transition from conventional armed conflict at the end of the Chinese Civil War to civil resistance in the intervening

---

[151] State Council Information Office (2019).
[152] Duchâtel (2019); Global Times (2016); Marty (2017).   [153] Putz (2019).
[154] State Council Information Office (2019).

period to political violence through 2014. The current equilibrium is held in place by very high levels of repression.

As we contemplate what comes next, we envision a potential return to violence, this time concentrated abroad in Central Asia along China's Belt and Road investments. In other words, the political violence is likely not over but rather temporarily suppressed and displaced at great social and economic cost. Uyghur militants simply do not have the capacity to mount a full-scale civil conflict, and the extent of Chinese power in the region makes it unlikely that Uyghurs will obtain a state sponsor that could help close that gap. In the present political climate in China, it also seems unlikely that authorities would be willing to cede the political space necessary to make any form of serious accommodation possible. However, as we will demonstrate in Chapter 4, it is also unlikely that Chinese authorities will be able to indefinitely sustain the levels of repression they have used since 2014 to stamp out violence. Indeed, evidence suggests that repression has already receded slightly from the high-water mark. This indicates the potential for violence along the "Belt" of the Belt and Road.

3 | Political Sensitivities

The cycle of repression and political violence in Xinjiang over the past three decades reveals a CCP caught between contradictory impulses.

On the one hand, there are strong incentives for retrenchment – to clamp down and pull back. In Chapter 2, we documented the contemporary CCP's profound intolerance for dissent, particularly dissent that challenges the primacy of the Party or the territorial integrity of the country. The Party has postured itself as the guarantor of stability since the end of the civil war, but the appeal grew dramatically after the 1989 Tiananmen Square massacre and again with the rise of Xi Jinping beginning around 2012.

The rhetorical positioning of the Party as the country's firewall against another century of humiliation makes Party officials extremely allergic to the internal opposition and external criticism that can accompany news of flareups and crackdowns in Xinjiang. This impulse to repress even the acknowledgment of political violence, not to mention the violence itself, permeates the Party and government bureaucracies from top to bottom.

On the other hand, the CCP has equally strong and well-documented incentives to trumpet the threat posed by violence when it occurs and the potential for violence when it does not. Drawing attention to terrorist threats can lend legitimacy to the Party by stoking patriotic sentiments. A similar logic holds internationally – if the CCP is to successfully reframe Uyghur unrest (or the threat thereof) as a manifestation of global extremism, it can best do so by exaggerating the threat rather than obscuring it. Acknowledging the realities of the situation in Xinjiang can also bolster the credibility of the Party domestically as an honest broker of information, which is increasingly vital in a single-party autocracy where public perceptions matter.

The political calculations that govern the management of this trade-off can be opaque, but one available window into them is the official Party media. Discussion of Uyghur violence and unrest in China's official media oscillates dramatically between prompt, transparent reporting and nearly complete censorship. The dramatic variation highlights the strategic tension between the desire to downplay the threat of violence emanating from Xinjiang and the desire to exaggerate it.

There are, however, consistent patterns governing policymakers' choice to highlight or obscure incidents of domestic political violence, and these patterns reveal official priorities more broadly.[1] This chapter unpacks the strategic considerations that shape these patterns to clarify political sensitivities and red lines.

The short version of that longer story is that the Party's near-term considerations consistently take precedence – the official press reflexively suppresses information and promptly acknowledges incidents only when *both* international and domestic conditions are highly favorable toward the Party's standing and legitimacy.

When domestic conditions are broadly favorable, particularly when economic indicators are favorable, Chinese citizens are less likely to challenge the government's handling of attacks. And, if some citizens do question the government, the government is better positioned to tolerate the dissent.

When international diplomatic conditions are favorable, particularly in terms of China's standing globally and with the United States, China is less likely to receive external criticism for its minority policy, which the Party has long viewed as a direct threat to its legitimacy. A favorable international diplomatic environment also presents an opportunity for the CCP to tie Uyghur militancy to the global terrorism trends that call for an international response – thereby shielding domestic policies in Xinjiang from scrutiny.

---

[1] For example, *Radio Free Asia* reported an incident in which a high-ranking newspaper editor was fired and prosecuted for terrorism coverage that displeased those higher up in the bureaucracy. According to another official, Zhao Xinwei was fired for "publishing stuff that a party newspaper isn't supposed to publish; it's as simple as that" (Pa et al. 2015).

Only when both conditions hold are authorities sufficiently confident that prompt disclosure will not risk the Party's immediate grip on power and individual officials' paths toward promotion. In contrast, when these conditions are not in place, delays allow time for authorities to gauge political sensitivities and let passions cool.

Official media is therefore highly revealing of the deep wells of caution that keep the CCP locked in a trap of its own making in Xinjiang.

Regime Type, Information Control, and Terrorism

As we have done throughout this volume, it is valuable to contextualize the role of information and media coverage of political violence in China alongside our broader understanding of how these forces typically function in autocracies. Despite persistent debate, a relative consensus has emerged in the literature that powerful authoritarian governments possess a counterterrorism tool that democracies lack – information control.[2] China is, of course, one such autocracy, so it stands to reason that its approach to information control would illuminate its sensitivities toward terrorism and the security policies engendered by the threat of terrorism.

According to Hoffman, a defining feature of terrorism is that attacks are "designed to have far-reaching psychological repercussions beyond the immediate victim or target."[3] In order to instill this fear and panic in a broader audience or society, terrorists usually need publicity and media coverage to reach their intended political audience.[4] As Schmid and De Graaf conclude, "For the terrorist, the message matters, not the victim."[5] Publicity can also help terrorist groups recruit potential supporters and can contribute to the spread of successful terrorist tactics.[6]

---

[2] Many empirical studies have indirectly established this positive relationship between publicity seeking and terrorist attacks. For instance, Ross (1993) finds that wealthy countries are actually more likely to experience terrorist attacks because they have well-developed mass media that allow terrorists greater chances to publicize their activities. Li (2005) tests this and finds a significant and positive relationship between press freedom and terrorist attacks.

[3] Hoffman (2006: 43.)

[4] See, for example, Crenshaw (1981); Sandler, Tschirhart, and Cauley (1983); Atkinson, Sandler, and Tschirhart (1987); Wilkinson (2001).

[5] Schmid and De Graaf (1982: 14).

[6] Nacos (2002, 2006); Chenoweth (2010); Horowitz (2010).

Democracies, for their part, are poorly adapted to control information, even when it might be in the best interest of their citizens. Former UK prime minister Margaret Thatcher, cognizant of the amplifying role that media could play in the cycle of political violence, famously asked the media to stop providing terrorists with the "oxygen of publicity." Her entreaties, however, were hopeless in a democracy with a free and competitive media market.[7] Publics typically have a voracious appetite for this type of information and a fundamental right to it in an open society. Of course, no such right is acknowledged or extended in an autocracy.

Given these dynamics, it is widely thought that powerful authoritarian regimes – which are capable of controlling, censoring, and manipulating information – enjoy a strategic advantage in combating terrorism because they can order state-controlled media to deprive terrorists of a forum.[8] By contrast, not only is such information control nearly impossible in democracies, but the privatized and commercialized news industry can also develop a symbiotic relationship with terrorism.[9] Violence attracts eyeballs and helps media outlets compete for readers and viewers. As the adage goes, "if it bleeds, it leads."[10]

While autocracies have informational advantages, there are a couple of reasons why this does not lead to immunity to terrorism.

First, autocratic regimes may have incentives to not only acknowledge but also to overstate the number of terrorist attacks in order to justify hardline policies against political foes or dissidents – a phenomenon that has been noted in contexts well beyond China and the Global War on Terror (GWOT).[11] This tendency has become more

---

[7] Thatcher (1985).

[8] However, many scholars argue that this empirical pattern is not driven by autocracies' better performance in combating terrorism; they contend that it simply reflects the fact that autocracies that conduct information control and censorship tend to underreport terrorist attacks. See, for example, Drakos and Gofas (2006) and Sandler (1995).

[9] A minority of empirical studies find no robust link between press freedom and terrorist attacks, though they tend to attribute the null result to the fact that press freedom is almost entirely collinear with regime type. See, for example, Gaibulloev, Piazza, and Sandler (2017) It is possible that, as Brian Jenkins of the RAND Corporation put it, "The news media are responsible for terrorism to about the same extent that commercial aviation is responsible for the airline hijackings." Quoted in Farnen (1990: 113–114).

[10] Martin (1985); Crelinsten (1989); Farnen (1990); Wilkinson (1997); Rohner and Frey (2007).

[11] Gaibulloev, Piazza, and Sandler (2017).

prevalent in the post-9/11 era, during which the United States' stance against terrorism overtook the notion that one person's terrorist could be another's freedom fighter. Regardless of whether this moral absolutism represents a durable shift in global norms, it created the opportunity for autocracies to couch their domestic terrorism problems in strategically advantageous ways, at least for a time.

Second, the argument that autocracies can effectively combat terrorists by muting their voices tends to overlook the informational dilemmas faced by many modern, institutionalized autocracies, particularly given evolving technological and media environments.

While muting news coverage of terrorist attacks can discourage perpetrators from adopting a propaganda-through-violence strategy, such censorship comes with other risks for the regime. Strict information control may exacerbate the grievances that motivate terrorist violence in the first place. A potential consequence is that terrorists may not be discouraged but rather pushed to make their voices louder by killing more people, projecting violence against highly visible soft or symbolic targets, and adopting more sophisticated tactics.

Furthermore, if they have access to even partially independent information through the Internet or other means, domestic audiences can interpret silence from the state as incompetent counterterrorism policy. This, in turn, can contribute to a larger loss of legitimacy than would occur by simply acknowledging an attack in the first place.

Finally, absent credible information, rumors about attacks can prove worse than the reality. The advent of the Internet and the penetration of social media into middle income autocracies such as China make these potentially negative political consequences ever more likely.[12] As a consequence, despite the authorities' best efforts, information control becomes partial rather than absolute, and strategies must be correspondingly more nuanced.

China's Media Dilemma

Through the 1990s, absent the Internet and social media to contend with, China was able to almost completely obscure news of terrorist attacks, thereby removing much of their appeal by removing the

---

[12] For a more general discussion of media control in autocracies, see Gehlbach, Sonin, and Svolik (2016).

audience. For example, Western media reported a bombing campaign that targeted public transportation and cinemas in Urumqi in February 1992, but emphasized that "China's state-run media have not mentioned the bombings, although they happened almost three weeks ago."[13] Even today, government control over the reporting of terrorist attacks is explicitly written into the 2015 counterterrorism law, which states, "The Counter-Terrorism Leading Group is responsible for releasing information on terrorist incidents, their developments and the government's responses ... No other units or individuals are allowed to disseminate details of the incidents that may lead to copycat actions, nor may they spread cruel or inhuman images of the incidents."[14]

Despite the government's pervasive surveillance, China is nonetheless an increasingly connected society where information can spread organically and unpredictably, and the CCP is deeply sensitive to public opinion and domestic pressure.[15] Rapid evolution in the means and effectiveness of social control intersects with equally momentous changes in both governmental media control policies and technology that makes communication easier and censorship more difficult. While these changes can be a positive development in many domains, the rewards are less clear when it comes to terrorism and counterterrorism.

The Long-Term Benefits of Transparency

The CCP has several compelling reasons – both international and domestic – to acknowledge terrorist violence promptly in its official media when it occurs.

As discussed in Chapter 2 – and at length by Roberts and others – the CCP has strategically emphasized (and overemphasized, embellished, and invented) incidents of Uyghur-initiated violence in order to link its policies in Xinjiang and Central Asia to the broader GWOT.[16] Pursuit of this

---

[13] Sampson (1992).
[14] Counterterrorism Law of the People's Republic of China (Order No. 36 of the President of the PRC) (2015).
[15] According to Lampton (2001: 155), "The government cares about public opinion because it is concerned with political stability, suggesting that the role of public opinion is mostly a negative one. Nevertheless, the effort the government puts into understanding public opinion suggests that the role of public opinion is somewhat broader."
[16] Roberts (2020); Potter (2013).

goal weighs in favor of loudly and rapidly highlighting Uyghur violence when it occurs.

In the post-9/11 context, the Chinese government clearly recognized the long-term benefits of internationalizing domestic terrorism in Xinjiang by linking it to global counterterrorism efforts, thereby insulating China's policies from critique.[17] The global fixation on militant Islamist movements provides a useful and easy rhetorical context for Uyghur violence – this is, after all, emanating from a Muslim minority bordering Afghanistan in the heart of Central Asia. In that context, it was difficult for Western leaders to credibly condemn Chinese policies, and particularly for the United States to do so, if the situation in Xinjiang could be successfully framed in terms of terrorism and international jihadism.

International attentiveness to violence in China is, however, generally short-lived, so authorities risk wasting an opportunity if they obscure an incident by delaying official acknowledgment.

Framing violence in terms of terrorism also provides justification for China's expansive military, political, and economic ambitions in Central Asia. The Shanghai Cooperation Organization (SCO) was formed with the explicit charge to fight against the "three evils" of separatism, extremism, and terrorism.[18] It is rhetorically useful for the Chinese government to promptly and officially acknowledge terrorist attacks in order to highlight the severity of these "evils" and bolster the SCO's credibility as a nascent collective security institution. This is particularly important because, while the "three evils" are the organization's stated raison d'être, there has always been suspicion that China's regional policies are actually driven by larger strategic concerns – the desire to dominate Central Asia, counter US influence, and bolster the Belt and Road Initiative.[19]

Finally, and most importantly, information transparency bolsters the Party's long-term legitimacy. The link between transparency and Party legitimacy is well documented in the Chinese context. Stockmann and Gallagher note that exposing Chinese citizens to news regarding labor disputes promotes the perception that the Party and Chinese law favor workers, which helps increase the Party's popular legitimacy.[20] Similarly, studies by Huang, Boranbay-Akan, and Huang find that Chinese

---

[17] Potter (2013).   [18] Chung (2004: 990–991).
[19] Cohen (2006); Swanstrom (2005).
[20] Stockmann and Gallagher (2011) label this type of media representation "bad apples but happy endings," as the reported disputes are usually resolved positively in favor of the rights of workers.

citizens give the Party higher marks when state media acknowledges social protests.[21]

The Party has grown increasingly explicit in the linkage it draws between transparency and legitimacy, and it is clearly cognizant of the positive returns that can accompany quick, official acknowledgment of negative events. Chinese policy circles talk about avoiding the "Tacitus Trap" – shorthand for a permanent loss of credibility, as the Party's every subsequent action after some threshold would be viewed as a lie. The Roman senator and historian Tacitus once said, "Indeed, when a ruler once becomes unpopular, all his acts, be they good or bad, tell against him."[22]

For example, as a kindergarten abuse scandal came to light at the end of 2017, Chinese "netizens" blamed the government for failing to release enough information about the investigation process in a timely manner.[23] Internally, Chinese officials referred repeatedly to the kindergarten incident's potential to mar the Party's credibility in the long-term – explicitly invoking the Tacitus Trap.

In 2014, Xi Jinping touched on the problem of eroding credibility at an enlarged meeting of the Lankao County Party Committee convened to discuss corruption. Xi is quoted as saying, "We are certainly not there [falling into the Tacitus Trap] yet, but the current problem facing us is not trivial either; if that day really comes, then the Party's legitimacy foundations and power status will be threatened."[24]

The problem is not entirely hypothetical – the CCP's failure to acknowledge officially high-profile incidents has proven costly in some key cases, with public outrage outstripping the official response and risking stability.

The school collapses in the Sichuan earthquake and a high-speed rail crash in 2011 are well-known examples of the risk of seeming to ignore incidents that are highly relevant to the public.[25] But the issue continues to plague the Party.

---

[21] Huang, Boranbay-Akan, and Huang (2016).
[22] Li (2017: 5).   [23] Quackenbush (2017).
[24] *CPC News (2016)*; emphasis added.
[25] This insight is echoed by recent work on China's social media, which has revealed that the scale of censorship of sensitive materials on the Chinese microblogging platform (*Sina Weibo*) is more limited than commonly appreciated – a pattern attributed to the government's desire to gauge bottom-up public opinion and provide an outlet for it (Qin, Strömberg, and Wu 2017).

For example, the fallout from the initial response to the corona-virus outbreak in Wuhan starkly illustrates the risks the Party runs, both domestically and globally. In December 2019, Li Wenliang sent a message to fellow doctors warning them that he had noticed several cases of a virus that looked like SARS. A few days later, according to the BBC, members of the Public Security Bureau ordered Li to sign a letter that accused him of "'making false comments' that had 'severely disturbed the social order.'"[26]

Li himself then started exhibiting symptoms of the virus, which he described on social media in January 2020. He was hospitalized and diagnosed with COVID-19 on January 30, the same day the World Health Organization declared the virus's outbreak a global health emergency. He died a few days later.

The public's reaction to Li's death was initially overwhelming. Observers were hard-pressed to recall an event that had led to such a significant outpouring of "online grief, rage and mistrust against the Chinese government."[27] A copy of the statement Li was forced to sign quickly circulated around the Internet,[28] and social media exploded with posts about his death, with defiant hashtags such as "Wuhan government owes Dr. Li Wenliang an apology" and "We want freedom of speech."[29] In an effort to mitigate the damage, the country's anti-corruption body, the National Supervisory Commission, announced that it was sending a team to Wuhan to "thoroughly investigate issues related to Dr. Li Wenliang."[30]

Chinese officials' initial repression of information about COVID-19 caused a clear loss of legitimacy – both within China and abroad. Beyond the stifling of Li, the public sensed that the government was suppressing information because it had failed to control the outbreak.[31] To mitigate this loss of legitimacy, the CCP relied on two strategies that, according to Mattingly, have helped it stay in power for decades: deflecting blame to local officials and mobilizing massive government resources to ameliorate the crisis, if not the underlying problem.[32]

---

[26] *BBC News* (2020a).   [27] *BBC News* (2020a).
[28] Neuman, Feng, and Huo (2020).   [29] *BBC News* (2020a).
[30] Neuman, Feng, and Huo (2020).   [31] Felter and Maizland (2020).
[32] Mattingly (2020).

One sees the same response pattern when political violence threatens the CCP's legitimacy. The Wuhan fallout, however, magnified by social media, illustrates the increasing fragility of these strategies and the increasing value of transparency. While the central government did admit that it was responsible for some "shortcomings and deficiencies,"[33] most firings fell on local officials. State media, according to the BBC, reported "hundreds of sackings, investigations and warnings across Hubei and other provinces," and officials in Hubei were replaced by the deputy director of China's National Health Commission.[34] This, however, only serves to incentivize future coverups and the withholding of information lower down in the system.

Scapegoating tactics only work for so long. In the Wuhan case, some local officials pushed back on the narrative that mistakes were made solely at the local level. The mayor of Wuhan complained that the "rules imposed by Beijing limited what he could disclose about the threat," suggesting that "the central government was partially responsible for a lack of transparency."[35] In addition to these top-down disclosure rules, local officials may also have feared repercussions from the central government if they disclosed the coronavirus problem before they had the virus under control locally – thus depriving the central government of information about a credible threat that it could have helped address.

While the CCP seems to appreciate the role that transparency can play in bolstering its legitimacy, its response to the coronavirus crisis reveals a governance structure that is poorly equipped to foster the transparency required for optimal policy responses at the local and national levels.

These costs of opacity increase as it becomes easier for Chinese citizens to know when the government is *not* talking about issues. The decentralization of the flow of information, stemming from the rise of internet forums and social media, has made it increasingly difficult and costly for the Chinese government to control sensitive information, including information about terrorist attacks. Government censors find themselves often playing catch-up to clamp down on internet message boards and text messages.

---

[33] Felter and Maizland (2020).   [34] *BBC News* (2020b).   [35] Chin (2020).

Twitter-style microblogs, which have exploded in popularity, have upended the information ecosystem due to their sheer volume and speed, coupled with the decentralization that characterizes social media. Whereas Chinese authorities once were able to keep terrorist incidents out of the public consciousness, thereby devaluing the tactic for potential perpetrators, technology has made this increasingly difficult to accomplish in an absolute sense. In other words, the CCP now finds itself in a "leaky" information environment due to media fragmentation, semiprivatization, technological change, and the proliferation of camera-equipped smart phones. The government might elect not to discuss an incident in the official media, but news of it may still reach segments of the public.

Gaps between what official voices choose to engage with and what the people are concerned with can contribute to the erosion of legitimacy.[36] While it is broadly understood that the Party heavily influences what is and is not discussed in the semi-independent press, acknowledgment in the state-controlled press sends a distinct and important signal about the Party's commitment to certain issues. It is therefore important not just that information is released but that the government is seen as the source and conveyor of that information.

The Short-Term Risks of Transparency

There remain, however, strong countervailing incentives for leaders to delay the acknowledgment of terrorist incidents in the official media until risks can be mitigated and passions cool. As we have noted, since Deng Xiaoping's "reform and opening" strategy, "stability above everything else" (*wending yadao yiqie*) has been a cornerstone of domestic policy. Prompt acknowledgment of violence in the official media has the potential to undermine that stability. Green-lighting public discussion and further media coverage may, for example, intensify the ethnic tensions between Han and Uyghurs by triggering – and even seeming to sanction – violent reprisals against Uyghurs. For instance, the July 2009 Urumqi riot was reported on extensively, coverage that likely contributed to the deadly protest by Han Chinese that immediately followed.[37]

---

[36] Lorentzen (2014).   [37] Wong (2009).

Public opinion surveys on these sensitive matters are few and far between, but those that exist underscore why the government treads carefully. For example, Hou and Quek found in 2019 that 96 percent of Chinese citizens thought the government should *increase* efforts to prevent Uyghur violence, raising the possibility that popular demands could outstrip what the government is able or willing to deliver.[38] Further, while a 2014 survey suggested that citizens do not primarily blame the government for incidents of political violence, 69 percent of Chinese citizens did think ethnic policies needed to be modified.[39]

In that study, there was a lack of consensus on the appropriate response to Uyghur political violence, with 28 percent strongly agreeing with forceful suppression and 40 percent strongly disagreeing.[40] In this context, official discussion of attacks can invite critiques of government policy, push policy in directions that authorities would prefer that it not go, or expose rifts in public consensus. The direction of the reaction can be unpredictable and therefore threatening to domestic stability and national solidarity.

Disincentives also arise from international considerations, particularly because highlighting Uyghur violence can invite foreign criticism of China's highly repressive ethnic policies.[41] Although global fixation on militant Islamist organizations can provide China with a useful rhetorical frame for Uyghur violence, Western suspicion that China cloaks human rights violations against its ethnic minorities behind the war on terror has never faded. Indeed, even when China's support at the United Nations was urgently needed shortly after the 9/11 attacks, President George W. Bush nonetheless cautioned the then Chinese president, Jiang Zemin, that "the war on terrorism must never be an excuse to persecute minorities."[42]

The risk to diplomatic relations also diminishes the incentive to acknowledge terrorist incidents, if doing so is more likely to engender international critique than deflect blame or elicit sympathy. The CCP has long perceived critiques of its human rights record and minority policies to be a threat to the regime and a barrier to international prestige, which Beijing uses to nurture its legitimacy at home. As a

---

[38] Hou and Quek (2019).   [39] Chen and Ding (2014).
[40] Chen and Ding (2014).   [41] Jacobs (2016).   [42] Lam (2001).

consequence, a key concept that underpins China's diplomatic posture on political violence and terrorism is that "double standards" should not be allowed.[43]

Balancing Short- and Long-Term Priorities

Given these incentives and constraints, Chinese authorities' long- and short-term preferences are inconsistent and mutually exclusive. Legitimacy at home and abroad are long-term priorities for the CCP, and the erosion of that legitimacy is perceived as a fundamental threat to power.[44] Domestic instability and international pressure, however, are usually of more immediate concern. The Chinese government therefore confronts a dilemma: prompt official coverage of terrorist violence is an investment in long-term legitimacy, but fear of instability in the short-term favors delay or silence.

The way in which Chinese authorities have approached this dilemma reveals a strong preference for short-term stability, even at the expense of long-term priorities. Incident data show that unless both domestic and international conditions are favorable, Chinese authorities consistently prioritize short-term stability by delaying or forgoing official coverage of Uyghur-initiated violence. This bias arises from the foundations of the Party's claim to authority. As we have noted, China's longstanding prioritization of social stability dates to the collapse of Communist regimes in Eastern Europe and the democracy movement sparked by the 1989 Tiananmen Square protests and the subsequent government crackdown.[45]

Even before the Tiananmen protests, Deng Xiaoping reportedly told President George H. W. Bush, "Before everything else, China's problems require stability."[46] Shortly after the crackdown, Deng reemphasized that "stability is of overriding importance," and a front-page *People's Daily* article titled "Stability above Everything Else," published on the first anniversary of the Tiananmen crackdown, cemented this as the bedrock of China's domestic policy.[47]

The third generation of China's leadership, led by Jiang Zemin, continued this prioritization, stating that "stability is the premise, reform

---

[43] Duchâtel (2016).   [44] Shambaugh (2008); Holbig and Gilley (2010).
[45] Wang and Minzner (2015).   [46] Bandurski (2012).   [47] *People's Daily* (1990).

is the driving force, and development is the goal."[48] Hu Jintao, in turn, repackaged this idea as "building a harmonious socialist society." Hu's core principles were to "promote harmony through reform, consolidate harmony with development, and guarantee harmony through stability."[49]

Finally, and most relevant to the issues at hand, in the Second Xinjiang Work Forum held in 2014, Xi Jinping declared that "social stability and lasting peace and order is the general objective."[50]

Why does the CCP delay coverage in the face of international condemnation rather than expediting it? One might plausibly (but mistakenly) suppose, for example, that Beijing would be more likely to report on terrorist incidents when diplomatic conditions are otherwise adverse. This strategy would supposedly enable China to convince other countries that it is a victim of terrorism and needs their support.

The answer lies in China's history, rapid rise, and current emphasis on nationalism, increasingly tinged with elements of Han-centric ethnonationalism. China's emergence from a "century of humiliation" has left it with an arguably outdated, but still very real, intolerance of outside critique, particularly in moments of perceived weakness.[51]

As Anand notes, the CCP's claim to authority is built upon the assertion that only it can protect the nation from "various threats to its security and territorial integrity." In this telling, for China to take its rightful place on the international stage after its "century of humiliation," the CCP must "safeguard 'national unity and social stability' from hostile external forces." Through this lens, Anand argues that Uyghurs and Tibetans are labeled as threats to security and territorial integrity by the "state and its (Han) majoritarian nationalism." Complaints by these groups are portrayed as "products of separatism, extremism and terrorism associated with Uyghur and Tibetan identities."[52]

Citing the shift toward a market economy in the 1980s that muted the Party's communist rhetoric, Dupre argues that nationalism,

[48] *People.com* (2001).
[49] Resolutions of the CPC Central Committee on Major Issues Regarding the Building of a Harmonious Socialist Society (2006).
[50] Leibold (2014).   [51] Kaufman (2009).   [52] Anand (2019).

alongside economic development, has "become a crucial pillar" of the CCP's legitimacy. Centered on the Han majority and territorial integrity, the foundation of the nationalism promoted by the CCP is based upon the acceptance of its rule. The CCP's brand of nationalism merges the concept of state, nation, and Party, allowing the Party to create a narrative in which it is the "only legitimate defender of national interests and state sovereignty." This merger of state, nation, and Party enables the CCP to label any criticism of its policies as "traitorous and seditious" activities.[53] This legitimation strategy becomes particularly attractive as economic growth slows, but it comes at the expense of the nation's minorities.

Expanding on this logic, Leibold argues that Xi Jinping is driving state policy "away from a previous tolerance of ethnocultural heterogeneity, and towards a virulent form of cultural nationalism that pathologizes dissent and diversity as an existential threat to the Party and the nation." In making this argument, Leibold examines a speech Xi delivered to an audience of "national role models for ethnic unity" on September 27, 2019. Touting the "uniquely embracive and absorbent character" of Chinese civilization, Xi emphasized the development of the "communal consciousness of the Zhonghua nation" enabled by the fusion of ethnic groups. Xi declared that cultural identity is "the deepest level of identity" and "the root artery of national unity" and that the love for Zhonghua must be placed "deep in the soul of each and every child." Leibold notes that Xi's urging of officials to increase their efforts in forging ethnic unity was relayed in policy directives immediately after his speech. Recalling the 1994 patriotic education campaign launched after the Tiananmen crisis, the CCP Central Committee and the PRC State Council issued a directive "promoting patriotic education in the new era." The directive includes the "promotion of 'red tourism,' flag raising ceremonies, commemorative activities, and the celebration of traditional Zhonghua festivals and culture." The enactment of this directive requires that Uyghurs, Tibetans, and other ethnic minorities "conform to Han norms."[54]

Chinese authorities have been particularly sensitive to accusations of human rights violations, which are generally viewed as a pretext

---

[53] Dupré (2002).   [54] Leibold (2019a); Anand (2019).

for interference and a means of delegitimizing the Party. International critiques on these matters also tend to play poorly with Chinese domestic audiences and inflame popular passions in the wake of a terrorist incident. Most significantly, because China has thus far been unable to garner consistent international approval of its policies in Xinjiang, there is little reason for Chinese authorities to think that the international response will be favorable when the diplomatic situation is otherwise bad.

In this sense, Western attitudes and China's corresponding responses are contingent on the bigger picture. When disagreements are high, the Uyghur issue becomes a human rights issue with which to pressure and delegitimize Beijing, but when diplomatic relations are in a more cooperative mode, Western governments are more likely to avert their eyes and go along with the terrorism narrative. The result is that when Chinese leaders make decisions about reporting domestic political violence, they carefully evaluate international conditions, and they are much more likely to report quickly when these conditions are favorable.

This bias toward caution is baked into the Chinese governing system's structure and incentives, from the lowest levels on up to the highest. For individual bureaucrats and lower-level officials, poor performance on social stability targets has an immediate impact on promotion prospects and typically cannot be outweighed by good performance on other targets.[55]

At the same time, top-level leadership is perennially fearful of popular unrest and accustomed to exercising strong controls over information. The combination of these forces leads players in the system to default to caution and opacity – a strategy that the Party has long employed to enforce compliance with single-party rule.[56]

Media Coverage (and Censorship) of Political Violence in China

Official media sources in China are no longer simple propaganda mouthpieces – instead they reflect the government's increasingly sophisticated strategies for information control.

---

[55] Minzner (2009: 68).   [56] Stern and Hassid (2012).

China's media landscape during the first decades of CCP rule was defined by state ownership and control; citizens were even required to subscribe to (and pay for) the official newspaper. This media landscape was significantly altered in the early 1980s as the CCP allowed some media outlets to sell advertisements and retain profits, creating a semi-privatized marketplace. By 2003, the state eliminated mandatory subscriptions, and most official newspapers lost their state subsidies and were forced to compete with commercial outlets. As the media marketplace became more privatized, consumers were increasingly drawn to the "lively and colloquial" language of commercial outlets and began to view commercial publications as more credible than the official press.[57]

While semiprivatization reduced public consumption of official media, the state retains effective control through both censorship and self-censorship. The Communist Party's Central Propaganda Department, along with several other government bodies, ensures that traditional media content does not stray too far from the Party line.

The State Council Information Office has taken the lead in monitoring the massive surge in internet traffic over the last decade. Over two million workers, employed by the state and commercial media outlets, monitor internet posts and "compile reports for 'decision makers.'"[58] Most media outlets also maintain their own in-house censors to prevent their content from running afoul of the official state censors, and the cost of censorship is increasing for both the state censors and media outlets. Observers estimate that the country's eighteen leading social media outlets spend more than $2.5 billion (combined) each year on internal censors.[59]

Over the past decade, scholars have been able to develop a better understanding of the media content that is more likely to be deemed impermissible by censors. King, Pan, and Roberts, for example, argue that media censorship is primarily aimed at suppressing collective action rather than content that is critical of the state.[60] Extending this argument, Shao finds that censors tolerate criticisms of the

---

[57] Shirk (2011: 9).   [58] Xu and Albert (2017).
[59] Yuan (2018).   [60] King, Pan, and Roberts (2013).

government's performance but block any content "questioning the Party's leading role."[61]

Other scholars have noted distinct structural differences between the central and local propaganda authorities. Kuang finds that the central propaganda authority is more concerned about content that is critical of the "image of the central state and leadership," while the local propaganda authorities focus on news that is "harmful to social stability and the image of the local government."[62] This comports with the distinction between concerns over legitimacy at higher levels and paths to promotion at lower ones.

The state maintains significant censorship capabilities, but self-censorship plays an even greater role in the control of the media. The CCP Central Propaganda Department (or Publicity Department) and the Bureau of Internet Affairs have historically sent media outlets weekly guidelines to promote self-censorship among editors; however, the exact boundaries of permissible content are often uncertain. Stern and Hassid argue that the state uses this uncertainty to promote self-censorship among journalists.[63] In an environment in which there are unclear limits on permissible actions, editors and journalists conservatively police their own content to ensure that they do not run the risk of crossing any invisible boundaries.

There are serious consequences for those who fail to censor themselves. Editors and journalists face "dismissals and demotions, libel lawsuits, fines, arrests, and forced television confessions."[64] Editors who fail to censor their outlets according to regulators' standards are frequently ordered to "write 'self-examination letters.'" Commercial outlets that go too far may be temporarily shut down by authorities, and the lack of ad revenue during these temporary shutdowns may lead to permanent closures.[65]

This systemwide self-censorship, buttressed by rigorous official state censorship, creates a media landscape that is effectively controlled by the state. Operating in an industry with indefinite boundaries and definite punishments, editors and journalists generally follow the lead of Party media outlets. When contending with particularly sensitive subjects such as terrorist attacks, commercial outlets are even more likely to adhere to the limits exhibited by official state reporting.

---

[61] Shao (2018).   [62] Kuang (2018).   [63] Stern and Hassid (2012).
[64] Xu and Albert (2017).   [65] Hancock (2018).

By the numbers, the semiprivatized media dominates the Chinese media landscape, but official media retains an outsized role because it clarifies CCP priorities and guardrails. Among official outlets, the *People's Daily* (*Renmin Ribao*) retains pride of place as the most authoritative. Its editorials and commentaries not only represent official opinion but also enjoy hegemony in shaping Chinese public opinion. Shambaugh points out that while the reach of the CCP Propaganda Department is opaque, the *People's Daily* is one of the institutions over which it has absolute and uncontested authority.[66] Coverage in the *People's Daily* is therefore an unambiguous indication that a topic is acceptable for popular discussion and further media coverage. As a result, the acknowledgment of an attack in the *People's Daily* can amplify broader coverage because it is a strong signal to both traditional and social media.[67]

Official Media Coverage of Uyghur-Initiated Violence

To identify whether an attack was acknowledged in the *People's Daily* we searched for coverage of each of our identified incidents of militant violence with a combination of the timing, location, and available details of the attack (weapons, targets, perpetrators, casualties, etc.).[68] For those incidents for which we lacked sufficient information (or if initial searches failed to turn up any coverage), we searched for phrases or words that the Chinese media commonly use when reporting terrorist attacks: "violent/terrorist attack" (*baokong xiji*), "East Turkestan Movement" (*dong yi yun* or *dong tu*), and "three evils" (*sangu shili*). As a final check, we scanned the physical pages of the paper for coverage of each identified incident.

---

[66] *People's Daily*'s editorials are usually directly drafted by the Propaganda Department, and news coverage is carefully considered and vetted (Shambaugh 2007: 53).

[67] While the terrorism coverage of more independent, audience-driven newspapers is not our dependent variable of interest, we searched these resources in the course of gathering our original data on all terrorist incidents. That survey indicated that these outlets generally wait for an official green light before reporting.

[68] To generate this measure, we rely on both the newspaper's digital database (*Renmin Ribao Shujuku*) and its print version. We rely on the University of Michigan's *Renmin Ribao* full-text database (with PDF images of the original print version) for 1990–2008 data. For 2009–2014 data, we rely on China National Knowledge Infrastructure (CNKI).

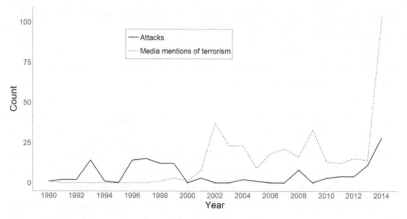

Figure 3.1 Attacks, reports, and number of articles

Figure 3.1 summarizes the resulting data from 1990 to 2014, plotting the number of attacks (solid line) and the number of articles published in the *People's Daily* that mentioned Uyghur-related violence (dashed line), even if the article did not refer to a specific incident.[69]

Official discussion of violence in and emanating from Xinjiang is sparse throughout the 1990s. The very first *People's Daily* article that mentions Uyghur separatism and the associated violence was published in 1990 and does so in the context of a general introduction to China's ethnic minority policy. An article from 1998 illustrates the nature of delayed disclosure of terrorist incidents. It discusses a press conference held by Wang Lequan, the head of the Xinjiang delegation to the First Session of the Ninth National Party Congress, in which he mentions two attacks that occurred in 1997.[70] Reflecting the same broader pattern, Uyghur separatist violence was also mentioned twice after Li Peng, chairman of the National People's Congress Standing Committee, visited Turkey in 1999.[71]

The relatively peaceful period from 2002 to 2007 marks an important turning point in the Chinese government's public relations strategy toward domestic political violence in Xinjiang. Despite the relative

---

[69] The correlation between attack and mentions is 0.54.
[70] *People's Daily* (1998).
[71] *People's Daily* (1999a); *People's Daily* (1999b). Li Peng labeled the "East Turkestan terrorist organization" (*Dongtu kongbu zuzhi*) an anti-China separatist organization.

calm that prevailed in Xinjiang at the time, the number of *People's Daily* articles that mentioned "East Turkestan terrorism" jumped to thirty-seven in 2002 – an increase of more than 300 percent – and has remained high since, particularly after 2013.

This shift reflected the growing incentive to publicize violence and frame it around terrorism after 9/11, as well as the changing domestic media environment. In 2002, *People's Daily* published "East Turkestan Terrorist Forces Cannot Get Away with Impunity," which acknowledged for the first time many Uyghur-related attacks that occurred in the 1990s (alongside many that appear to have never occurred at all). The article also publicly identified many purported Uyghur-related terrorist organizations, including ETIM, the East Turkestan Islamic Party, the East Turkestan Islamic Party of Allah, and the East Turkestan Liberation Organization.

These revelations (and in some cases constructions) were the starting point of Chinese attempts to internationalize Uyghur-related terrorist attacks by claiming a connection between East Turkestan terrorists and Osama bin Laden and al-Qaeda. The article states,

The "East Turkestan" terrorist organization based in South Asia has the unstinting support of Osama bin Laden, and is an important part of his terrorist forces. The "East Turkestan Islamic Movement" headed by Hasan Mahsum is supported and directed by bin Laden. Since the formation of the "East Turkestan Islamic Movement," bin Laden has schemed with the heads of the Central and West Asian terrorist organizations many times to help the "East Turkestan" terrorist forces in Xinjiang launch a "holy war," with the aim of setting up a theocratic "Islam State" in Xinjiang.[72]

Eight months later, the *People's Daily* reported that the United Nations had designated ETIM a terrorist organization.[73]

Counterterrorism cooperation is also frequently highlighted in *People's Daily* articles covering meetings between high-level Chinese officials and foreign leaders, especially those between China and other members of the SCO.

US–China counterterrorism cooperation also became a hot topic in the *People's Daily* for a brief period after the 9/11 attacks. On December 12, 2001, the *People's Daily* reported on the first US–China counterterrorism meeting, which was held in Beijing. Subsequent US–China

---

[72] *People's Daily* (2002a).   [73] *People's Daily* (2002b).

counterterrorism meetings were held in 2002, 2003, and 2004; they were mentioned three times in 2002 and two times each in 2003 and 2004. Counterterrorism cooperation was also mentioned in 2005 during President Hu Jintao's visit to the United States.

Another feature of the coverage is repeated flip-flopping between internationalizing the issue by linking militancy in Xinjiang with the war on terror and insisting that Uyghur terrorism is a domestic concern shielded by sovereignty. For example, one article about the annual report of the Congressional-Executive Commission on China cited the spokesman of China's Foreign Affairs Ministry stating that "fighting against East Turkestan terrorist organizations is based on China's law and is aimed to protect the fundamental human rights of Chinese citizens, which is welcome by Chinese people ... We urge the [United States] to stop intervening in China's domestic affairs."[74]

In contrast, another article about Chinese Uyghurs detained at Guantanamo Bay stated that "East Turkestan terrorism is part of international terrorism, which poses threats to the whole international society, including both Chinese people and American people."[75]

Assessing the Timing of Official Coverage

By the numbers, China's official media has clearly increased its coverage of Uyghur-related violence over time. However, it remains unclear whether the inconsistent timing of official acknowledgments is deliberately nuanced. To answer this question, we turn to a more systematic analysis of the timing of reporting in the official media to clarify whether prompt coverage is associated with favorable domestic and international conditions.[76]

As a first cut, it is clear from the data that violence tends to be rarely reported immediately following an attack but is more likely to be disclosed later. Event-history models are able to capture this time-to-coverage dynamic. We measure duration as the number of days (up to one year) between the occurrence of an attack and the

---

[74] *People's Daily* (2002c).   [75] *People's Daily* (2004).
[76] King, Pan, and Roberts (2013: 5). After the 2011 Wenzhou train wreck, some categories of events were cleared for immediate reporting, but terrorism was not among them.

date it first appears in the *People's Daily*.[77] To avoid bogging down the reader with the details of these models, we provide only their broad structure and key takeaways here. Details can be found in the appendix to this chapter.

Measuring Domestic and International Conditions

There is no perfect single indicator for a concept as abstract and multifaceted as domestic conditions in China. Our approach is first to rely on multiple formulations of what is broadly deemed to be the best indicator – economic performance – before establishing robustness across a wide array of alternative measures, including natural disasters and machine-coded events data from the Integrated Crisis Early Warning System (ICEWS) database.[78]

We prioritize economic performance as a measure of domestic conditions for a few reasons. First, Chinese officials themselves treat economic performance as foundational. Despite China's tremendous economic growth over the past few decades, the income of Chinese citizens as a percentage of gross national income remains relatively low. Increasing it remains a top official priority and doing this without substantial turmoil requires growing the overall "economic pie."[79] Given the size of China's population and the extent of urban–rural inequality, high growth rates are seen as important to broader social stability and cohesion. It is unsurprising, then, that since Deng Xiaoping's "open and reform" strategy, much of the CCP's legitimacy stems from its ability to deliver economic growth.[80] While there have been preliminary indications of a shift from purely growth-based Party legitimation to a strategy that takes social equality and welfare more seriously, such refinements are still based on the prerequisite of overall growth.[81] Finally, economic performance is broadly felt across the whole of the society and it is therefore more difficult for Beijing to

---

[77] The complete data and summary statistics are available in the appendix of this chapter.
[78] Boschee et al. (2018).   [79] Zhu (2011).
[80] Womack (2005); Schubert (2008); Laliberté and Lanteigne (2007). In a meta-analysis of 168 articles on the subject, Gilley and Holbig (2009) find that most treat economic growth as foundational to Party legitimacy.
[81] Gilley and Holbig (2009); Holbig and Gilley (2010).

shape public perceptions of it. Citizens have firsthand experience with and are highly responsive to the job market, the cost of living, wages, and the stock market. The government is therefore sensitive to any negative signals from the economy.

To address concerns regarding the accuracy of official Chinese statistics, we rely on three indicators: annual GDP growth rate (*Growth*), the annual Consumer Confidence Index (*CCI*),[82] and the "Li Keqiang Index" (*Li-Index*).[83] In 2007, Li Keqiang, then a provincial governor and later the Chinese premier, reportedly told an American diplomat that he focused on three indicators to evaluate the true economy: electricity consumption, railroad freight, and bank loans.[84] We construct the *Li-Index* as the annual average of the growth of these three indicators.[85]

There is wide skepticism about the accuracy of China's official GDP statistics, but the debate primarily centers on whether the official figures overstate or understate the reality.[86] The fluctuation in the GDP is still seen as informative. For example, Owyang and Shell note that "while the level of Chinese GDP may remain overstated ... the recent growth rate numbers for Chinese official data are more reliable."[87] The CCI and Li-index measures sidestep this concern entirely.

It is equally challenging to measure how Chinese government officials evaluate the international environment, but as Ikenberry argues, "Chinese leaders understand that globalization has changed the game and that China accordingly needs strong, prosperous partners around the world."[88] To measure the state of international relations for China, we analyze the extent to which China is diplomatically isolated or allied in the United Nations, using General Assembly voting data.[89]

---

[82] According to the OECD (2019), "This consumer confidence indicator provides an indication of future developments of households' consumption and saving, based upon answers regarding their expected financial situation, their sentiment about the general economic situation, unemployment and capability of savings."

[83] We also considered the unemployment rate and found similar results, but we do not report these models because these statistics are generally considered highly unreliable.

[84] Rabinovitch (2010).   [85] Clark, Pinkovskiy, and Sala-i-Martin (2017).

[86] Holz (2014).   [87] Owyang and Shell (2017).   [88] Ikenberry (2008).

[89] Bailey, Strezhnev, and Voeten (2017).

The variable, *Majority Frequency*, measures the proportion of each year's significant UN votes in which China is a member of the majority.[90] To further address the concern that Beijing may value relations with some countries more than others, we also assess two variants of the *Majority Frequency* measure: China's majority votes among G20 countries and China's majority votes with the Security Council.

Because our theory implies a conditional relationship between China's domestic and international environments, we include the interaction term between them in all models.[91]

We also address incident attributes that would increase public awareness and/or newsworthiness. We account for attacks that *Target Civilians* or involve a *Bombing*. It is also reasonable to anticipate that attacks are more likely to be reported when they happen in densely populated *Urban* areas. Finally, we include a measure of *Casualties* per attack. Our models also address politically delicate periods for the CCP (*Sensitive Period*), when authorities are likely to be systematically biased toward stability maintenance (*wei wen*). We identify these periods as (1) a month in which annual sessions of the National People's Congress and National Committee of the People's Political Consultative Conference (*liang hui*) are held; (2) a month in which the National Congress of the CCP is held; (3) a year in which there are leadership transitions; or (4) the 2008 Olympics year.[92] Finally, we include *Internet Penetration* (the ratio of the number of internet users to the total population in each year) to address the possibility that the costs of delayed transparency grow with technological change, particularly social media.[93]

---

[90] This results in a continuous variable, ranging from about 26.7 percent to 77.8 percent, with larger values indicating a more favorable international diplomatic environment.

[91] Because both indicators are continuous and lack a substantively meaningful zero, we center these variables by subtracting the mean value from the observed value.

[92] For a more comprehensive discussion of sensitive political moments and how the Chinese government preemptively represses to preserve stability, see Truex (2019).

[93] The number of internet users in China grew from about 620,000 in 1997 to approximately 632 million in 2014 (China Internet Network Information Center 2014).

Results

Table 3.1 presents the results of seven event history models. Model 1 is a streamlined test of the interaction between the domestic and international environments, measured in terms of GDP growth and UN voting majority frequency. Model 2 adds country-level control variables. Model 3 contains both country-level and incident-level controls. Models 4 and 5 replicate Model 3 but with the Li-index and CCI as alternate indicators of economic performance. In Models 6 and 7, we use two variants of UN voting majority frequency that focus exclusively on G20 countries and Security Council members respectively.[94]

In all the models the results indicate that Chinese authorities promptly cover violence in the official media only when both domestic and international conditions are favorable. This relationship is clearest when shown graphically.[95]

Figure 3.2 shows the probability that a terrorist incident will remain unreported over time for: (1) high economic growth and high frequency of voting with the UN majority, (2) high growth and low frequency, (3) low growth and high frequency, and (4) low growth and low frequency.[96]

The figure demonstrates that it is a near certainty that a violent incident will be omitted in the official media unless both the domestic and international political environments are favorable to the CCP. When these conditions are favorable, the probability of omission drops to about 80 percent one day after a terrorist incident and continues to decline over time, dipping to about 60 percent after four days. In contrast, the probabilities of omission under all other combinations of

---

[94] Figures corresponding to Models 6 and 7 are available in the appendix.

[95] Figure 3.2 is generated from Table 3.1, Model 3; we provide graphical representations from Models 4–7 in the appendix.

[96] We characterize low growth and high growth as one standard error below and above the mean value of the centered value of *Growth* (which are –2.14 and 2.14 respectively), which are equivalent to a growth rate of 6.95 percent and 11.22 percent. Similarly, we characterize low frequency and high frequency as one standard error below and above the mean value of the centered value of *Majority Frequency* (which are –12.61 and 12.61), which are equivalent to 36.96 percent and 62.18 percent respectively. All other control variables are held at their mean values.

Table 3.1 Models of time to reporting in the People's Daily *after attacks*

	Cox PH models						
	(1)	(2)	(3)	(4)	(5)	Majority Frequency G20 countries (6)	Majority Frequency SC members (7)
Growth	-0.454	0.302	0.150			0.854***	0.349*
	(0.291)	(0.268)	(0.362)			(0.219)	(0.180)
Majority Frequency	0.074***	0.062*	0.108***	0.073***	0.16***	0.070*	0.001
	(0.018)	(0.025)	(0.034)	(0.028)	(0.058)	(0.039)	(0.047)
Growth × Majority Frequency	0.030**	0.040***	0.048**			0.063***	0.045**
	(0.014)	(0.015)	(0.021)			(0.023)	(0.018)
Li-Index				0.027			
				(0.120)			
Li-Index × Majority Frequency				0.033*			
				(0.015)			
CCI					1.135		
					(1.583)		
CCI × Majority Frequency					0.031**		
					(0.015)		
Internet Penetration		0.095***	0.071***	0.052***	0.160	0.077***	0.059***
		(0.014)	(0.012)	(0.012)	(0.130)	(0.014)	(0.014)

Table 3.1 (*cont.*)

			Cox PH models			Majority Frequency G20 countries	Majority Frequency SC members
	(1)	(2)	(3)	(4)	(5)	(6)	(7)
Sensitive Period		1.188** (0.533)	0.731 (0.521)	1.079** (0.500)	0.710 (0.450)	1.404** (0.620)	1.346** (0.550)
Casualty			0.023*** (0.007)	0.021*** (0.006)	0.021*** (0.005)	0.018*** (0.006)	0.017*** (0.005)
Urban			0.357 (0.485)	0.327 (0.518)	0.340 (0.582)	0.281 (0.520)	0.295 (0.540)
Target Civilian			−0.897 (0.547)	−0.750 (0.541)	−0.532 (0.560)	−0.877 (0.571)	−0.664 (0.580)
Bombing			0.317 (0.470)	0.624 (0.486)	0.673 (0.441)	0.522 (0.541)	0.353 (0.505)
Observations	137	137	122	122	122	122	122
Max. possible R^2	0.702	0.702	0.734	0.734	0.734	0.734	0.734
Log likelihood	−75.530	−67.193	−58.289	−60.235	−58.069	−61.571	−63.213
LR test	14.675***	31.349***	45.015***	41.123***	45.454***	38.451***	35.166***

Note: Table entries are coefficients obtained from Cox proportional hazards models. Robust standard errors clustered on the incident are in parentheses. *p<.10, **p<.05, ***p<0.01

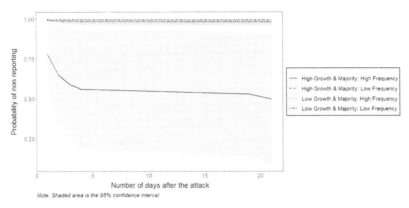

Figure 3.2 Probability of nonreporting for combinations of growth and majority (Model 4)

domestic and international conditions remain statistically indistinguishable from one another, hovering at or near 100 percent.

In further assessments (found in the appendix to this chapter), we account for a variety of alternative explanations. First, we address the possibility that both *Majority Frequency* and days until coverage may be confounded with underlying elements of Chinese foreign policy. Put differently, a change in China's foreign policy may simultaneously lead to voting in the majority at the United Nations and just happen to coincide with the willingness to acknowledge attacks in the official media.

Given that our data cover the tenures of three different Chinese leaders – Jiang, Hu, and Xi – there might be systematic differences in their foreign policies that must be considered. To address this, we include an estimate of China's ideal point from the General Assembly voting data,[97] which has been widely used as a measure of foreign policy position.[98] We also include *Global Terrorist Incidents,* measured as the logged value of the total number of successful terrorist attacks in a given year around the world. This is to account for the possibility that trends in global terrorism may both induce Uyghur attacks and make the international climate more favorable for transparency.

[97] Bailey, Strezhnev, and Voeten (2017).
[98] See, for example, Mattes, Leeds, and Carroll (2015).

To further address concerns about the way we have used key variables, we use alternative measures of domestic and international conditions: natural disasters and diplomatic relations with the United States (while controlling for GDP growth).[99] The Chinese government has long been sensitive to natural disasters because they disrupt regional economic development, threaten social stability, and present openings for critiques of government performance.

The 2008 Sichuan earthquake exemplifies this concern. Days after the earthquake, local residents, especially parents who lost children, turned from grief to anger and started protesting the poor workmanship and government corruption that led to the collapse of several schools.[100]

We posit that a year with more natural disasters indicates a more challenging domestic environment, during which the Chinese government would be more reluctant to report other negative events, including domestic terrorist attacks. To measure the severity of natural disasters, we calculate the total number of days in a given year during which China experienced natural disasters that caused ten or more deaths. A further advantage of these data is that natural disasters are outside the government's control and therefore plausibly exogenous to the mechanisms we are exploring.[101]

As an alternative measure of the international environment, we focus on China's relationship with the United States. It is reasonable to anticipate that this bilateral relationship might factor more prominently in official calculations than the global average, given the primacy of the United States in the international system, the salience of

---

[99] In the appendix, we provide an additional model in which GDP growth is not included as a control. The results are substantively equivalent to those in the main body of the chapter. Because economic growth remains the ultimate objective for the Party, any model that excludes it entirely runs the risk of being seriously underspecified. Notably, the theoretical action in our model is coming through the interaction term, and it is, therefore, the movement of alternative measures in and out of that interaction term that is relevant rather than the movement of independent variables such as GDP in and out of the model entirely.

[100] Blanchard (2008); Branigan (2008).

[101] To account for the number of major natural disasters per year (*Natural Disaster*), we rely on the EM-DAT database. For a disaster to be entered into the database, at least one of the following criteria must be fulfilled: ten or more people reported killed; one hundred or more people reported affected; state of emergency declared; international assistance requested.

the United States in Chinese foreign policy calculations, China's sensitivity to American human-rights critiques, and the United States' particular centrality to global counterterrorism policy.[102]

We further assess the robustness of the finding with machine-coded measures of domestic and international conditions from the ICEWS event data.[103] All our previous models of domestic and international conditions vary only by year, which may be insufficiently granular to capture the decision-making environments facing the Chinese government when attacks happen. The ICEWS data allow us to address this with monthly "intensity scores" of both domestic and international conditions.[104]

Finally, as we have noted, the aftermath of the 9/11 attacks provided a strategic opportunity for Beijing to reframe the Uyghur militancy as part of the war on terror. In addition, internet penetration and social media use began to take off in China at that time. To explore this dynamic, we limit the analysis to the post-2000 period in Model 11 using the ICEWS data.[105]

The probabilities of nonreporting (i.e., censorship), which can be found in the appendix, remain consistent across these models. Regardless of the nuances of particular models, there is prompt acknowledgment of terrorist incidents in the *People's Daily* only when both international and domestic conditions are favorable to the Party.

---

[102] The variable *US–China Distance* is the absolute distance between the ideal points of China and the United States based on their UN voting. Bailey, Strezhnev, and Voeten (2017).

[103] Boschee et al. (2018). Since the ICEWS data only go back to 1995, Model 10 is based on a truncated 1995–2014 sample.

[104] For more details see Computational Event Data System (2013). The intensity score ranges from –10 to 10 with lower values indicating hostile interactions and higher values indicating cooperation. To assess Internal Conditions, we calculate the mean value of the intensity scores of all China's domestic events that happened within ninety days before each violent attack. External Condition is calculated in the same way for all international events, in which China is on the target side. We normalize both variables to a 1–10 scale and lag each by one month. Mattes and Rodrıguez (2014) adopt a similar strategy to measure the degree of cooperation between two states using the 10 Million International Dyadic Events data (1990–2004).

[105] Unfortunately, the narrow time window of the ICEWS data prevents us from using them for an equivalent pre-9/11 analysis that would further clarify this point.

Conclusion

The coverage of political violence in the official media reveals a Party that is highly sensitive, both to Uyghur-initiated incidents and to discussion of them. While there are clear incentives for transparency, the depth of these sensitivities leads to conservatism when conditions are even marginally suboptimal. Of course, China's media landscape is far more complex than just the official media, though official media gives the clearest insight into CCP sensitivities and priorities. As we have noted, the country now features a partially competitive media market. In this context, news outlets are forced to navigate the difficult task of providing content that appeals to the Chinese public without crossing the obscure red lines and third rails laid down by Party officials.[106] This creates an incentive to get as close to these lines as possible without crossing them, leading to both a relative increase in controversial stories that challenge government priorities and to substantial self-censorship.[107] This tension between the Party line and the bottom line is particularly stark in the traditional media's coverage of political violence occurring within China. The public has a powerful appetite for such information, so news outlets attempt to provide it without crossing the line.

A similar story is unfolding online. With over 420 million internet users, China has more people surfing the web than any other country and new web-based technologies are increasingly drawing eyeballs. Since the advent of widespread internet penetration in China, numerous incidents first reported online generated such outrage that traditional news media were compelled to report on them, often leading to changes in the government's policies toward the incident in particular and the withholding of information more generally.[108] Any technology-driven democratization of information challenges the current model of media control in China, which relies on a combination of self-censorship and official oversight.[109]

---

[106] Stockmann and Gallagher (2011).   [107] Liu (2011).

[108] Famous incidents include one involving Sun Zhigang, a migrant graphic designer beaten to death by police (Yu 2006). Another incident, known as the "Wanzhou uprising," was in response to a violent encounter between a "lowly porter" and a "self-proclaimed" government official (Zhao 2009).

[109] Weber and Jia (2007).

These developments have created a dilemma that the Chinese government has never encountered before in its handling of Uyghur violence. Transparency can boost the government's legitimacy by satisfying the public's appetite for information, demonstrating the government's competence and justifying its position internationally. But publicizing attacks immediately risks social and political stability by intensifying ethnic tensions, encouraging copycat attacks, engaging public opinion, and prompting international criticism.

These trade-offs lead Chinese decision-makers to attend to the short-term risks at the expense of longer-term goals. Chinese policymakers' decisions regarding official coverage of terrorist incidents are indeed highly politicized and available evidence indicates that this political calculus is governed by caution and risk avoidance.

4 | *Securitization and Repression in Xinjiang*

The CCP's prioritization of stability extends far beyond media policy. The imperative for social stability has arguably informed every major policy initiative in Xinjiang since the Tiananmen Square protests. And this is far more than a local matter.

For decades, the Party has drawn a direct line between the stability of Xinjiang and the stability of the country as a whole. A leaked March 1996 politburo document on the "maintenance of stability in Xinjiang" spells out the linkage; "Document No. 7" would come to define and drive the government's Xinjiang security policy for years to come:

If we do not increase our vigilance and strengthen work in every respect, large-scale incidents might suddenly occur and confusion and disruption could break out and affect the stability of Xinjiang and the whole nation.[1]

According to the director of the Xinjiang Academy of Social Science, Li Xiaoxia, Document No. 7 was issued after a meeting of the politburo – the top twenty-five or so Party officials – to discuss the series of insurrections, bombings, and other attacks that had erupted in the wake of the collapse of the Soviet Union.

Document No. 7 elevated the stability of Xinjiang to a national priority, exhorting officials to "dam the river before the floods come."[2] That is exactly what they did, through a series of repressive and ever-tightening policies. The underlying problems, however, remained unresolved, and more than two decades later Chinese leaders seem to

---

[1] Chinese Communist Party Central Committee Document Central Committee (1996) No. 7 (https://caccp.freedomsherald.org/conf/doc7.html), which refers to the Record of the Meeting of the Standing Committee of the Political Bureau of the Chinese Communist Party concerning the maintenance of stability in Xinjiang.

[2] Chinese Communist Party Central Committee Document Central Committee (1996). Li (2018); Becquelin (2000); Hastings (2011); Liu (2019).

be more attuned than ever to potential threats to the region's stability. A dam can hold the water back, but it doesn't make it go away.

When violence peaked in 2013 and 2014, authorities responded by expanding security-related expenditures, manpower, and high-tech surveillance systems to unprecedented levels. To get in or out of town by car or train, travelers must pass guarded security checkpoints and show identification. Smartphones might be searched for encrypted chat apps, politically charged videos, and other "suspicious content." Drivers can't even fill up with gas without swiping an ID card and showing their face to a camera. Facial scanners also monitor pedestrians at hotels, shopping malls, and banks.[3]

Despite these unprecedented measures, it was not until the exposure of "reeducation" camps in Xinjiang in late 2017 that it became apparent that China's strategy had undergone a deeper change. These camps – which the Chinese government describes as "vocational education and employment training centers" – marked a shift from reactionary crackdowns to a preventive approach aimed at a complete social transformation.[4]

This strategy now underpins much of China's policies in Xinjiang and the region. The rationale is laid out most explicitly in the writings of Hu Lianhe, one of the architects of the ongoing "de-extremification" campaign. Although Hu has disputed the existence of reeducation camps, he has also argued publicly that the "standardizing of human behavior" is a prerequisite of stability.[5]

What accounts for this excessive response? Some have attributed the escalation to the policies of Chen Quanguo, the newly appointed Party chief in the Xinjiang Uyghur Autonomous Region (XUAR) who had been the Party's secretary in Tibet. Others point to the potential transnational terrorism threat stemming from the radicalized Uyghur networks.[6]

While there are elements of truth to both of these arguments, they leave three important questions inadequately addressed. First, why does the new strategy take this specific form – one that relies on mass internment and political indoctrination? Second, why are Chinese leaders so threatened, given that the militants' capability remains quite

---

[3] Chin and Burge (2017), citing a 2017 *Wall Street Journal* article.
[4] Doyon (2019); Greitens, Lee, and Yazici (2020).   [5] Doyon (2019).
[6] Zenz and Leibold (2017); Greitens, Lee, and Yazici (2020).

low (see Chapter 2)? And, third, why did the Chinese government dramatically escalate repression after the violence and militant capability in Xinjiang had already declined?

We argue that the strategic shift was driven by three key forces.

First, the carrot-and-stick approach – economic incentives combined with harsh reprisals – failed to deliver the absolute stability that Beijing required. At points, officials have expressed frustration that Uyghurs in Xinjiang were insufficiently appreciative of improved standards of living (the carrots). This frustration, of course, overlooks the reality that such improvements were small and hugely outpaced by those enjoyed by Han Chinese in the same region.

Second, Chinese officials anticipated that an economic slowdown could create intolerable political upheaval among the Han majority. This led the regime to rely more heavily on populism (or "mass line" in the Chinese context) and ideological unity for its legitimacy. At the same time, Xi Jinping's rise and consolidation of power reintroduced an element of personalism into the regime. Any instability is viewed as a personal affront to Xi and a direct challenge to Party legitimacy. This reduces officials' room for tolerance still further.

Finally, China perceived a deterioration in the international conditions that had previously supported its preferred policies in Xinjiang, particularly as the United States pivoted away from its fixation with terrorism and jihadist extremism and toward competition with China.

All of these forces transcend Xinjiang, though their manifestations there have been particularly harsh. As such, they have broader implications for China's security and foreign policies. The same factors that drive repression and securitization in Xinjiang echo through the ongoing crackdown on Hong Kong. Will those echoes ripple through China's policies toward Taiwan in coming years? With that possibility in mind, it is vital that we understand the forces and factors at play.

In this chapter, we attempt to do that by introducing the organizations and investments that have driven the securitization of Xinjiang over time. Our account partially diverges from the widely held belief that 2017 marked the inflection point in China's Xinjiang policy; we instead demonstrate a strategic reorientation that dates earlier to 2013–2014. We then provide a detailed analysis of what drove that shift and assess the sustainability of these security policies.

Security in Xinjiang

Security and stability in today's Xinjiang are enforced by a composite force with differentiated responsibilities.[7] A massive security force of police and assistant police staff (*xiejing or fujing*) comprise the frontline of the everyday patrol, surveillance, rapid reaction, and intelligence collection. Backing them is the People's Armed Police (PAP), whose training, equipment, and placement allow it to crack down quickly, effectively, and often brutally, on protests and violence. The last line of defense is the colossal military power projected into the region by the People's Liberation Army (PLA), which primarily performs a traditional military role defending borders shared with states that have been plagued by instability and militancy for decades. However, the PLA's role in internal security, despite ongoing professionalization, has never completely gone away.

Police and assistant police staff comprise the vast majority of security forces in today's Xinjiang. Xi Jinping has referred to them as the "fists and daggers" in the fight against "extremism." The assistant police staff do not have official enforcement rights, but the enormous manpower they represent enables the government to penetrate communities and set up a seamless surveillance network that covers the region almost entirely. Initially, this was a ragtag group, but the government has made extensive investments in their equipment, training, and compensation (see Table 4.1.)

According to Wayne, the shift toward local policing dates all the way back to early 1997, shortly after the declaration of the first strike-hard campaign to crack down in Xinjiang. The aforementioned Document No. 7, which prioritized security in the region, had already directed authorities to "[s]trengthen the democratic dictatorship organizations, such as Public Safety and National Security, and fully utilize their functions in fighting separatism and sabotage activities."

The region's then Party secretary, Wang Lequan, pledged to "reorganize the entire police system of Xinjiang in the villages and small towns."[8] Motivated by the belief that insurgency arises from

---

[7] Since our main focus is the functionalities of the security forces, we exclude Xinjiang Production and Construction Corps (XPCC) from this discussion. The XPCC is an administrative authority with subprovincial powers that also relies on the military, the PAP, and the police to maintain stability and security.

[8] Wayne (2008: 98).

Table 4.1 XUAR public security expenditures by category, 2015–2018

	2015	2016	2017	2018
			Unit: 10,000 Yuan	
Total public security expenditures	2,519,645	3,009,036	5,763,869	5,669,604
Subcategory public security expenditures				
People's Armed Police	174,383 (7%)	149,039 (5%)	167,400 (3%)	123,725 (2%)
Public security (Police)	1,442,954 (57%)	1,744,759 (58%)	3,083,085 (53%)	3,109,622 (55%)
State security	59,667 (2%)	78,050 (3%)	70,580 (1%)	78,989 (1%)
Procuratorial system	133,513 (5%)	128,242 (4%)	136,549 (2%)	129,766 (2%)
Court system	214,417 (9%)	227,907 (8%)	224,999 (4%)	219,479 (4%)
Judicial system	82,760 (3%)	86,753 (3%)	188,980 (3%)	190,036 (3%)
Prison system	239,334 (10%)	240,145 (8%)	465,103 (8%)	629,920 (11%)
Coercive isolated detoxification	45,227 (2%)	55,947 (2%)	85,446 (1%)	94,573 (2%)
National Administration for the Protection of State Secrets	585 (0.02%)	643 (0.02%)	912 (0.01%)	799 (0.01%)
Uncategorized	126,805 (5%)	297,551 (10%)	1,340,815 (23%)	1,092,695 (19%)

Source: XUAR Finance Department (final accounts)

the grassroots and that successful counterinsurgency depends on the government's ability to penetrate and gather intelligence from local communities, the XUAR government established new police stations and sent experienced police officers to rural areas where they had historically been few and far between.[9] And, again, early roots can be found in Document No. 7, which called on authorities to "[m]ake southern Xinjiang the focus of attention; establish a sensitive information net and manage to get information on a deep level which can covertly alert beforehand. Establish individual files; maintain supervision and vigilance."

The new XUAR administration formed after the Urumqi riot in 2009 further invested in local policing. Zhang Chunxian announced a new "one village, one policeman" strategy, which would require 8,000 new officers to strengthen local stability maintenance (*wei wen*) capability.[10] That recruitment target actually understated the impact of this policy; each officer was accompanied by at least three assistant police staff and six militia soldiers at a village police station.[11]

Zenz and Leibold's seminal analysis of XUAR public and civil service jobs advertised on the Chinese internet shows that most of the growth in manpower happened in this period – there were two massive spikes in police recruitment in 2012 (11,559 security-related positions, a 57 percent increase compared to 2009) and 2016 (31,687 security-related positions, more than a 300 percent increase over the previous year).[12]

The truly explosive growth in the number of assistant police staff came in the second surge in 2016, which, according to Zenz and Leibold's data, contributed more than three quarters of the newly posted security-related jobs.[13] This boost was largely driven by the establishment of the omnipresent "convenience police stations" brought to Xinjiang by Chen (who replaced Zhang in September 2016). These were set up every three hundred to five hundred meters on the streets across the populated areas to enable police officers to theoretically reach any location within one minute.[14] Given the extraordinary number of these

---

[9] Wayne (2008: 98).   [10] People.com (2012).   [11] *Boxun News* (2012).
[12] Zenz and Leibold (2017).   [13] Zenz and Leibold (2017).
[14] *Sohu News* (2017).

stations, the expansion of comparatively low-paid assistant police staff allowed the government to manage the considerable costs.

Drawing on data from the XUAR Department of Finance, Table 4.1 shows the breakdown of XUAR annual domestic security expenditures by different departments from 2015 through 2018. Expenditures by public security departments (*gong an*) – the regular police force – have consistently accounted for more than 50 percent of the total regional security-related spending. Another interesting feature is the sharp jump in expenses for uncategorized public-security-related affairs in 2017, in terms of both absolute number (a 351 percent increase) and the share of total public security expenditures (from 10 percent in 2016 to 23 percent in 2017).

It is worth noting, however, that the PAP's true reach is obscured because most of its expenses are funded by the central government instead of provincial governments.[15]

Established in 1982, the PAP is the paramilitary branch of China's domestic security apparatus. Its primary mission is to provide internal security and domestic stability, particularly in response to "mass incidents."[16] The PAP was under the dual command of both the Central Military Committee and the State Council for most of its existence. However, since 2018, in another major move to centralize authority over Chinese forces, the Central Military Committee (chaired by Xi Jinping) assumed sole command of the PAP. This move stripped provincial and local officials of control over the deployment of the PAP in the event of emergencies, underscoring the importance of this function to the central government.[17]

In terms of equipment and capability, the PAP is equivalent to light infantry and therefore has long been described as the "twin brother" of the PLA.[18] And when it comes to the on-the-ground handling of large-scale riots in Xinjiang, the PAP has certainly been no less brutal

---

[15] Zenz (2018).

[16] Department of Defense, Office of the Secretary of Defense (2018).

[17] Regarding this reform, the Ministry of Defense spokesman emphasized in a press conference that "the fundamental function and responsibility of the PAP is not changed" (Xinhua 2017). For analyses of the strategic considerations behind and consequences of this reform, see Zenz (2018) and Wuthnow (2019).

[18] Yang (2016).

than the PLA. Tear gas, mass arrests, and beatings have been widely employed, and the PAP reportedly fired live ammunition in their response to both the 1997 Yining and 2009 Urumqi riots.[19]

In addition to riot control, the PAP is the designated force for counterterrorism combat operations. This role is explicitly written into the 2009 Law of the People's Republic of China on the People's Armed Police Force and repeatedly emphasized in China's national security white papers.[20] For example, on January 5, 2007, the PAP, equipped with helicopters, led the largest operation to that date against militants in the Pamir Mountains, which reportedly killed eighteen militants and led to the arrest of seventeen others.[21]

The PAP also has two specialized counterterrorism units, the Snow Leopards and the Falcons, the former of which reportedly conducted a hostage rescue mission in Iraq in 2005.[22] Although information regarding the size of the PAP forces deployed in Xinjiang is not publicly available,[23] the PAP XUAR General Detachment (*zongdui*) and the Beijing General Detachment are the only two Army Grade (*zheng jun ji*) units, while all other provincial PAP general detachments are Secondary Army Grade (*fu jun ji*). This suggests that PAP forces in Xinjiang have a special status in terms of both size and equipment.[24]

The Xinjiang region falls under the PLA's Western Theater Command,[25] which consists of the Thirteenth Army from the former Chengdu Military Zone and the Twenty-First and Forty-Seventh Armies from the former Lanzhou Military Zone. Together, these account for

---

[19] Millward (2004); Dillon (2004); Wayne (2008); Kang (2019).
[20] Ministry of National Defense (2011); The State Council Information Office (2011).
[21] Sohu News (2007).   [22] *Sina* (2009); Blasko (2015).
[23] China's 2006 defense white paper revealed that the PAP has a total force of 660,000 across the country.
[24] While the PAP Tibet General Detachment is a Secondary Army Grade unit, the commander and the political commissar of Tibet PAP enjoy benefits (salary and welfare) equivalent to those of the heads of Army Grade units (Zhong 2016).
[25] In 2016, as one of President Xi Jinping's major moves to reform the military, the PLA reduced its seven military zones to five Theater Commands – Eastern Theater Command, the Southern Theater Command, the Western Theater Command, the Northern Theater Command, and the Central Theater Command. Before the reform, Xinjiang was an independent military zone from 1954 to 1985; it was part of the Lanzhou Military Zone from 1985 to 2016.

more than a third of China's land-based military. According to Chan, the Western Theater Command is charged with "threats in Xinjiang and Tibet and other minority areas close to Afghanistan, and other states that are home to training bases for separatists, terrorists and extremists."[26]

That said, the PLA's role in internal security affairs has been curtailed by design.[27] The PLA's last direct operations in Xinjiang were more than thirty years ago in response to the 1990 Baren unrest, in which the PLA reportedly used airpower to support the response and airlifted in forces to deal with rebels who had fled into the mountains.[28] In later violent mass events, such as the 1995 unrest in Hotan, the 1997 Yining riot, and the 2009 Urumqi riot, the PLA played a supporting role to the PAP or was not involved at all.

The PLA's reduced role in domestic stability maintenance extends beyond Xinjiang. Since the Tiananmen crackdown in 1989, concerns over legitimacy and fears of international backlash have made Beijing increasingly reluctant to involve the military directly in internal unrest. The PLA is, however, playing an increasingly salient role in China's counterterrorism efforts abroad (a point that we will return to in detail in Chapter 5). As such, the PLA's reduced role should be viewed as part of the broader professionalization of the force rather than any kind of conciliatory measure.

After all, as Document No. 7 laid out in 1996: "A stronghold against ethnic separatism should be formed by greatly strengthening the construction of the People's Liberation Army in Xinjiang. *The military forces in Xinjiang will only be strengthened, not weakened.*"[29]

The Securitization of Xinjiang

These same three forces – police, PAP, and PLA – are the backbone of domestic security and stability maintenance throughout China, but particularly along the border regions where there are significant

---

[26] Chan (2015).
[27] Historically, the PLA was intensively involved in the consolidation of both security and political control over the Xinjiang region. For a comprehensive review of the history of the PLA's deployment and function in Xinjiang (1949–1980s), see Shichor (2004).
[28] Wayne (2008: 81).   [29] Emphasis added.

minority populations. Thus, while the breakdown of the domestic security expenditures provided in Table 4.1 is informative, the short time span of the data and the lack of comparison between Xinjiang and the rest of China limits insight into how securitization efforts have evolved over time or the extent to which Xinjiang is policed relative to other places. To address this, we turn to aggregate provincial-level public security expenditures, data for which are available over a longer time period and for more provinces.

As we discussed in Chapter 3, there is much debate as to whether official Chinese economic data are reliable or accurate. There are equally good reasons to extend these suspicions to public expenditure data. When it comes to security expenditures in particular, the Chinese government (and especially the Xinjiang government) has significant incentives to underreport because internal security spending is likely to be interpreted as government efforts to boost social control and repression.[30] However, underreporting would bias against the detection of the divergent securitization efforts between Xinjiang and the rest of China. In other words, the patterns we observe likely understate the reality.

The most complete information on these expenditures comes from China's *Statistical Yearbooks*, which itemize general public expenditures by category and by province. Although China started publishing its *Statistical Yearbooks* in 1982, the provincial-level data begin in 1995. Since 2007, there has been an independent entry in the *Statistical Yearbook* for "Public Security Expenditures," which, according to official documents, includes the PAP, the public security police, state security, the procuratorate, the court system, the judiciary system, the prison system, the reeducation through labor system, state secrets protection, and "others."[31] To allow for an apples-to-apples comparison, for the 1997–2006 period, we add two separately reported domestic security-related items together: (1) expenditures for the public security system, the procuratorate system, the court system, and the judicial system (PPCJ) and (2) expenditures for the PAP. For the 1995–1996 period, the *Statistical Yearbook* reports only expenditures for the PPCJ.[32]

[30] Greitens (2017).   [31] Ministry of Finance (2016).
[32] The public security system, the procuratorial system, the court system, and the judicial system are all independent agencies but under the administration

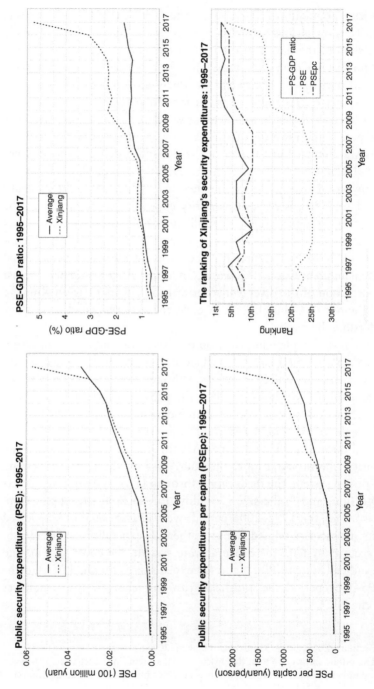

Figure 4.1 Security expenditures in Xinjiang

The upper-left graph in Figure 4.1 shows the annual public security expenditures (PSE) in Xinjiang compared to the nationwide average. Surprisingly, when it comes to the total amount of money spent on security, Xinjiang did not catch up with the provincial/regional average until 2014 – the year that marked a series of deadly attacks and the launch of the third strike-hard campaign. This steady spending pattern changed abruptly in 2017 when Xinjiang's total security expenditures spiked by about 92 percent to 576 million yuan – nearly double the average per province/region. This jump in security expenditures reflects the previous year's massive expansion in police manpower noted by Zenz and Leibold.

Focusing solely on *total* security expenditures, however, can lead to the mistaken conclusion that Xinjiang's police presence has only recently exceeded that found in the rest of China. Spending in more populous, wealthy provinces inflates the national average. For example, in every year within the 1995–2017 period, Guangdong Province (which has been the most populated province since 2006, and the wealthiest province in terms of local GDP) ranked first in total security expenditures.

To account for these issues, we plot the public security expenditures per capita (PSEpc) (bottom left of Figure 4.1) and the provincial-level PSE–GDP ratio (upper-right graph). These clearly demonstrate that security spending in Xinjiang began pulling away from the pack much earlier, in 2009. That year marked the outbreak of the July 5 Urumqi riot, which caused the deaths of over 150 people in the bloodiest known unrest in China since the Tiananmen Square protests.[33]

The bottom-right graph in Figure 4.1, in which we plot the ranking of Xinjiang among thirty-one provinces and direct-administered municipalities by all three security expenditure measures, also shows that after 2009 Xinjiang quickly became one of the top five most heavily policed regions, both per capita and as a ratio of spending to GDP. Xinjiang's PSE–GDP ratio has been second only to Tibet's since 2011.

Given the eye-catching jump in all three spending categories in Xinjiang in 2017, it is helpful to see what was happening across China in that year. Map 4.1 plots a snapshot of the cross-province comparison

of the local and central Political and Legal Affairs Commission of the CCP. In the statistical yearbooks, these agencies' expenditures are reported in one category – "PPCJ."

[33] *The Economist* (2009).

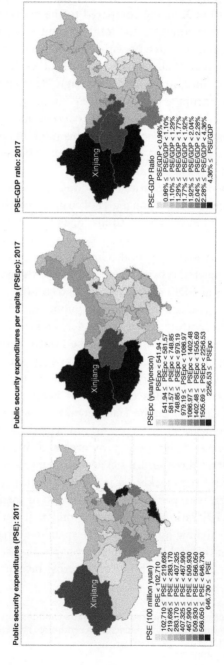

Public security expenditures (PSE): 2017

PSE (100 million yuan)

PSE < 102.710
102.710 ≤ PSE < 219.695
219.695 ≤ PSE < 283.170
283.170 ≤ PSE < 407.325
407.325 ≤ PSE < 467.990
467.990 ≤ PSE < 509.930
509.930 ≤ PSE < 566.050
566.050 ≤ PSE < 646.730
646.730 ≤ PSE

Xinjiang

Public security expenditures per capita (PSEpc): 2017

PSEpc (yuan/person)

PSEpc < 541.94
541.94 ≤ PSEpc < 581.57
581.57 ≤ PSEpc < 748.85
748.85 ≤ PSEpc < 979.19
979.19 ≤ PSEpc < 1086.97
1086.97 ≤ PSEpc < 1402.48
1402.48 ≤ PSEpc < 1505.69
1505.69 ≤ PSEpc < 2256.53
2256.53 ≤ PSEpc

Xinjiang

PSE-GDP ratio: 2017

PSE-GDP Ratio

PSE/GDP < 0.96%
0.96% ≤ PSE/GDP < 1.10%
1.10% ≤ PSE/GDP < 1.29%
1.29% ≤ PSE/GDP < 1.77%
1.77% ≤ PSE/GDP < 1.92%
1.92% ≤ PSE/GDP < 2.04%
2.04% ≤ PSE/GDP < 2.28%
2.28% ≤ PSE/GDP < 4.36%
4.36% ≤ PSE/GDP

Xinjiang

Map 4.1 A cross-province comparison in 2017

of the three security spending indicators in 2017, with the darker areas indicating higher spending. Xinjiang is the only region in either the darkest (at or above the 95th percentile) or the second-darkest (between the 90th percentile and 95th percentile) category in all three maps.[34]

Strategic Reorientation: Ethnic Mingling and De-extremification

The exposure of the mass internment of Uyghurs in the reeducation system led scholars to posit that 2017 marked Beijing's shift to preventive repression.[35] However, a careful examination of official speeches, meetings, and policy actions indicates that the seed of this more coercive and assimilatory approach was planted somewhat earlier.

Early forays into these more repressive policies focused on elites, particularly prominent Uyghurs in civil society. Many received draconian prison sentences for criticizing the government while others have disappeared on tenuous charges (or no charges at all). Among the most prominent of these cases is that of Ilham Tohti, an economics scholar at Beijing's Minzu University who was detained in 2014 after criticizing Beijing's response to the 2013 Tiananmen Square attack.

Tohti was sentenced to life in prison after being accused of "separatism and stoking ethnic tension." Human Rights Watch countered that Tohti has "consistently, courageously and unambiguously advocated peacefully for greater understanding and dialogue between various communities, and with the state." In 2019, the EU Parliament awarded Tohti its highest human rights award for his efforts to "foster dialogue" between ethnic Han and Uyghurs.[36]

Another prominent case is that of Ekpar Asat, a Uyghur social media tech entrepreneur and philanthropist who went missing in April 2016. He disappeared three weeks after returning to Xinjiang from the United States, where he attended a State Department leadership program – a program for which he was nominated by Chinese authorities. After several inquiries from US Senators, Chinese authorities said Asat had been sentenced in a secret trial to fifteen years in prison for "inciting ethnic

---

[34] With an average of 2,357 yuan spent on each Xinjiang resident and about 5 percent of its regional GDP spent on security, Xinjiang was the second-most heavily policed region in terms of both PSEpc and PSE-GDP ratio, following Tibet.

[35] Greitens, Lee, and Yazici (2020). [36] *BBC News* (2019).

hatred and ethnic discrimination." It is unclear what actions, if any, these charges were based upon. Asat's parents are CCP members and he had participated in events organized by the Chinese authorities before he went missing, according to Amnesty International, which has been lobbying for his release or the disclosure of the evidence against him.[37]

After first targeting the elites, the CCP turned to the suppression of even measured dissent from the masses. Shortly after the 2014 Kunming and Urumqi attacks, the Second Xinjiang Work Forum was held in Beijing on May 28 and 29 and was attended by all seven members of the Standing Committee led by President Xi Jinping.[38] Comparison of the language used in this policy meeting and Hu Jintao's language and priorities in the First Xinjiang Work Forum in 2010 (a year after the Urumqi riot) sheds light on how Beijing fundamentally altered its strategic approach to the region. In Table 4.2, we compare Hu's and Xi's guiding principles as delivered in these two meetings, arranged in order of appearance of each principle in the respective speeches.

In 2010 Hu prioritized economic development and enhancing the standard of living for the region, but just four years later Xi unambiguously shifted the priority to stability maintenance and ethnic unity. Xi also highlighted the importance of religious regulation and assimilation into Chinese culture, which were not mentioned at all by his predecessor.[39] Four months after the Second Xinjiang Work Forum, Xi reaffirmed this new strategic orientation in the Central Ethnic Work Conference by putting less emphasis on diversity and more on increasing efforts to bind together the people of China proactively.[40] In other words, there is a clear shift from politics based on the notion that rising economic tides would placate Uyghur grievances to approaches based on forced assimilation and, eventually, cultural genocide.

These changes manifested in large part as "de-extremification" policies. As commonly occurs in China, once the official signal was sent, this policy shift became an instant object of academic inquiry. A survey of the China National Knowledge Infrastructure – the leading national research and information repository – reveals that the number of Chinese language research articles on "de-extremification" ("去极端化") rose sharply beginning in 2014 (Figure 4.2).

---

[37] Amnesty International (2020).
[38] *BBC News* (2014).
[39] For a detailed documentation of China's new religious regulations, see Famularo (2018: 46–53).
[40] Leibold (2019a).

Table 4.2 *A comparison of speeches on Xinjiang*

Order	Hu Jintao 2010	Xi Jinping 2014
1	Promote leapfrog development in Xinjiang; the fundamental approach to the Xinjiang problem is to adhere to the Scientific Outlook on Development and speed up development.	Social stability and long-term peace and order is the overall objective; must treat cracking down on terrorist and violent activities as the priority of current struggle.
2	Treat enhancing the standard of living of people of all ethnic groups as the starting point and end goal.	Among the problems of Xinjiang, the longest-term problem is still ethnic unity; all ethnic groups should get together like "seeds of a pomegranate"; need to promote interethnic interaction and mingling, promote bilingual education, establish social structure and community environment where all ethnic groups are embedded with each other.
3	Hold high the banner of the unity of the people of all ethnic groups.	Work hard to promote a more harmonious religious relationship; actively guide religions to adapt to the socialist society.
4	Effectively combine the promotion of reform and development with the maintenance of social stability; adhere to the principle of "two hands to grasp, both hands must be hard."	Unswervingly continue promoting better and faster development in Xinjiang; make sure that development policies are implemented in a way that can effectively improve the standard of living, benefit the locals, and enhance unity.
5		Strengthen the sense of belonging to China, to the Chinese nation, to the Chinese culture, and to the path of socialism with Chinese characteristics.
6		The key to Xinjiang work is to uphold the Party's role as the core of leadership in directing the overall situation and coordinating the efforts of all quarters.

Source: Baidu Encyclopedia on the First and Second Central Meetings on the Work of Xinjiang.

Chinese scholars eager for professional advancement tend to study topics that will please the Party and thereby attract state funding; therefore, it's reasonable to assume that this jump in the number of publications on such a narrowly defined topic reflects the official preference change during that period.

The lurking explanation behind all these transitions is the consolidation of power by Xi Jinping, which took hold at this same time. As the most powerful leader in China since Mao, Xi's thoughts were taken as orders by local leaders. As early as February 2014, even before the Second Xinjiang Work Forum,[41] XUAR's then Party secretary, Zhang Chunxian, had already launched a plan to "explore the people's conditions; benefit the people's livelihood; and fuse with the people's sentiments," known as *fanghuiju* for short.[42] In an effort to strengthen grassroots governance and promote ethnic unity, this plan would rotate over 200,000 Party members to take up part-time residence in 8,635 administrative villages, 754 state-owned farm and ranch village groups, and 931 communities over the next three years.[43] This policy set objectives to be achieved over three years:

1. 2014 – promote ethnic unity and religious harmony;
2. 2015 – strengthen grassroots organizations, speed up de-extremification, and improve standards of living;
3. 2016 – achieve "One-Two-Three-Five."

The "One-Two-Three-Five" policy requires explanation. In Zhang's formulation "One" referred to establishing *one* standardized style of village, with an office for the village committee, a service center and group activity room for villagers, an interim housing service, a police station, a Chinese-language kindergarten, and a clinic. "Two" referred to resolving *two* key problems: the "slackness" of grassroots Party organizations and local dissatisfaction with these organizations. "Three" referred to eliminating *three* types of incidents: violent "terrorist" attacks, "extremist" religious activities, and mass incidents (protests and riots). "Five" referred to building local Party branches with *five* features: good leadership, good Party members, good working channels, good development ideas, and a good reputation among people.[44]

---

[41] On December 19, 2013, after being debriefed on the work of Xinjiang, Xi Jinping had commented on the guiding principles on Xinjiang work, which conveyed signals similar to those he sent five months later. *China Daily* (2016).
[42] *China Daily* (2016).   [43] Zheng (2016).   [44] Zhang (2016).

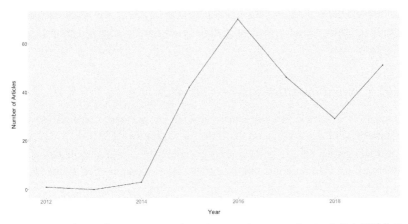

Figure 4.2 Chinese-language journal articles on "de-extremification" ("去极端化")

Later in 2014, reports began to circulate in international media that the XUAR under Zhang had begun offering cash incentives to promote interethnic marriage. According to *The Guardian*, Chinese authorities in Qiemo County began to offer a generous "gift package" to couples in which one member was an ethnic minority and the other was Han Chinese. The package included annual cash payments of 10,000 yuan (about $1,600 in 2014) during the first five years of the marriage, as well as housing, healthcare, and education subsidies.[45]

Also, under Zhang, the now infamous reeducation system began to take shape. According to Zenz, three-tiered "transformation through education bases" were established at the county, township, and village levels in Xinjiang's Konashahar (Shufu) county in late 2014. These reeducation centers were the forbearers of the detention facilities that came to international attention in the years that followed.[46]

Despite Hu Lianhe's insistence that reeducation camps did not exist, a former XUAR Commission Secretary for Discipline Inspection, Fu Qiang, confirmed them in a 2015 *Xinjiang Daily* article. In the article, Fu described visiting the "de-extremification education center in Hotan City." He claimed the center "can hold up to 3,000 people" and has "already trained five batches of students."[47] However, during Zhang's tenure the scale of the reeducation campaign remained limited

[45] *The Guardian* (2014).   [46] Zenz (2018).   [47] Fu (2015).

in comparison to what was to come, targeting only the small subset of the population that authorities viewed as deeply affected by religious extremism.[48]

From Internment to Cultural Genocide

Despite these measures, sporadic violence continued, culminating in a knife attack at a coal mine in Aksu on September 18, 2015, in which, according to *Radio Free Asia,* fifty people, including five police officers, were killed.[49] In response, Beijing sent Chen Quanguo, the former Party secretary in Tibet, to replace Zhang Chunxian. While some believed Beijing was second-guessing Zhang's "soft approach" (*rouxing*) to Xinjiang, relying more on incentives than coercion, he was subsequently promoted to vice director of the Central Coordinating Group on Xinjiang Work – suggesting that his policies were not fully rejected.[50]

In line with this interpretation, Chen did not actually abandon Zhang's policy framework so much as implement it more coercively and at larger scale. In terms of the *fanghuiju* policy – "Visit the People, Benefit the People, and Get Together the Hearts of the People" – Secretary Chen also established a control center in Urumqi where higher-level officials were required to contact Party members dispatched to village-level working groups twice a day by video.[51] This policy was aimed at both checking whether working groups were on duty and ensuring that officials in Urumqi could respond to local situations.[52]

Under Chen, Xinjiang authorities also took steps toward fulfilling another of President Xi's guiding policy principles – "binding together" the people of China. Secretary Chen took President Xi quite literally.

The XUAR government held a mobilization convention on October 16, 2016, where it called for ethnic unity.[53] Shortly thereafter, XUAR launched a new campaign, officially named "Pair Up and Become Family," or *jie dui zi*.[54] According to the government, the idea behind this program was to increase and deepen the cultural exchanges between different ethnic groups by sending over one million Han, mostly Party

---

[48] Leibold (2019b).   [49] *Radio Free Asia* (2015).
[50] Uyghur Human Rights Project (2017); Yu (2016).
[51] Author interview (2019), PRC.   [52] Author interview (2019), PRC.
[53] *People's Daily* (2018).   [54] *People's Daily* (2018).

members who are civil servants and employees of state-owned enterprises, to spend about a week every two months living in the home of Uyghur host families as "relatives."[55]

According to Darren Byler, who conducted fieldwork in southern Xinjiang in spring 2018, the daily work of the "relatives" usually consists of four types of activities: (1) poverty alleviation; (2) conveying and explaining state policies to their host families; (3) promoting Chinese culture, Mandarin, and patriotic education, especially to children in their host families; and (4) reporting signs that their host family's attachment to Islam might be "extreme."[56]

While these forced "relative ties" are described by the government as voluntary, reports suggest that, at least for the Uyghur hosts, the "voluntary behavior" was induced by their belief that refusing any state initiative could lead to being branded a potential extremist.[57]

Xinjiang's new government also tweaked the interethnic marriage incentives. Beginning in 2019, bonus points on the national college entrance exam replaced the annual cash payments for interethnic couples. The XUAR Education Department slashed the bonus points previously awarded to candidates whose parents are both ethnic minorities, from thirty-five bonus points down to fifteen.[58] But, if one of the candidate's parents is Han Chinese and the other is an ethnic minority, then the candidate is entitled to a twenty-point bonus. The authorities were not subtle about the intention underlying this policy change – a widely circulated article on the policy was titled "Another Heavy Punch to Promote Ethnic Mingling."[59]

Chen's best-known policy change was the dramatic expansion of the reeducation system that first sprang up under Secretary Zhang. However, according to Leibold's documentation, Zhang's more limited strategy of targeting known extremists was under pressure before the arrival of Chen in 2016. Other high-level XUAR officials (most notably Justice Department secretary Zhang Yun) and scholars (such as the Urumqi-based sociologist Li Xiaoxia) were already arguing that as much as 30 percent of southern Xinjiang's residents were "infected" by extremist ideology.

---

[55] *People's Daily* (2018). [56] Byler (2018) [57] Withnall (2018).
[58] This policy applies to eleven ethnic groups in Xinjiang (excluding Hui): Uyghur, Kazakh, Mongolian, Kyrgyz, Tajik, Sibe, Uzbek, Tatar, Daur, Tibetan, and Russian.
[59] Sohu News (2019).

In February 2017, shortly after three Uyghur militants killed five civilians in a knife attack near Hotan, Secretary Chen appeared in Beijing to attend a National Security Commission meeting in which the new reeducation strategy appears to have been discussed and approved by President Xi.[60]

Almost immediately after Chen's return from Beijing, the XUAR Justice Department issued a document that recommended establishing "five centers and three talent pools" in southern Xinjiang. Among other things, the five types of centers would include "centers for centralized transformation through education and training" – the widely decried reeducation camps – and the talent pools included "teachers" for the reeducation centers.[61] The March directive for northern Xinjiang, considered less volatile and less Muslim than the south, called for just "four centers and two talent pools," excluding reeducation centers and the accompanying teachers from that directive.[62]

After the government published the De-extremification Regulations, the regional government fired off requests for reeducation-related procurement and construction bids at a quick clip. The number and value of such government projects rose to unprecedented levels, and the demand for construction services and supplies remained high until September of that year.[63]

The rapid expansion in the reeducation system through 2017 led directly to the mass incarceration of over one million Muslim Chinese citizens in up to 1,200 reeducation centers in Xinjiang – a scale that exceeds the size of the entire Chinese reeducation-through-labor system as it existed prior.[64] The strategic logic of CCP policy in Xinjiang had clearly changed – as one local official put it: "You can't uproot all the weeds hidden among the crops in the field one by one – you need to spray chemicals to kill them all."[65]

Understanding the Strategic Reorientation

What explains this radical shift in China's Xinjiang policy? Drawing on a wide range of official statements, speeches, and documents, Greitens, Lee, and Yazici conclude that the answer lies in the Party's

---

[60] Leibold (2019b).   [61] XUAR Department of Justice (2017).
[62] XUAR Department of Justice (2017).   [63] Leibold (2019b).
[64] Zenz (2018).   [65] *Radio Free Asia* (2018).

mounting concern over transnational terrorism.[66] They argue that this change in China's internal security strategy was driven by "its desire to prevent terrorism from diffusing into China via radicalized transnational Uyghur networks, particularly those with links to terrorist groups in Southeast Asia, Syria, and the broader Middle East."[67]

Yet despite the mounting threat imposed by transnational terrorism, the ability of any militants – Uyghur or otherwise – to penetrate Chinese borders from the outside remains relatively low in comparison to China's defensive capability. Moreover, Uyghur militants have demonstrated only a muted desire to return to China to carry out attacks, according to Mumford and others.[68] China's policy changes are clearly a reaction to the increasing instability in the region, but Beijing's fears of instability and secession clearly exceed the facts on the ground.[69]

We argue that this unprecedented intensification of assimilation and de-extremification efforts were fueled by three additional factors: frustration with the failure of ineffective prior policies, changes in domestic situations and institutions, and deteriorating international conditions.

For decades, Beijing's approach to Xinjiang can be best understood as a "sticks and carrots" strategy. However, the "sticks" repeatedly failed to deter violence, while the "carrots" were unable to induce the compliance that Chinese officials sought.

The "stick" policy has its roots in the March 1996 politburo meeting we introduced at the beginning of this chapter. From that point forward, "strike-hard" campaigns featuring rapid mass arrests and harsh sentences became a nearly automatic reaction to any surge in Uyghur-related violence in the region, with the first initiated immediately after the issue of "Document No.7" and the second following the July 5 Urumqi riots in 2009.[70]

The authorities' initial response to the most recent wave of violence in 2013 and 2014 came from the same playbook. According to official media, three days after a deadly May 22, 2014 attack on a street market in Urumqi, a strike-hard campaign code-named Zero Point "swiftly

---

[66] Greitens, Lee, and Yazici (2020).
[67] Greitens, Lee, and Yazici (2020: 10–11).
[68] Mumford (2018: 22)   [69] Leibold (2019a and 2019b).
[70] In this chapter, and throughout the book, we restrict our focus on strike-hard campaigns that specifically target Uyghurs. The first nation-wide strike-hard campaign targeting general criminal activities was initiated in 1983 under Deng Xiaoping.

overthrew several groups that were involved in terrorism and religious extremism, arrested a batch of suspects, and seized large quantities of tools and materials that can be used to make explosive devices."[71]

The problem with sticks is that they increase discontent and may even cause violence. The causal, cyclical relationship between repression and violence is a subject of heated debate. The official line insists that strengthened security measures in Xinjiang are a necessary response to the increasing terrorist threats in the region and a show of the government's commitment to stability.[72] Uyghur dissidents, however, argue precisely the reverse – that the repression triggers violence.[73]

Variants of this debate are abundant in the literature on terrorism and counterterrorism.[74] An important component of this body of research assesses the efficacy of state repression in deterring domestic political violence.[75] Some argue that harshly repressive measures such as police surveillance, mass arrest and detention, and stringent media control effectively curb violence.[76] In this view, state repression allows the government to demonstrate its resolve, collect intelligence, and increase the cost of terrorist plots – thereby limiting options for potential perpetrators. Others, however, conclude that state repression is at best ineffective and at worst counterproductive; it not only closes off nonviolent avenues for political expression but also delegitimizes the government in the eyes of the broader population.[77]

Xinjiang is a laboratory for this debate.

On the one hand, as a powerful institutionalized authoritarian regime, China has been able to successfully keep the region under tight control through an increasingly intense police presence, periodic crackdowns, and the strategic manipulation of information. Despite the simmering tension, violence has been sporadic and casualties per

---

[71] *Legal Daily* (2014).   [72] Leading Industry Research (2020).   [73] *DW* (2014).

[74] Although the primary interest here is counterterrorism, we also refer to studies of counterinsurgency, civil war, civil unrest, and repression, for they share similar theoretical logics.

[75] For a helpful review of the literature, see Piazza (2017) and Sanchez-Cuenca and de la Calle (2009).

[76] Schmid (1992); Eyerman (1998); De Figueiredo and Weingast (2000); Lyall (2009); Nacos (2016).

[77] Gurr (1970); Crenshaw (1981); Li (2005); Siqueira and Sandler (2006); Bueno de Mesquita and Dickson (2007); Piazza (2017).

attack have remained relatively low compared to global averages. Since 2015, violence within China has been essentially nonexistent. As discussed in Chapter 2, this is primarily due to the difficulties that militants in Xinjiang face in coordinating and accessing lethal weapons. Through this lens, China seems to typify the "autocratic advantage" against terrorism.[78]

On the other hand, the underlying potential for violence in Xinjiang has never been eradicated and each round of forceful pacification seems to require more repression than the last. This reality is apparent in the attack trends we discussed in previous chapters – with escalating waves of intense violence interrupted by periods of comparative quiet – as well as the rising security expenditures in the region. The data imply a tragic feedback loop between citizen violence and state repression.

Indeed, many studies of Xinjiang note this spiral of grievance and crackdown. For instance, Hastings finds that the months following the first strike-hard campaign in 1996 were accompanied by a rise in logistically sophisticated violent incidents.[79] Focusing on the same time period, Millward argues that the February 1997 unrest in Yining was likely a response to the mass arrests during the strike-hard campaign the previous year.[80] Looking at the post-9/11 period, Smith Finley draws on interview data and analysis of representative violent incidents to argue that China's increasingly indiscriminate preemptive policing against Uyghur minorities in that period not only triggered retaliatory violence but also resulted in a broader deterioration in interethnic relations in the region.[81] Finally, Tschantret finds that repressive securitization measures in Xinjiang have been ineffective because separatists adopted tactical innovations to circumvent policing.[82]

While this body of work contributes to our understanding of the relationship between repression and violence in Xinjiang, it is limited to comparatively short periods of analysis and anecdotal evidence. We remedy this with a more robust assessment of the statistical interdependencies between militant violence and repression. We employ vector autoregressive (VAR) models but only present the key results and takeaways here while leaving discussion of data preparation, model

---

[78] Wilson and Piazza (2013); Gaibulloev, Piazza, and Sandler (2017).
[79] Hastings (2011).   [80] Millward (2004: ix).
[81] Smith Finley (2019).   [82] Tschantret (2018).

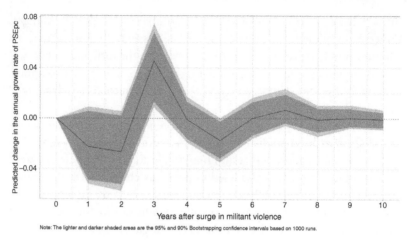

Note: The lighter and darker shaded areas are the 95% and 90% Bootstrapping confidence intervals based on 1000 runs.

Figure 4.3 The impact of violence on security spending

specifications and diagnostics, and robustness check models to this chapter's appendix.

Figure 4.3 plots the impact of an increase in militant violence on the annual growth rate in public security expenditures per capita in Xinjiang (PSEpc).[83] The figure shows a delayed increase in security measures in response to violence – a roughly 4.3 percent increase in the annual growth rate in PSEpc in the third year after the shock.[84]

There are three explanations for this delayed response.

First, this chart captures only local government security expenditures, which fails to capture the countermeasures provided by other levels of government. Take the 2009 Urumqi riot as an example. In addition to the dispatch of local PAP forces, two days after the incident the Ministry of Public Security ordered the emergency-response SWAT forces from thirty-one cities to support local police in Xinjiang. These forces landed in Urumqi within eleven hours on thirty-seven chartered airplanes.[85] It is unlikely that the local government in

---

[83] In all of the impulse response function analyses, we use the orthogonalized unit shock, which is equal to one standard deviation of the residuals in the VAR equation that corresponds to the shock variable.

[84] The fact that the initial response (*time 0*) from the annual growth rate in PSEpc to a shock in violence is zero is by design – the ordering of the model is (PSEpc, PVEs).

[85] *Sina* (2009).

Xinjiang bore the costs associated with this large-scale mobilization of forces. In other words, even if the government reacts quickly to violence, the increase in *local* security-related expenditures takes longer. Second, much of the responsibility for many large-scale, quick reactions in Xinjiang (e.g., riot control, searches for suspects, and combat missions) are undertaken by the PAP, which is primarily funded by the central government. Third, except in cases of large-scale unrest, local leaders have career incentives to address problems quietly rather than calling on Beijing for help, but doing so leaves them constrained by local revenue. While maintaining stability is the de facto priority for any regional government, especially for places such as Xinjiang and Tibet, it can be slow and painful to divert limited resources from other departments – and the lag in local public security expenditures reflects this reality.

To examine the flip side of the repression–violence cycle, Figure 4.4 plots the change in violence that occurs in response to increased security and repression (measured with the annual growth rate of PSEpc). The plot demonstrates that securitization generates a rapid but brief decline in violence. However, this initial decline quickly gives way to an increase in violence – albeit a statistically insignificant one. This pattern – an initial drop in violent attacks followed by a roughly equal-sized *increase* in attacks in the third year after the securitization shock – is consistent with other academic studies that suggest repressive securitization tactics are effective for a short while but are soon followed by hardened long-term grievances and more violence.

To confirm these findings, we run two additional models. First, as we have noted, securitization measures changed three times in the period covered by the expenditures analysis, which we account for in the models by assessing each independently. Second, in his study of the relationship between Xinjiang's local public goods spending and ethnic conflicts, Liu finds that counties with higher government spending on education were significantly less likely to experience conflict.[86] Promoting education in Xinjiang, especially in Chinese, is one of the key cultural integration policies that Xi Jinping emphasized in his speech at the 2014 Xinjiang work forum.[87] (See Table 4.2.) To account for these potential confounding effect of education on violent events,

[86] Liu (2019). [87] *BBC News* (2014).

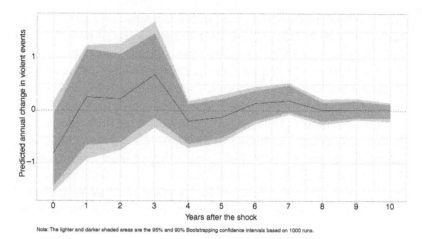

Figure 4.4 Response of violence to securitization

we add an additional time series – the annual growth rate of XUAR expenditures on education. The results, which are available in this chapter's appendix, are consistent with the findings presented here.

Finally, some might wonder if the modest increase in violence in response to securitization could result from the annual frequency of the data, which makes it challenging to pick up any granular variations that might occur immediately after the policy change. To address this, we run an intervention model using monthly violence data (January 1990–December 2014) with three step-interventions (dummy variables coded 1 for the intervention period and 0 otherwise), capturing three strike-hard campaign periods separately: *SH1* (June 1996–December 1997), *SH2* (August 2009–May 2010), and *SH3* (June 2014–December 2014). The result of this intervention model shows that the coefficient of *SH2* is negative (curbing violence) and both *SH1* and *SH3* have positive coefficients (provoking more violence). None of these coefficients, however, are statistically significant.[88]

In sum, Xinjiang has long been trapped in a cycle of repression and violence (Figure 4.5). The Chinese government has consistently reacted to any surge in Uyghur unrest by flooding the region with troops, police, and technology. However, while hardened security delivers stability

---

[88] Model specification, diagnosis, and regression tables are available in this chapter's appendix.

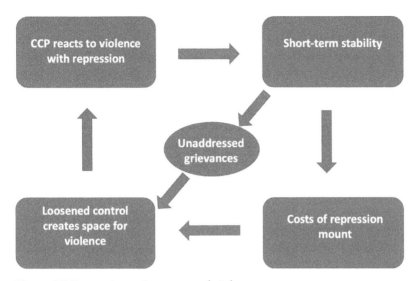

Figure 4.5 Repression, grievances, and violence

initially, the associated costs are challenging to sustain. With grievances deepening and largely unaddressed, violence tends to reemerge when control is loosened, triggering yet another round of repression.

We have demonstrated the inefficacy of the "sticks" used in Xinjiang, but in the eyes of the Party, there was deeper disillusionment with the "carrots." The most notable among these was the Western Development Strategy (WDS). In October 2000, the CCP Central Committee launched the WDS, which covered twelve provinces, autonomous regions, and municipal cities, including Xinjiang – a strategy aimed at reducing regional economic and security disparities and transforming the western region into "a new one with a prosperous economy, advanced society, stable living, united nationalities and beautiful sceneries at the middle period of the 21st century."[89]

In Xinjiang, this strategy failed to deliver what Beijing expected. The gap between Xinjiang's GDP per capita and the national average actually increased from 646 in 1999 to 14,694 yuan in 2017. Per capita,

[89] Specific tasks and objectives include "speeding up the construction of infrastructure facilities; improving the protection and development of environment; consolidating the basic status of agriculture, adjusting the structure of industry, and developing characteristic tourism; developing undertakings of science and technology, education, culture and sanitation."

Xinjiang's GDP declined from 91 percent of the national average to just 75 percent over that same span. Correspondingly, the share of Xinjiang's contributions to the national GDP also dropped slightly, from 1.32 percent in 1999 to 1.28 percent in 2017, according to data released by the National Bureau of Statistics of China. This demonstrates that Xinjiang's high economic growth, which averaged 13.4 percent in the 2000–2017 period, was outpaced by even faster development in the east, worsening interregional inequality and breeding resentment.

Moreover, several studies have underlined that while Uyghur minorities benefited from what growth there was, the program disproportionately favored Han living in the region. This is evidenced by the sizable and growing income gaps between ethnic groups, which are exacerbated by labor market discrimination.[90]

Corruption made these disparities even worse. This was a particular problem under Wang Lequan (1994–2010). During this period, substantial money for new projects poured into Xinjiang as part of the Western Development Strategy. Corruption and rent-seeking activities grew in kind.[91] This generated grievances among Uyghur officials, whose typically lower-ranking positions did not afford them many opportunities to "earn" their own under-the-table fortune.[92]

President Xi's speech at the 2014 Xinjiang work forum (Table 4.2) seemed to reflect Beijing's concern over the feeble economic results delivered during Secretary Wang's rule, as he emphasized that development policies need to be implemented in a way that "can effectively improve the standard of living, benefit the locals, and enhance unity."[93]

Further exacerbating this growing inequality, the WDS led to an influx of new Han migrants into Xinjiang, which was viewed by the local Uyghur population as further colonization.[94] Unlike the state-orchestrated Han immigration into Xinjiang during the 1950s and 1960s, which rapidly increased the Han population in Xinjiang from less than 7 percent in 1949 to over 40 percent by 1978, this new wave of migration was fueled by self-motivated temporary immigrants who entered Xinjiang from poor areas in the interior of China searching for work.

[90] Iredale et al. (2001); Gladney (2004c); Pannell and Schmidt (2006); Liu and Peters (2017); Wu and He (2018).
[91] Author interview (2019), PRC.   [92] Author interview (2019), PRC.
[93] Xinhua News Agency (2014).   [94] Liu and Peters (2017).

These "temporary" workers – who benefited from discriminatory hiring practices – increased from 2.25 percent of Xinjiang's total population in 1990 to 8.21 percent in 2010.[95] State orchestrated or not, this new influx was congruent with China's decades-long cultural and ethnic assimilation strategy in Xinjiang, which hinged on increasing the proportion of Han Chinese in the region. According to a draft manuscript by Ilham Tohti, who was imprisoned before finishing it, Han migration into the region in all its forms resulted in ethnic segregation that had "a profound impact on the Uyghur sense of ethnic and national identity."[96]

The CCP also faced domestic challenges during this period, which contributed to the dramatic escalation of repression. As discussed in earlier chapters, economic performance remains the most important source of legitimacy for CCP. However, according to the World Bank data, the year 2015 marked the first time since 1990 that China's GDP growth rate dropped below 7 percent.[97]

The transition from Hu to Xi also marked one of the most challenging political transitions in CCP governance. The prosecution of Bo Xilai, among others, exposed to the public both the corruption among top-ranked officials and a fractured political elite. The dual economic and political difficulties led to heightened efforts to maintain stability across the country, as well as a massive anti-corruption campaign and the enactment of the 2015 National Security Law. These moves, according to Daniel Blumenthal, revealed a Party that felt "more besieged than at any time since Tiananmen Square."[98]

These domestic challenges also triggered a deeper shift in the Party's legitimation strategy – from one that highlighted the material improvement of people's lives to an emphasis on ideological unity and purity. While there is little doubt that the economic growth of the past three decades considerably strengthened the Party's legitimacy, the problems associated with this rapid development and its globalizing forces raised alarm among the ruling elites.

As early as 2010, China began to ban newspapers, publishers, websites, radio, and TV from using foreign words, particularly English

---

[95] Wu and Song (2014). [96] Tohti (2013).
[97] China's GDP growth rate in 2014, 2015, 2016, and 2017 were 7.3 percent, 6.9 percent, 6.7 percent, and 6.8 percent respectively.
[98] Blumenthal (2019).

ones, in an effort to protect the Chinese language and the country's "cultural environment and character."[99] To take one small example, in its live broadcast of the 2010 NBA playoffs, the CCTV 5 commentators were not allowed to refer to the "NBA" but had to use *mei zhi lan*, a Chinese abbreviation of the direct translation of "National Basketball Association."

This campaign intensified with the rise of Xi Jinping, a "second-generation red" – a child of the original revolutionary elite (*hong er dai*).[100] Even when he was still the vice president, Xi advocated to keep China's educational institutions more closely aligned with Communist Party ideology.[101] Upon becoming president, Xi formally declared "ideological war" against Western values. The 2013 *Briefing on the Current Situation in the Ideological Realm*, an internal Party document, explicitly warned that "Western forces hostile to China and dissidents within the country are still constantly infiltrating the ideological sphere."[102]

Following Xi's declaration, Education Minister Yuan Guiren told attendees at a conference of college academics that they should "by no means allow teaching materials that disseminate Western values in our classrooms."[103]

This focus on ideological unity translated directly into policies in Xinjiang. One of Xi's guiding principles from the 2014 work forum emphasized the need to strengthen "the sense of belonging to China, to the Chinese nation, to the Chinese culture, and to the path of socialism with Chinese characteristics" in the region.[104] Through this lens, while the ethnic mingling and "de-extremification" campaign is specific to Xinjiang, this shift in emphasis away from growth also reflects the same deeper concerns that drove the nationwide campaign promoting nationalism, cultural revival, and the achievement of the "China Dream" – a campaign whose core idea was the rejuvenation of the Chinese nation.[105]

As the Chinese government encounters inevitable difficulties in delivering prior levels of economic growth, providing safety and

---

[99] *BBC News* (2010).
[100] Xi Jinping's father, Xi Zhongxun, was a leading revolutionary in Yan'an in the 1930s and played a central role in the CCP through the 1980s.
[101] Simpson (2012).   [102] Buckley (2013).   [103] Beech (2016).
[104] See Table 4.2.   [105] BBC News (2013); Yang (2017).

security becomes a necessary move to preserve legitimacy. There has been a clear trend in recent years in state propaganda, promoting the notion that China is one of the safest places in the world to live. For example, for three consecutive days in early 2018, *People's Daily* published commentaries trumpeting China's safety.[106] As a consequence, any continued violence, even if it is sporadic and of low intensity, calls into question official competence. That in turn drives the government's tolerance for violence to zero.

All of this has a profound impact on security policies in Xinjiang. Authorities have the domestic political capital to crack down on Uyghurs because Han public opinion is generally hawkish toward containing Uyghur violence and broadly dismissive of Uyghur grievances. Moreover, exposure to violence in the news makes Chinese citizens more likely to approve of harshly repressive tactics, particularly among less wealthy Han, as Hou and Quek found after conducting an online survey using a national sample of Chinese citizens.[107]

Though systematic data are lacking, anecdotally, it seems that many in Beijing saw the mass detainment of Uyghurs as an unfortunate, but necessary step toward stability in Xinjiang.[108] As noted in Chapter 3, these hawkish opinions have pushed China to pursue a cautious media strategy when reporting terrorist attacks, for fear that such reporting may fuel interethnic tension or drive the public to make demands that exceed what even this government is able to deliver. When the government does decide to push beyond policing norms, this same set of hawkish and volatile sentiments can both spur and legitimize the government's more severe policies.

Chinese citizens can be hawkish about maintaining stability in Xinjiang because the security tactics employed there are not replicated in most other areas of China. In most of China, stability maintenance targets the whole population and must therefore be more calibrated to prevent backlash and preserve public support. For example, authorities have historically blocked portions of the Internet but still tolerate some open discourse on less sensitive matters and have even tolerated the use of virtual private networks (VPNs), which enabled citizens to access the uncensored internet. (That said, China began cracking down on VPNs in 2017.) More recently, there has been a crackdown on online gaming but not an outright prohibition.

---

[106] People.com (2018).   [107] Hou and Quek (2019).   [108] Author interviews (2019).

But in Xinjiang, the perceived threat comes from a specific minority segment that is increasingly vilified by the government and also viewed suspiciously by the Han majority. The result is that harsh enforcement in the name of stability becomes a way for the Party to cultivate approval among Han Chinese at the expense of the minority. This also fits into the populist strategy the Party has long pursued, originally under Mao but now under Xi.[109]

Beijing also sees Xinjiang's stability as a clear prerequisite for national economic growth and justifies securitization on those grounds. As China's gateway to Central Asia, Xinjiang is the key to a trillion-dollar trade, investment, and infrastructure development project. The region hosts railroads that connect China to Europe and to several critical gas pipelines. As Tsinghua University professor Cao Feng stated at a 2018 conference, "The stability of Xinjiang is the basic guarantee for the implementation of China's BRI."[110]

Last but not least, as President Xi has continued to consolidate power at the national level, XUAR's local officials have more forcefully implemented Xi's guiding principles for Xinjiang policy. Through a series of moves – including the nationwide anti-corruption campaign that swept out even some of the most senior officials in the Party, the government, and the military; the establishment of the National Security Commission Xi himself heads; the largest reform of the PLA and the PAP in decades; and the removal of presidential term limits – Xi has become China's most powerful leader since Mao. Xi's status was cemented when the Party adopted his treatise, "Xi Jinping Thought on Socialism with Chinese Characteristics for a New Era," into the CCP's constitution.[111]

Xi's unprecedented consolidation of power reordered the relationship between local authorities and the central government in Beijing. Traditionally, local officials could, at times, afford to be lax about enforcement. With new monitoring and accountability measures in place, officials are now much more likely to overshoot Beijing's

---

[109] Dai and Shao (2016).   [110] Qu (2019).

[111] It is worth noting that Deng Xiaoping's "Theory on Socialism with Chinese Characteristics" was formally written into the Party constitution only after Deng's death in 1997. Xi is the second leader after Mao who secured an eponymous reference in the constitution while still in power (Hornby and Mitchell 2017). See also Lau (2018) and Ruwitch (2018).

intentions for fear of coming up short. As a *New York Times* headline put it, when President Xi speaks, "Chinese officials jump, maybe too high."[112]

Increasingly, paths to national promotion within the Party run through Xinjiang and ambitious officials are expected to demonstrate toughness. In a study of cases of official overreach (which was later censored online) the Tsinghua University–based sociologist Sun Liping warned that "this mobilizing form of government sometimes evolves into a race between officials. 'If you're tough, then I'll be even tougher. If you go to extremes, I'll go further.'"[113] This arms race of getting tougher and going further drives securitization without much thought to the long-term consequences.

As we have noted, the mistreatment of the Uyghur minority does incur one cost to which the Party had previously been highly sensitive – international condemnation. So why *are* Chinese leaders more willing to risk the potential international outcry over Uyghur human rights violations?

Counterintuitively, the answer lies in part in China's deteriorating external relationships, which led to a certain fatalism among Chinese leaders in their expectations for future diplomatic conditions. Foremost, this relates to the rapidly worsening relations with the United States. The leadership transition in Taiwan from the more pro-Beijing Kuomintang to the more pro-independence Democratic Progressive Party created friction, along with the 2016 South China Sea Arbitration and emerging resistance among neighboring states that are increasingly apprehensive about rising Chinese power.

This ongoing deterioration has heightened the CCP's fear of foreign interference. Such fear has long been a feature of "official tone" and propaganda, but Chinese political elites authentically and increasingly perceive Xinjiang, alongside other contentious issues as varied as LGBT rights and the disposition of Hong Kong, to be especially vulnerable to Western interference. Chinese leaders have consistently feared that these issue areas could be "weaponized" by their foreign adversaries. For instance, when Chinese state councilor and foreign minister Wang Yi met with US deputy secretary of state Wendy Sherman in Tianjin on July 26, 2021, he reiterated that the first of China's three bottom lines for US–China relations is that "the United States

---

[112] Buckley and Bradsher (2018).   [113] Buckley and Bradsher (2018).

must not challenge, slander or even attempt to subvert the path and system of socialism with Chinese characteristics."[114] As Nathan and Scobell put it, one of Chinese policymakers' top concerns is that the United States "maintains a host of official and unofficial programs that seek to influence Chinese civil society and politics."[115]

When it comes to Xinjiang in particular, we have presented suggestive evidence that Uyghur violence tended to intensify when China faced international headwinds (Chapter 2) and that officials became particularly sensitive to violence under those same circumstances (Chapter 3).

In that light, China's intensification of security and repression in Xinjiang could signal resolve and toughness but also serve as a preventive measure – not only against the penetration of transnational terrorism as Greitens and her colleagues argue but also against hostile foreign intervention amid intensified competition among the world's great powers.

Beyond a certain threshold, further diplomatic deterioration may not figure into the political costs associated with repressive policies. Once relations hit rock bottom, any action in Xinjiang cannot further damage an already adversarial relationship. And critique from abroad is already flowing at full volume. Similar fatalistic reasoning may also explain why China decided to unilaterally and forcefully implement its Hong Kong National Security Law in mid-2020, despite the international outcry.[116]

The Path Forward

Even with support from the central government, the scale of the de-extremification campaign at its height was a painful burden for the regional government, especially as China's economic growth slowed. The burden was even heavier in opportunity costs – the securitization of Xinjiang enormously disrupted local economic activities. Xinjiang's economy was paralyzed in the two years after the policy reorientation that followed the 2014 Xinjiang work forum. Over that period, the region's local GDP growth rate was just 0.6 percent and 3.5 percent in 2015 and 2016 – the lowest and the third-lowest regional growth rates

---

[114] Ministry of Foreign Affairs of PRC (2021a).
[115] Nathan and Scobell (2012: 90).
[116] Hass (2020).

since 1978.[117] Costs – measured in both Renminbi and international outcry – mounted still further with the expansion of the mass detention system to its apex in 2020.

Likely even more alarming to Party leadership was emerging evidence that concern over the approach had penetrated into the cadres. The leak of the "Xinjiang papers" to *The New York Times*, which consisted of more than 400 pages of internal Chinese documents on Xinjiang's de-extremification works, may have signaled resistance to the hardline approach among at least some officials.[118] The *South China Morning Post* reported that China's chief Xinjiang policy coordinator, Wang Yang, informed Xi Jinping that "even the Han people are deeply dissatisfied" with the security measures in Xinjiang and that "life is harsh [in Xinjiang] even for cadres" as "nobody is allowed days off [even after working for weeks]."[119] A statement from an official, placed in this outlet was a clear signal that a pivot was underway.

The heavy hand of the state limited growth and made life so unpleasant for Han Chinese migrants to the region that some began to leave (or attempt to leave) the region. For example, the population of Korla, where the presence of PetroChina once drew multitudes of Han immigrants, dropped by half after the government implemented its harshest security measures.[120] Explaining Korla's loss of a quarter million people, Yang said people leave because "it's difficult to find labourers now and there's no money to be earned."[121] This stood in sharp contrast to the decade prior when outsiders flooded into the region in such numbers that they reduced Uyghurs to minority status in the XUAR.

These developments cast serious doubts on the sustainability of the maximalist version of the "de-extremification" strategy. Responding to mounting monetary and reputational costs, authorities predictably declared victory and slightly dialed back the pressure. The State Council Information Office published a white paper in August 2019, claiming that "remarkable results" had been achieved as these measures have succeeded "to an enormous extent in eliminating the conditions in which terrorism and religious extremism breed," and "no terrorist incidents have occurred in Xinjiang for nearly three years since the

---

[117] The second-lowest GDP growth rate was 2.2 percent in 2009. It is also possible that the low growth was caused by the surge in violence in previous years, which severely hurt Xinjiang's tourism.

[118] Ramzy and Buckley (2019).   [119] Lau (2019).   [120] Yang (2019).

[121] Yang (2019).

education and training."[122] Our findings confirm the latter of these claims – but with perhaps 20 percent of Uyghurs forcibly detained (at the height) and a police state harshly suppressing the activities of the remainder, it is unsurprising that there has been a lull in violence. Truly "remarkable" would be a sustained reduction in violence over the longer term if state repression of local communities was substantially eased.

Furthering this trend, on May 18, 2020, a "guideline on advancing western development in the new era" issued by the CCP Central Committee and the State Council was published on the front page of *People's Daily*. The opening paragraph made the obligatory head nod to the "still heavy tasks in terms of safeguarding the ethnic unity, social stability, and national security [in the western region]," but the vast majority of the article focused on development.[123] Suddenly, official focus returned to industrial, environmental, technological, and economic policy suggestions for promoting high-quality development so that the western region "will basically realize socialist modernization by 2035, with its public service level, infrastructure connectivity and people's living standard on par with the eastern regions."[124] And for Xinjiang specifically, the document calls for accelerating the work to transform the region into "the core district of the Silk Road Economic Belt as well as a center for westbound transportation."[125]

At some moments, officials seem to recognize that these developmental objectives cannot be achieved in tandem with mass detention and repression. But, at the same time, a sudden move away from repression could lead to an outburst of violence, which is unacceptable to Beijing. The reality is that while policymakers have identified growing inequality and geographically uneven development patterns as pressing policy problems, no solution can be achieved if Xinjiang is so heavily policed and repressed. The inability of the state to cut through this Gordian knot means that Xinjiang is likely to revert by default to a version of its 2014–2016 policies – fewer reeducation camps but even heavier everyday security, arbitrary detention, and monitoring of the population.

Rather than solving the problem, these measures will further entrench the divide between the "two Chinas": a relatively open East

---

[122] Information Office of the State Council (2019).   [123] People's Daily (2020).
[124] *People's Daily* (2020).   [125] *People's Daily* (2020).

in which comparatively more liberal commerce and political behavior fuel one another's growth, and a highly authoritarian and centrally planned West.[126] As we have noted, the "two Chinas" approach incentivizes cross-border linkages and puts a premium on the ability to take the fight to eastern China, where the government's capacity to disrupt it is lower and the rewards of an attack are higher. Thus, the more Beijing tries to bottle up grievances in the West, the higher the rewards for groups that can strike in the East or abroad.

The reversion to past policies is, however, also an acceptance of reality by the CCP. The entire concept of reeducation, in the way that it is explicitly discussed in Chinese policy, is suspect. Even if, for the sake of argument, we were to take Chinese authorities at their word that there were substantial numbers of militants, radicals, and religious extremists among those detained, there is little evidence to suggest that "deradicalization" programs produce the desired effects, especially at the scale applied in Xinjiang. There is, in fact, a substantial body of scholarship that points to the near-universal ineffectiveness of such programs in a variety of international contexts.[127]

Detention and repression generate resentment at a mass scale and breed militancy among a minority.[128] Detention centers and prisons played starring roles in the origin stories of the Irish Republican Army, Hamas, al-Qaeda, Islamic State, and many other militant organizations.[129] As such, it is safe to assume the recent detention and repression of Uyghurs have not actually changed many hearts and minds, regardless of what the Party claims.

As a result, it will be hard to meaningfully reduce repression without risking violent unrest. Centuries ago, Tocqueville noted what has become a consistent finding in the understanding of repressive politics:

---

[126] The "two Chinas" concept emphasizes the relative difference between the East and West of China. It is undeniably the case that security and repression have tightened across all of China. Xu (2021) has shown that repression increasingly substitutes for co-optation as a consequence of enhanced capability in digital surveillance. Nonetheless, we hold to the point that the level of security in Xinjiang dwarfs anything experienced by average citizens on a day-to-day basis in places like Shanghai, Beijing, and Guangzhou.

[127] Rabasa et al. (2010); Horgan and Altier (2012); Zhou (2019).

[128] Dalacoura (2006); Cronin (2009); Comolli (2015); Shadmehr (2015).

[129] Hannah, Clutterbuck, Rubin (2008); Mulcahy, Merrington, and Bell (2013); Speckhard and Shajkovci (2018).

[I]t is not always when things are going from bad to worse that revolutions break out. On the contrary, it oftener happens that when a people which has put up with an oppressive rule over a long period without protest suddenly finds the government relaxing its pressure, it takes up arms against it.[130]

The capacity for revolution does not appear to be present in Xinjiang as of this writing, but the notion that there will be a response to "oppressive rule over a long period" seems close to inevitable.

The result is a tragic deadlock. "Long-term peace and stability (*chang zhi jiu an*)," which is required by President Xi, is unlikely to follow on the heels of a repressive "reeducation campaign."

[130] De Tocqueville (1955 [1856]: 176–177).

5 | *Foreign Policy*

In sharp contrast to its hardline response to Uyghur-related violence at home, China's counterterrorism policies abroad have long relied more on carrots rather than sticks. They are, however, still governed by the same cautious tendency to avoid risk. In their conversations with regional partners, Chinese officials speak of cooperatively eradicating the "root causes" of terrorism, which they attribute to a lack of social and economic development and the absence of dialogue between different countries, religions, and ethnic groups. For instance, Chinese premier Li Keqiang has painted the China–Pakistan Economic Corridor, a signature Belt and Road project, as a means of "weaning ... the populace from fundamentalism."[1]

China's expansion abroad, however, has put stress on these traditional positions and sparked a new military component to China's international counterterrorism cooperation. Behind the self-effacing rhetoric on cooperation lurks the reality of China's mounting economic and military strength. Increasingly, that strength has translated into new forms of militarized regional engagement.

For example, in late 2016 reports began to circulate that People's Liberation Army (PLA) forces were regularly patrolling inside Afghanistan's far eastern Wakhan Corridor.[2] Beijing quickly denied infringing on its neighbor's sovereignty but did note that "the law enforcement authorities of the two sides have conducted joint law enforcement operations in border areas to fight against terrorism." Experts, however, were quick to point out that "law enforcement and military patrols are rather blurred terms" in a place like Afghanistan.[3]

More recently, evidence emerged that Chinese troops were stationed in Tajikistan near the border with Afghanistan and were regularly

---

[1] Small (2018).   [2] Gibson (2016); Marty (2017).   [3] Clover (2017).

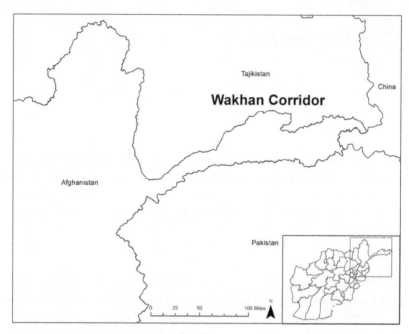

Map 5.1 The Wakhan Corridor

conducting counterterrorism missions there – well before US and North Atlantic Treaty Organization forces withdrew from the country.[4] These deployments are indicative of the tightening link between China's economic and security relationships in Central Asia.

If China continues to prioritize security and stability in the region, it may increasingly find itself pulled into the vacuum produced by the US withdrawal from Afghanistan. Those in the United States who lament the withdrawal from Afghanistan often express the concern that it will again become a haven for terrorists who might then target the United States.[5] What generally goes unappreciated is that, in the present environment, militants would be just as likely to strike China or Chinese interests. In other words, a haven for militants in Afghanistan is at least as much a Chinese problem as an American one.

---

[4] Shih (2019). As indicated in Map 5.1, the idiosyncrasies of the geography make Tajikistan a more preferable location from which to monitor this region than China itself.

[5] Ciorciari et al. (2020).

Concern over this risk is evidenced by China's rapid engagement with the Taliban in the wake of the US withdrawal from Afghanistan and the expansion of those discussions into matters of counterterrorism. Uyghurs in Afghanistan increasingly worry that China will make desperately needed financial assistance to Afghanistan contingent on their repatriation.

The counterterrorism operations in Afghanistan are not isolated incidents. China increasingly prioritizes regional stability to protect its foreign investment. Moreover, counterterrorism cooperation allows China to extend its political reach abroad, a longstanding goal. However, China's emergence on the world stage also introduces vulnerabilities for the aspiring great power.

Until relatively recently, China was able to hew closely to Deng Xiaoping's admonition to "keep a low profile" internationally. Limited foreign policy kept China off the radar of international terrorist organizations such as al-Qaeda. This situation is rapidly evolving for two reasons.

First, ambition has pushed China to expand abroad in search of economic growth. Abroad, China finds the resources, market access, productive destinations for accumulated capital, and the prestige it seeks. But China's expansion into Central Asia, the Middle East, and North Africa places it squarely in the regions of the world that are most contested by violent extremist groups, for whom foreign incursion is a particularly egregious offense.[6]

Second, as China increases its prominence as a stakeholder in the global order – starting with its accession into the World Trade Organization but extending more recently to cooperative security efforts abroad – militants opposed to elements of that order will increasingly see the country as a legitimate target for terrorist attacks. China may chafe at US dominance in the existing global order and seek to reshape it to better suit the country's interests, but one way or another it is increasingly an owner of that order – and with ownership comes risk.

In this chapter, we systematically explore the heightened role of counterterrorism in China's foreign policy. We identify the inherent trade-off between engagement and vulnerability to violent nonstate actors that confronts the country and the policies that China employs to manage these competing risks.

---

[6] These grievances include both the economic and military presence of foreigners.

Counterterrorism in Chinese Foreign Policy

China has only recently come to view militancy abroad as a top-tier foreign policy issue. This prioritization is the product of two distinct but converging trends. On the one hand, the elevation of counterterrorism was used instrumentally to diffuse heightened tension with the United States. On the other, it was a response to very real concerns over both internal violence emanating from Xinjiang and regional threats to China and Chinese investments.

China's strategic use of counterterrorism in its foreign policy can be traced to the early days of the George W. Bush administration. During his 2000 presidential election campaign, Bush promised that he would shift from treating China as a "strategic partner" (as it was under Clinton) and instead treat it as a potential "strategic competitor."[7] For their part, Chinese policymakers – long accustomed to hawkish rhetoric from American candidates that turns more benign upon entrance into office – seem to have shrugged this off as rhetoric.

While China may have anticipated the same pragmatic transition from the Bush administration, instead the campaign threats escalated into what Beijing saw as ominous policy signals once the new administration assumed office. For example, immediately following his inauguration, Bush telephoned every major world leader except Chinese president Jiang Zemin, signaling an intent to downgrade Beijing's position.[8] This snub was taken seriously. As China's then foreign minister Tang Jiaxuan wrote in his memoir, "To a certain extent the word competitor implied the US position as being in opposition to China and it was disturbing to think about the possible adverse impact on China-US relations should the Bush argument become the China policy of the US government."[9]

It did not take long for diplomatic slights to give way to a real crisis: In April 2001, a US EP-3 reconnaissance aircraft and a Chinese fighter jet collided, leading to the death of the Chinese pilot, the detention of the twenty-four US crew members, and a nadir in bilateral relations.[10] The sides arrived at a mutually face-saving settlement over the course of ten days, but the damage was done. Shortly after the crew was

---

[7] Lippman (1999).   [8] Malik (2002).
[9] Tang (2011: 330).   [10] Keefe (2002).

released, the White House announced a multibillion-dollar weapons package for Taiwan and Bush pledged that the United States would do "whatever it took to help Taiwan defend herself" against China.[11] A month later, the US government granted Taiwanese president Chen Shui-bian permission to stop briefly in the United States on his way to and from Latin America.[12] Doubling down, the Bush administration also challenged another core interest of Beijing – Tibet – by hosting the Dalai Lama at the White House that same month.[13]

The 9/11 attacks fundamentally altered this downward trajectory in the US–China relationship. For Chinese leadership, this was a "heaven-sent" opportunity to prevent further deterioration in bilateral relations with the United States while executing a long-sought strategic pivot toward securitization.[14] Chinese decision-makers quickly recognized that reframing policies toward the Uyghur population in terms of a common threat posed by terrorism could divert the United States' focus away from competition while providing cover for China's preferred domestic counterterrorism policies and regional ambitions in Central Asia.[15]

Tang Jiaxuan wrote in his memoir that after exchanging views with Yang Jiechi (then the Chinese ambassador to the United States), they "agreed that 9/11 had forced the United States into a major foreign policy readjustment, and brought about a significant turning point for improving and developing China-US relations."[16] The vice premier and former foreign minister Qian Qichen expressed a similar view in a speech at Peking University in 2002, stating, "Since the end of the Cold War, the US government had been discussing who the primary enemy is ... [A]fter the 9/11 event, the answer became clear."[17]

Beijing wasted no time in seizing the opportunity. Jiang Zemin was among the first to reach out to President Bush to express his sympathy and condolences. Shortly thereafter, China voted to support UN Resolution 1368, authorizing the United States to use force in Afghanistan. This marked the first time it had voted in favor of authorizing the use of military force by the United States. The rewards were nearly instantaneous.

---

[11] Wallace (2001).   [12] Lacey (2001).   [13] Office of the Press Secretary (2001).
[14] Ching (2011).   [15] Potter (2013); Roberts (2020).   [16] Tang (2011: 367).
[17] Qian (2005).

The Bush administration not only dropped "strategic competitor" from its lexicon but also referred to China for the first time as a "great power" and called for more constructive and cooperative relations between the two countries.[18] In congressional testimony, Secretary of State Colin Powell praised Beijing's diplomatic support, saying that China "helped in the war against terrorism."[19]

In the year following the attack, Bush and Jiang held three bilateral meetings and emphasized the desire to strengthen cooperation every time they met.[20] This culminated in the establishment of an FBI legal attaché office at the US embassy in Beijing. In short, counterterrorism, as Chinese leadership had anticipated, stabilized US–China relations.[21]

Moreover, the new emphasis on terrorism provided China with a more reassuring context in which to pursue the modernization and internationalization of PLA activities. As we noted in Chapter 3, in the post-9/11 political context, even militarized counterterrorism cooperation could be framed as a contribution to the global commons, allowing China to achieve its aspirations while avoiding charges of revisionism.[22] The strategy parallels China's later use of "counterpiracy efforts" as a way for its blue-water navy to cut its teeth without provoking a strong counterresponse, particularly from the United States.[23]

---

[18] Office of the Press Secretary (2002).

[19] Senate Foreign Relations Committee (2002).

[20] Bush and Jiang met on October 20, 2001, during the APEC meeting in Shanghai; on February 21, 2002, in Beijing; and on October 25, 2002, at Bush's private ranch in Crawford, Texas.

[21] Kan (2010).

[22] Illustrating the point, three days after 9/11, the leaders of the six SCO members attending the prime minister–level meeting in Alma-Ata released a joint statement expressing "the determination of the multilateral group to stand with all countries and international organizations in waging a relentless war on all threats of terrorism around the world" (Pan 2004).

[23] Ericson and Strange (2015). These routine actions can aggregate into formidable operational experience. According to official records, "as of December 24, 2018, the Chinese navy has sent 31 escort fleets, 100 ships, 67 shipborne helicopters and more than 26,000 soldiers to escort more than 6,600 Chinese and foreign ships over the past decade. They successfully rescued and escorted more than 70 Chinese and foreign ships in distress and captured three pirates" (Li 2019).

These gains, however, came with two potentially disastrous consequences for China's core strategic interests.[24]

First, the war on terror led to an open-ended increase in the US
military presence in Central, South, and Southeast Asia. As Lampton
notes, Chinese leaders quickly sensed a millennia-old fear – encirclement – when they observed the trend that major states all around
China's periphery were "aligning with the US-led coalition against
terrorism to various degrees and for undefined duration."[25] Indeed,
Jiang feared from the start that a war on terrorism "had the potential to expand American power even further" and believed that "any
extension of U.S. armed forces would not be in China's long-term
interests, particularly if American troops took up long-term residence
near China's borders."[26]

Second, throwing in with the United States in the Global War on
Terror fundamentally shifted China's place in the eyes of the global
Salafist jihadist movement in a way that opened new vulnerabilities
to terrorism. Where China was once seen as a counterbalance to the
United States – and a patron of liberation movements around the
globe – jihadi propaganda suddenly characterized China as the "head
of the snake."[27]

These opportunities and challenges created a strategic conundrum
for China. Counterterrorism became the best vehicle for its ambitions
for regional expansion because it was the domain least likely to spur
American opposition. But the more that China availed itself of the
opportunity to expand, the more it actually needed counterterrorism
to deal with the emerging threats to its interests in Central Asia.

Managing the Benefits of Engagement
and the Risks of Blowback

China attempted to split the difference by engaging in international
counterterrorism cooperation and exercises, but in a targeted way
designed to limit blowback. Balanced in this way, counterterrorism moved to the center of Chinese security policy in Central Asia
and became the primary vehicle by which China pursued its broader

---

[24] Malik (2002).   [25] Lampton (2001: 108).
[26] Kuhn (2004: 472).   [27] Fishman (2011).

regional ambitions. It lies at the core of China's recent participation in regional institutions, beginning with the Shanghai Five. The Shanghai Five, the precursor to the Shanghai Cooperation Organization (SCO), was charged from its initiation in 1996 with targeting the "three evils" of terrorism, separatism, and religious extremism.[28]

The Shanghai Five's core mission transferred seamlessly to the SCO in 2001, even making its way into the title of the SCO's founding charter.[29] In both cases, the organizations' unspoken secondary purpose was to undercut the threat of US encirclement.

Under the auspices of the SCO, China began a robust program of counterterrorism cooperation with Central Asian partner countries, starting with its historic participation in joint SCO-sponsored anti-terrorist military exercises with Kyrgyzstan in October 2002.[30] China further tightened its grip on regional counterterrorism leadership with a 2003 addendum that established the SCO Regional Antiterrorism Structure.[31] Through this addendum, China expressed a strong preference that all members coordinate bilateral counterterrorism activities with the United States through the SCO, further limiting the United States' reach into the region. Similarly, the SCO–Afghanistan Contact Group was created in 2005 as a consultation mechanism between the organization and that country, but its larger purpose was to provide a vehicle for China's deeper engagement with Afghanistan as a counterbalance to the United States.[32]

While the SCO remains the preeminent regional organization, China's Belt and Road Initiative (BRI) has largely superseded it strategically. This shift has not, however, diminished the centrality of counterterrorism in China's regional foreign policy. As analysts have been quick to recognize, many countries along the Belt and Road route are located in high-risk areas where terrorists gather and terrorist activities are common.[33]

---

[28] The Shanghai Five consists of China, Kazakhstan, Kyrgyzstan, Russia, and Tajikistan and emerged from early cooperation over border demarcation and demilitarization after the fall of the USSR.

[29] The SCO's founding charter is titled the "Shanghai Convention on Fighting Terrorism, Separatism, and Extremism."

[30] China chaired the SCO's meeting at the deputy foreign ministers' level in Beijing. These exercises addressed a scenario involving the elimination of terrorists operating across regional borders (McDermott 2004: 16).

[31] Deng and Wang (2005: 81).   [32] Shi (2018).   [33] Zi (2018).

China has emerged on the world stage and with exposure comes vulnerability. Thousands of Chinese workers have gone to Pakistan following Beijing's pledge to spend $57 billion on BRI projects. These investments give rise to local complaints and are at constant risk of terrorist attacks.[34] For example, in March 2019, the Baloch Liberation Army (BLA) attacked a convoy of Chinese engineers near Karachi. The organization's spokesman made it clear the BLA would not react kindly to further outside incursion:

This attack is the continuity of the BLA's policy of not allowing any force, including China, to plunder the Baloch wealth in Balochistan. Our fighters had carried out deadly attacks on Chinese interests and engineers in the past and a series of such attacks will continue with intensification until China terminates the nexus with Pakistan, regarding Baloch land.[35]

Chinese leadership is defensive about the criticisms and threats that investment can generate, noting that the BRI could also promote further counterterrorism cooperation and security-enhancing economic development.[36] For example, Zhuang Jianzhong, Vice Director of the Shanghai Jiao Tong University's Center for National Strategy Studies, argues that improving the region's economy would weaken the root cause of terrorism and stabilize Central Asia and that the United States should therefore be more positive about the initiative as a stabilizing force for good in the region.[37] That said, the link between development and the reduction of terrorism is tenuous at best and these arguments sound disturbingly similar to those made about development and pacification within Xinjiang (where that policy came to naught).[38]

Rhetoric and political sensitivities aside, Chinese authorities are keenly aware that investment and expansion in Central Asia have the potential to produce undesirable side effects and they are actively managing those risks. The problem takes three basic forms:

1. threats against Chinese nationals and assets abroad;
2. threats against China itself from international terrorist organizations; and
3. the integration of Uyghur grievances in Xinjiang into the global Salafist/jihadist movement.

---

[34] Martina (2017). [35] Chaudhury (2019). [36] Dang (2017).
[37] Minnick (2015). [38] See, for example, Piazza (2006).

Managing the repercussions of foreign policy adventures is certainly not a uniquely Chinese problem and there are lessons to be learned from other contexts.[39] The 9/11 terrorist attacks in the United States were unprecedented in their magnitude and devastation, but according to some critics of US foreign policy, they were also predictable consequences of heavy-handed US engagement in the Middle East and support for leaders in that region.

Terrorist attacks in the United Kingdom and Spain since 2003 further support the notion that a blowback mechanism might be a process by which states become the targets of transnational terrorist organizations. For states potentially in this position, managing that possibility is essential to a comprehensive foreign policy. Both countries joined the United States in Iraq as participants in the "coalition of the willing" and both subsequently experienced devastating terror attacks (the Madrid train bombings in 2004 and the London tube bombings in 2005). Spain's government was voted out of office in part due to the public perception that its foreign policies had invited this blowback.[40]

A substantial body of work supports the validity of this mechanism, both theoretically and empirically. Much of that discussion originates with an influential paper from the Defense Science Board that argues that foreign engagement is a primary motivation for terrorist attacks against nations.[41] It states,

As part of its global power position, the United States is called upon frequently to respond to international causes and deploy forces around the world. America's position in the world invites attack simply because of its presence. Historical data show a strong correlation between U.S. involvement in international situations and an increase in terrorist attacks against the United States.[42]

Developing this logic, Eland notes a relationship between American foreign intervention and terrorist attacks.[43] The fundamental question is whether countries become targets of international terrorism because of "what they are" or "what they do."

Betts noted in 1998 that "as the only nation acting to police areas outside its own region, the United States makes itself a target for states

[39] Johnson (2001).   [40] Baum and Potter (2015).
[41] This analysis focused on the United States.
[42] Defense Science Board (1997: 15).   [43] Eland (1998).

or groups whose aspirations are frustrated by U.S. power."[44] Driving the point home, Osama bin Laden's original grievance against the United States was "the existence of US forces in the Arabian Peninsula."[45]

As China takes on a more prominent role in Central Asia, it also confronts these potential consequences. As a result, China's regional foreign policy, increasingly focused on investment in counterterrorism, must be carefully managed to optimize a series of competing priorities. China seeks to develop a credible reputation as a regional hegemon, maintain military readiness, and safeguard Chinese nationals and investments abroad; at the same time, it must minimize blowback. In practice, this means that China invests deeply in counterterrorism in places where it has substantial direct investment *and* militant violence threatens those investments, but it maintains a comparatively light footprint where one or both of those conditions do not hold.

In the sections that follow, we explore China's selection of partners for counterterrorism joint military exercises (CT-JMEs) as a demonstration of this strategy in action. These exercises, which began in 2002, have become a pillar of China's regional relationships and the most visible manifestation of the PLA's engagement abroad.[46] Drawing on an original and comprehensive dataset of China's CT-JMEs between 2002 and 2016, we show that China has consistently prioritized partners where both the threat of militant violence is high and there are significant Chinese economic interests at stakes. When only one (or none) of these conditions hold, China has been inclined to keep a lower profile.

While these exercises reveal the strategic nature of China's use of counterterrorism in its foreign policy, they also indicate yet another trade-off that Beijing must navigate as it confronts mounting terrorist threats. Specifically, the militarized interventions deemed necessary to protect Chinese political and economic investments in high-terrorism countries also increase that threat in the longer term.

---

[44] Betts (1998: 28).   [45] Orfy (2014).

[46] The start of these exercises in 2002 is notable, as it represents yet another example of China leveraging the post-9/11 political environment to internationalize its issues in Xinjiang and engage in activities that the United States would have found provocative under other circumstances.

Joint Counterterrorism Exercises

For most of its history, mystery has shrouded key elements of the Chinese military. The opacity comes from the PLA's penchant for secrecy, China's longstanding policies of nonintervention and non-alliance, and, most significantly, China's aforementioned "low profile" in international affairs. As a consequence, until quite recently, it was relatively rare to see the Chinese military in action outside China's borders. This posture has fundamentally changed under Xi Jinping – the country's strategic stance has fully shifted from "keeping a low profile" to "striving for achievements."[47]

To illustrate – on the seventeenth anniversary of the 9/11 attacks, Russia launched its most significant military exercise since the end of the Cold War in eastern Siberia. Named "Vostok-18," the exercise featured nearly a third of Russia's armed forces.[48] However, what alarmed the West was not only the scale of the exercise (which has been held every four years since 2010) but the involvement of Chinese forces for the first time in a strategic-level Russian exercise.[49] What is often missed is that China built up to its participation in Vostok-18 – an exercise led by a former foe – through a series of less provocative counterterrorism exercises over the preceding decade.

This process began with a two-day CT-JME with Kyrgyzstan in October 2002 – just a year after the 9/11 attacks. According to Chinese official media, this was their first joint exercise with foreign forces, and it "opened the door for the PLA to go out" and demonstrate that the "Chinese military has become more mature and more confident."[50] The PLA leveraged a steady stream of CT-JMEs in the ensuing years to further its internationalization and professionalization, gaining experience designed to prepare Chinese forces for more significant military action overseas.

The militarization of China's counterterrorism engagement abroad has also contributed to an ongoing shift in the regional balance of power. China has quietly emerged as the preeminent power in Central Asia on the back of its most potent weapon – direct investment. Extending military power in the context of counterterrorism cooperation as a follow-on to this investment further enables China to

---

[47] See, for example, Yan (2014).   [48] *The Economist* (2018).
[49] Higgins (2018); *DW* (2018).   [50] Mei and Yang (2002).

dominate a region critical to its ambitions. This transition is particularly significant as Russia confronts demographic decline and remains fixated on the West in its foreign policy and as the United States has withdrawn from Afghanistan and seems inclined toward a lower profile on the international stage – except when it comes to confronting China.

There are many reasons why China may want or need to hold CT-JMEs with foreign forces. The first and most straightforward among these is the training and experience such exercises can provide for PLA forces.[51]

The 9/11 attacks alerted the world to the significance of nontraditional security threats, and this warning was further distilled for China by its own experience with domestic political violence. According to Kuhn, shortly after the 9/11 attacks President Jiang Zemin "worried about restive Muslim populations in troubled Xinjiang province" and wondered "whether terrorists there might be plotting similar acts of violence."[52] In reaction, Jiang "ordered a review of security regulations and asked that more stringent procedures be enforced."[53] Beijing's initial audit revealed not only China's vulnerability but also a broader lack of counterterrorism capability.[54] Li Wei – arguably China's best-known counterterrorism expert – contended that "despite the long-standing terrorism threat facing China, when it comes to conducting effective counter-terrorism operations, China is still in its infancy."[55]

Since that time, China has invested heavily in enhancing its counterterrorism capabilities at home and abroad. In Chapter 4, we discussed the massive investments made in domestic counterterrorism capabilities, but the tallies are no less impressive on the international side. This includes agreements on law enforcement cooperation and intelligence sharing with dozens of countries, sending security personnel abroad to attend counterterrorism courses, and, of course, participating in CT-JMEs.[56]

---

[51] Blasko (2010). [52] Kuhn (2004: 472).
[53] Kuhn (2004: 472).
[54] Tanner and Bellacqua (2016). The seventy-fourth clause of the 2015 PRC Counterterrorism Law explicitly states that both the PLA and the PAP should establish professional counterterrorism forces and enhance their training.
[55] Xue (2015). [56] Tanner and Bellacqua (2016).

Chinese officials have never been shy about their willingness to learn from the experience of their CT-JME partners. For instance, in a press conference after the China–Pakistan "Friendship-2011" CT-JME, the PLA's Deputy Chief of the General Staff Hou Shusen reportedly said that the "Pakistani military has been in the front line for fighting terrorism since 2003 and has accumulated a lot of experience for China to learn."[57] China has proven willing to learn counterterrorism lessons from countries around the world, even from erstwhile strategic competitors such as the United States and India.[58]

The types of forces that China typically contributes to these joint exercises clarify its objectives. Reports indicate that the majority of counterterrorism exercises, both unilateral and joint, have involved PLA Special Operations Forces (SOF), providing them experience in a variety of operating environments.[59] Akin to the US Navy Seals, these forces are indeed the most likely to be used in targeted counterterrorism interventions, though they are also important domestically and would play a key role in any broader regional intervention.[60] China's particular interest in training SOF in terrorism scenarios is likely a reaction to the efficacy of American SOF in the US-led overthrow of the Taliban and al-Qaeda in Afghanistan, among many other engagements.[61]

China's growing overseas interests also incentivize CT-JMEs. As China's economic development strategy moved from "bring in" to

---

[57] Xinhua News Agency (2011).

[58] Jagannath P. Panda, a researcher from New Delhi's Institute for Defense Studies and Analyses, states that "Chinese authorities have expressed an interest in learning from the Indian military's tactics and methods in countering the insurgency in Kashmir" (Panda 2007).

[59] Chinese SOF have participated in almost every "Peace Mission" exercise within the SCO framework. Other notable examples include the China–Pakistan "Friendship" series CT-JMEs, the China–Indonesia "Sharp Knife" series CT-JMEs, and the China–India "Hand-in-Hand" series CT-JMEs, all of which prominently featured Chinese Special Operators (Blasko 2010; Duchâtel 2016; Allen, Chen, and Saunders 2017).

[60] Special Operations capabilities are of increasing importance in countries around the globe, and China's experience is certainly reflective of that broader trend. These capabilities are central to force modernization generally, but they are particularly important in a country without a bright-line civil/military divide because such forces can then be more readily deployed in domestic operations.

[61] "Special Operations Forces and Counter-Terrorism" (2006); Finlan (2003).

"go global," Chinese nationals and investments abroad have inevitably become more vulnerable to terrorist attacks as these individuals and investments become more prominent in terrorism hot spots around the world.[62]

A 2016 policy brief from the European Council on Foreign Relations reported a total of nineteen terrorist attacks causing forty-eight deaths of Chinese nationals overseas in the 2004–2016 period.[63] These incidents include both cases in which Chinese nationals were collateral victims (e.g., the 2013 Boston marathon bombing, the 2015 Bamako hotel attack in Mali, and the 2016 Brussels bombing) and cases in which they were the primary targets (e.g., the 2015 bombing at the Erawan Shrine in Thailand, the execution of Fan Jinghui by the Islamic State in 2015, and the suicide attacks on the Chinese embassy in Kyrgyzstan in 2016).[64]

This threat grows as the BRI extends China's presence deeper into the regions of the world where jihadist militant organizations are most active. Evidence suggests that Chinese leaders are keenly aware of this possibility and take it seriously. For example, at a high-level 2014 meeting on foreign affairs, Xi Jinping explicitly stated that "we should protect China's overseas interests and continue to improve our capacity to provide such protection."[65]

The CT-JMEs with foreign forces are a means by which to achieve this goal.[66] China's longstanding (though eroding) nonintervention policy, along with a regional strategy based on coopting local regimes, makes unilateral counterterrorism engagement undesirable. Some degree of cooperation with local forces is necessary for both legal and practical reasons. Indeed, one important reason why China abandoned its decades-old prohibition on training with foreign militaries,

---

[62] Zhao (2015).   [63] Duchâtel (2016: 3).

[64] Duchâtel (2016: 3).   [65] *China Daily* (2014).

[66] The PRC Counterterrorism Law specifies other rules to protect China's overseas interests. The forty-first clause requires the Ministry of Foreign Affairs, the Ministry of Public Security, the Ministry of State Security, the National Development and Reform Commission, the Ministry of Industry and Information Technology, the Ministry of Commerce, and the China National Tourism Administration to establish a risk assessment system for outward FDI and tourism. The fifty-ninth clause requires related ministries and agencies to establish contingency plans in response to terrorist attacks against Chinese agencies, nationals, and facilities abroad.

according to Dennis Blasko, was to "identify early-on problems inherent in multilateral operations" in the wake of the post-9/11 threat posed by al-Qaeda and other terrorist organizations on China's western borders.[67]

In addition to their importance for preparedness, CT-JMEs send an important signal to the region and beyond.[68] The visible presence of Chinese soldiers and weapons can deter potential challengers (terrorist or otherwise) by demonstrating China's capability to conduct military operations outside its borders. More importantly, exercises and joint training indicate local forces' willingness to cooperate with China in their commitment to protecting Chinese assets in their countries. An article published by the Office for International Military Cooperation of the Central Military Commission acknowledges this function: "[T]he regularization of the 'Peace Mission' series of counterterrorism joint military exercises has effectively deterred the 'Three Evils' and exerted positive and important impacts on regional security."[69]

Beijing also clearly leverages joint military exercises as a further means by which to internationalize Uyghur political violence and to legitimize its policies at home. As we have discussed here and elsewhere, the 9/11 attacks provided the CCP with an opening to place the Uyghur question firmly within the framework of the war on terror.[70] However, despite some immediate dividends, such as the United States' designation of the East Turkestan Islamic Movement as a terrorist group, Western criticism of China's repressive ethnic policies in Xinjiang has only grown alongside mounting mistreatment of the Uyghur minority.

The CCP has long bristled at this criticism and it has pushed back on perceived "double standards" when it comes to combating terrorism. For example, at an anti-terrorism conference at the Seventy-Second Session of the UN General Assembly, China's delegate, Shi Xiaobin, stated,

[67] Blasko (2010: 383).
[68] Blackwill and Legro (1989); Caravelli (1983); D'Orazio (2012).
[69] Office for International Military Cooperation of the Central Military Commission (2017).
[70] Potter and Wang (2022).

The international community must seek greater consensus and create stronger synergy in this regard. All parties concerned should unequivocally oppose and combat terrorism in all its forms and manifestations, and reject double standards and any attempt to link terrorism to any specific ethnicity or religion.[71]

Thus, CT-JMEs with foreign forces are integral to China's campaign to sell its framing of Uyghur unrest as terrorism and one of the "three evils" along with extremism and separatism. Countries that agree to participate in a CT-JME with China are expected to explicitly or implicitly accept China's expansive definition of terrorism.

China has, at times, faced criticism for its relatively modest contributions to broader international counterterrorism efforts.[72] Though it is perhaps not what Western critics had in mind, Chinese authorities see growing regional military-to-military cooperation, including CT-JMEs, as a way to refute this critique. For example, the Chinese official media trumpeted the 2016 establishment of the Quadrilateral Cooperation and Coordination Mechanism, a counterterrorism group that included China, Afghanistan, Pakistan, and Tajikistan. It was China's first multilateral cooperation mechanism and the state media called it a clear rebuttal to the West's depiction of China as a free rider in the international fight against terrorism.[73] In this light, CT-JMEs become a legitimacy- and image-building tool that demonstrates to domestic and international audiences that China has partners in its approaches to counterterrorism and is therefore acting as a responsible and constructive international stakeholder.

Finally, CT-JMEs were one of several mechanisms by which China could balance against the US military presence on its western periphery prior to the withdrawal from Afghanistan. Concern over strategic encirclement has agitated the CCP since its inception. A *People's Daily* article in 1966 accused "the United States, the Soviet Union, Japan, and India of collaborating in the military encirclement of China."[74] In the early 2000s, the locus of this worry shifted to Central Asia as Chinese officials fretted over the new presence of US troops on its western border after the invasion of Afghanistan. These fears have

---

[71] Shi (2017). [72] See, for example, Kan (2010).
[73] *Global Times* (2016). [74] *People's Daily* (1966).

deepened with the US pivot to Asia and renewed security cooperation among the United States, India, and Japan.[75]

While the benefits are clear, there are also costs associated with CT-JMEs. Most notably, these exercises are expensive. Although precise expenditures are unknown, a 2015 *Global Times* article cited the increasing number and scale of all types of joint military exercises held by the PLA and foreign forces as a significant contributor to the growth in China's defense expenditures in recent years.[76] The global economic recession of 2008–2009 was also blamed for the more modest Peace Mission 2009 CT-JME with Russia, suggesting some degree of cost sensitivity.[77]

Despite the significance of expenditures on CT-JMEs in yuan, the domestic political costs are likely a more significant concern for Beijing. China's ever-growing military expenditures, at the expense of domestic investment, have already triggered a national debate over "guns or tofu." In an interview with the *New York Times*, Shambaugh noted that "given other demands on state expenditures from various sectors – the stimulus, unemployment, insurance – to continue giving the military 15 percent increases year on year does cause some Chinese to raise questions."[78] Indeed, during the Peace Mission 2014 CT-JME, the CCP posted articles online to rebut the widely discussed rumor that China alone had paid for all SCO and Russia–China joint military exercises.[79]

While military cooperation on counterterrorism clearly has value, China has long been suspicious of exclusive reliance on military means to eradicate political violence – at least abroad. In his speech at the G20 summit soon after the 2015 Paris attack, Chinese foreign minister Wang Yi emphasized, "China holds that joint forces should be formed to fight against terrorism and that both the symptoms and root causes of the issue should be addressed."[80] A 2016 *People's Daily* article explicitly warned that China should not follow the Western "misunderstanding" of counterterrorism, arguing (without apparent irony) that the war on terror would only generate

---

[75] Chang (2016).   [76] Guo (2015b).
[77] Weitz (2015).   [78] Wines and Ansfield (2010).
[79] See, for example, *Sohu News* (2014).   [80] *China Daily* (2015).

more grievances.[81] For China, the long-term answer to militancy in unstable regions lies in economic development.[82] For example, in the Pakistani case, China has long insisted that the China–Pakistan Economic Corridor not only provides Pakistan with opportunities for social and economic development but also serves as the "route one must take" to tackle the root causes of violence and unrest.[83]

The same sensibilities are reflected to some extent in prior domestic policies in Xinjiang, which are heavy on sticks but also hinge on the belief that rising economic tides would resolve underlying grievances even for marginalized populations. There is reason to anticipate that this is as mistaken abroad as it is domestically – and for similar reasons. Even if there is local economic benefit, grievances will emerge if China is seen as benefitting disproportionately, and particularly so if an excess of the spoils go to Chinese nationals living on foreign soil (as has historically often been the case with Chinese investments and projects abroad).

In contrast to its regional engagement, China refrains from full participation in global counterterrorism efforts – particularly the more militarized efforts – in hopes of remaining a secondary target for international terrorist organizations.[84] Until the 2010s, China was largely able to achieve this goal as its status as a developing country and a potential challenger to the United States reduced its symbolic value as a target for the jihadist movement.[85] Osama bin Laden even saw the US–China rivalry as a strategic opportunity. For example, in an interview in 1997, bin Laden said, "The United States wants to incite conflict between China and the Muslims. The Muslims of Xinjiang are being blamed for the bomb blasts in Beijing. But I think these explosions were sponsored by the American CIA. If Afghanistan, Pakistan, Iran and China get united, the United States and India will become ineffective."[86]

But China's ability to keep a low profile is evaporating as it emerges as a global power. As we have demonstrated, China's growing global footprint has inevitably made its nationals and assets more vulnerable to international terrorism. However, what worries Beijing is

---

[81] Zhang (2016).   [82] Small (2018).
[83] He (2018).   [84] Small (2010).
[85] Potter (2013).   [86] Fishman (2011: 49).

the fundamental change in jihadist groups' strategic thinking about China. Shortly after the July 5 Urumqi riot, al-Qaeda in the Islamic Maghreb (AQIM) threatened to attack Chinese workers in Algeria and other projects in North African to avenge Uyghur deaths.[87] A few months later, a high-ranking member of al-Qaeda in Pakistan, Abu Yahya al-Libi, called on Uyghurs to prepare for a holy war against the Chinese government.[88] Islamic State leader Abu Bakr al-Baghdadi condemned China as a country in which "Muslim rights are forcibly seized."[89]

These countervailing incentives and constraints have led China to pursue international counterterrorism cooperation, but with a certain amount of caution. CT-JMEs can contribute to preparedness and secure investments against threats, but China focuses these efforts to allocate resources optimally and minimalize externalities. The ultimate goal is to reap the dividends from joint exercises while minimizing the risk of blowback. Thus, when selecting CT-JME partners, China prioritizes countries where the threat of terrorism and China's economic interests are both high.

The underlying logic is straightforward. Working with countries that face significant terrorist threats allows China to gain military experience while burnishing its image as a responsible actor. At the same time, limiting these activities to countries where China's economic interests are high allows China to concentrate its resources on protecting its overseas nationals and assets while mitigating the threat of blowback. Significantly, this dynamic only holds true when the partner country faces *domestic* terrorist threats rather than transnational terrorism. China's concern with Uyghur militancy may give Beijing an additional incentive to learn from countries that have experience dealing with domestic terrorism. However, there is a significant incentive to avoid drawing the ire of internationally oriented terrorist groups.

Assessing China's CT-JMEs

Assessing the strategic logic behind China's CT-JMEs requires a full inventory of these exercises. To accomplish this, we rely on three sources

---

[87] Moore (2009).   [88] Abedine (2009).   [89] Olesen (2014).

for China's military and diplomatic activities: D'Orazio's Global Joint Military Exercises Dataset (1970–2010),[90] Haas's dataset on SCO Military Exercises (2002–2015),[91] and the PLA Diplomacy Database (PLADD) managed by the National Defense University (2003–2016).[92] After merging the datasets and deleting duplicates, we analyzed each event to confirm that it was indeed a joint military exercise.[93] As a final check for possible missing events, we conducted an extensive search of online and primary sources in both Chinese and English, including China Military Online, *People's Daily* Online, *China Daily*, the Ministry of National Defense website, and China's biennial defense white papers. This process uncovered 190 joint military exercises between Chinese and foreign forces between 2002 and 2016.

We considered these exercises to be CT-JMEs if either Chinese officials or the host country identified counterterrorism as the primary purpose of the exercise. By this criterion, we identified 65 out of these 190 joint military exercises as CT-JMEs. Our coding differs from PLADD's categorization in important ways. PLADD narrowly defines counterterrorism exercises as "lower intensity, smaller unit activities that resemble conventional combat on the lower end of the spectrum of conflict."[94] While PLADD is focused strictly on the actual function of the forces, we emphasize the diplomatic language used to frame the activity. Two examples illustrate this distinction. The Shanghai Cooperation Organization's signature multinational joint military exercises, the Peace Mission series, are categorized by PLADD as "combat" rather than counterterrorism, due to their scale and the involvement of multiple military services.[95] We, however, code all Peace Mission exercises as counterterrorism because the Chinese Ministry of Defense explicitly states that the Peace Mission series should

---

[90] D'Orazio (2013).   [91] Haas (2016).

[92] Allen, Chen, and Saunders (2017).

[93] This leads us to drop observations that we are unable to verify or that do not qualify as joint exercises. For instance, D'Orazio recorded two joint military exercises between Pakistan and China in August 2004, but we are able to identify only one, code-named Friendship-2014. To consider another example, PLADD treats IMDEX-2015 as a maritime joint military exercise, but it was a warship exhibition that involved no exercise or training.

[94] Allen, Chen, and Saunders (2017: 22).

[95] By definition, PLADD counterterrorism exercises can only involve the army.

"deal with the threat imposed by the 'Three Evils' of terrorism, separatism, and extremism" and "enhance the capability of joint counterterrorism missions among participating countries' militaries."[96] Another example is the biannual AMAN multinational maritime security exercises held in Pakistan since 2007. While PLADD categorizes all AMAN exercises as "combat support," we treat these exercises as counterterrorism because Chinese official news sources clearly identify them as being focused on maritime terrorism and other nontraditional security threats. This approach to definition allows us to capture a broader range of Chinese transnational military activities that have been conducted in the name of counterterrorism so that we can probe more deeply into the motivations underlying China's counterterrorism foreign policy.[97]

Figure 5.1 shows the distribution of all types of PLA joint military exercises with foreign forces and demonstrates the extent to which counterterrorism has come to dominate the agenda. In the 2002–2016 period, counterterrorism scenarios accounted for more than a third of all exercises. The prominence of CT-JMEs is even more eye-catching in terms of the total number of days China spent on each type of exercise. Opaque PLA reporting and its culture of secrecy make it extremely difficult, if not impossible, to collect detailed information on the exact number of troops involved or the types of weapons used; however, the duration of exercises is almost always reported and serves as a relatively accurate proxy for size and scope.[98] From 2002 through 2016, the PLA spent 700 days on CT-JMEs, or about 44 percent of the total time it spent with foreign forces on joint exercises or training.

---

[96] Ministry of National Defense of People's Republic of China (2018).

[97] We categorize all identified CT-JMEs as *combat, combat support, competitions*, or *military operations other than war (MOOTW)*, according to definitions from Allen, Chen, and Saunders (2017: 12): "Combat activities capture exercises that emphasize combat skills on the high end of the conventional spectrum of conflict, including live-fire drills and combat simulations; combat support activities include communications, engineering, resupply, logistics, survival skills, and fleet navigation and maneuvers; competitions are exercises where the PLA sends forces to compete with those of other nations, typically simulating combat activities; MOOTW includes nontraditional security activities such as search and rescue, HA/DR, and medical exercises."

[98] For a more detailed discussion of how China's military institution and political culture prize secrecy, see Shambaugh (2000).

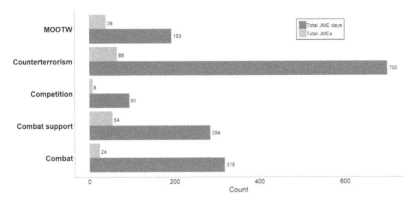

Figure 5.1 PLA joint military exercises, 2002–2016

Figure 5.2 plots the number of days China spends on CT-JMEs by year, and there is a clear upward trend over time.[99] This suggests an increasingly important role for the military in China's international counterterrorism policy.[100]

Map 5.2 illustrates the geographic distribution of China's partners in counterterrorism exercises. In the 2002–2016 period, thirty-nine countries from around the world had participated in at least one CT-JME with China. Unsurprisingly, China's CT-JMEs have been concentrated among its immediate neighbors. Among these partners, Pakistan leads with 181 days, followed by Russia with 138 days, Thailand with 124 days, and India with 111 days.

Even among neighboring states, China has consistently prioritized those countries where both terrorist threats and China's economic interests are high. For instance, despite China's relatively high foreign direct investment (FDI) in countries such as Vietnam and Mongolia, these countries are relatively insulated from terrorism, leading China to spend far less time with them on CT-JMEs. This strategic pattern holds at the other end of the spectrum as well. For example, while Afghanistan has been on the front lines when it comes to terrorism,

---

[99] The sharp temporary drop in 2013 and 2014 is a consequence of the most dramatic leadership turnover in China since 1949 (from Hu Jintao to Xi Jinping), which forced policymaking elites to focus on domestic affairs and consolidate their power at home (Shambaugh 2013).

[100] Duchâtel (2016); Small (2018).

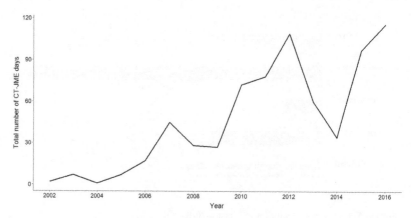

Figure 5.2 CT-JME days by year, 2002–2016

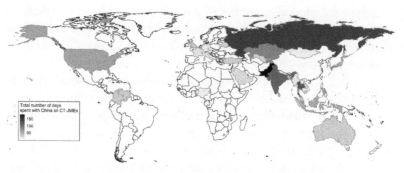

Map 5.2 China's CT-JME partners, 2002–2016

China's relatively low economic interests and fear of blowback there have led it to avoid high-profile CT-JMEs with Afghan forces in favor of quieter interventions, such as the patrols discussed at the outset of this chapter. It is also likely that China avoided such engagement with Afghanistan to forestall the inevitable tension with the United States that such exercises would have generated.

Western democracies (including the United States, the United Kingdom, and France) showed some early interest in training with China in the years after 9/11, but the incentives to do so rapidly waned. Due to mounting human rights concerns, Western democracies are increasingly reluctant to embrace China's definition of terrorism, especially as it relates to domestic policy toward the Uyghur minority.

China is also wary of being associated with Western democracies that remain the primary targets of current jihadist campaigns. Moreover, the growing geostrategic military competition between these parties further diminishes all parties' interest in any East–West joint training venture.

Digging Deeper

To examine the strategy underpinning China's CT-JMEs more systematically, we turn to a brief statistical analysis of the factors that drive cooperation.[101] To do so, we measure the extent of CT-JME cooperation in terms of the total number of days each country spent on exercises with China in a given year.[102] As we are primarily interested in assessing the interaction between the level of terrorist violence and Chinese investment in the potential host country, we have two primary explanatory variables in the model. The first, *Terror Attacks*, is a count of the total number of terrorist attacks that occurred in that country each year.[103] To capture investment, we generate *PRC FDI*, which is a measure of China's yearly outward direct investment in each country. For our purposes, FDI is a more appropriate indicator of overseas economic interests than bilateral trade, especially in terms of exposure to terrorist threats, because FDI typically involves China sending personnel to and establishing facilities in recipient countries.[104]

A secondary implication of our argument is that China should conduct more CT-JMEs with countries that face domestic terror

---

[101] The full dataset consists of 2,895 entries that cover 193 countries from 2002 through 2016, with country–year as the unit of analysis. However, one of our key independent variables, *PRC FDI*, only has records dating back to 2003. Thus, we sample 2003–2016 in our tests.

[102] We also construct an alternative measure of the intensity of CT-JMEs that takes account of whether the exercise was bilateral or multinational. Details are available in the appendix to this chapter.

[103] Data are drawn from the Global Terrorism Database (GTD) managed by the National Consortium for the Study of Terrorism and Responses to Terrorism (START, 2018).

[104] Data on China's FDI are drawn from China's *Statistical Yearbook*, published by the National Bureau of Statistics of China. As with terror attacks, log-transformed values are used to correct for right skewness.

threats, while avoiding those that are the target of transnational terrorists, so as to shield itself from becoming the target of terrorist
organizations with the demonstrated capacity to project violence
across borders. To capture this distinction, we further break down
the *Terror Attacks* variable into *Transnational Attacks* and *Domestic
Attacks*.[105]

We account for a variety of potentially confounding factors in our
analysis. *US Defense Pact* indicates whether or not a country in a
given year is in a defense pact with the United States, which, according
to Gibler, indicates the "highest level of military commitment, requiring alliance members to come to each other's aid militarily if attacked
by a third party."[106] The United States generally pressures its allies
to refrain from holding exercises with China (or at least to hold less
intensive ones). China itself may also have incentives to hold back
from engaging with these countries, in order to avoid intruding into
the US sphere or revealing capabilities and vulnerabilities.

We also control for *Regime Type*.[107] As we have noted, Western
democracies often view China's domestic counterterrorism measures
as a cloak for human rights violations, and we anticipate that such
democracies will generally hold less intensive CT-JMEs with China.

PRC Arms Transfer is an annual measure of the total value of
military technologies imported from and exported to the target state,
which we obtain from the SIPRI Arms Transfers Dataset. We anticipate a positive relationship between this measure and CT-JMEs for
two reasons. First, countries usually trade arms only with friends or
nonrival states. Therefore, a higher arms trade value should indicate
a closer security relationship. Second, from a technical perspective,

---

[105] GTD codes an attack as transnational if it meets any of the following
standards: "(1) the nationality of the perpetrator group is different from the
location of the attack, (2) the nationality of the perpetrator group differs
from the nationality of the target(s)/victim(s), and (3) the location of the
attack differs from the nationality of the target(s)/victim(s)." Conversely,
domestic attacks are those incidents that do not meet any of these standards. We use square root values of these variables to reduce right skewness. START (2021: 56–58).

[106] Gibler (2009).

[107] Based on Polity IV scores, which is a continuous variable scaled between
autocracy (-10 to -6) and democracy (+6 to +10) based on various regime
characteristics.

countries that share weapon systems have an added incentive to train together to practice using these weapons and potentially develop their capability for interoperability.

Extradition captures whether or not a country has an extradition treaty with China in a given year. We expect a positive correlation between this variable and CT-JMEs, given that extradition of Uyghur suspects overseas has been the primary component of China's international law-enforcement cooperation.[108]

Finally, we control for each state's *GDP per capita* (logged value), *SCO* membership, *BRI* membership (reflecting Belt and Road participants), and *Distance* to China (logged value). *GDP per capita* can have both positive and negative effect on the duration of CT-JMEs. On the one hand, richer countries may have more resources that allow them to participate in these expensive exercises. On the other hand, building and strengthening relationships with developing countries has long been the foundation of China's general diplomatic agenda.[109] Both *SCO* and *BRI* are expected to increase the number of days spent together in CT-JME, while *Distance* is expected to decrease those numbers.

Findings

We run a series of statistical models of increasing sophistication to clarify the strategic logic driving China's CT-JMEs.[110] Details about each model's specification and coefficient tables are available in the appendix. Here, we relay only the key findings.

Figure 5.3 clarifies the relationship between attacks and the number of CT-JME days as FDI varies. Each line represents a partner country receiving specific levels of FDI from China. We plot how the predicted number of CT-JME days changes as *Terror Attacks* increase while holding *PRC FDI* at one standard deviation below the mean, mean value, one standard deviation above the mean, and two standard deviations above the mean. The figure clearly demonstrates that China spends significantly more days on CT-JMEs with countries that

---

[108] Abuza (2017); Duchâtel (2019).   [109] Liu (2014).

[110] Because our dependent variable is a count and overdispersion is present, primarily due to an excessive number of observations with a count of 0, we perform our analysis using zero-inflated negative binomial (ZINB) models.

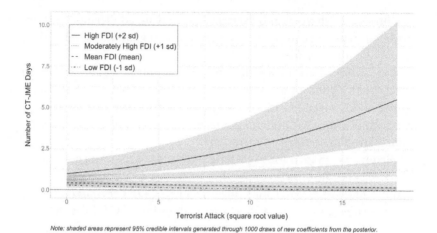

Note: shaded areas represent 95% credible intervals generated through 1000 draws of new coefficients from the posterior.

Figure 5.3 The conditional effect of attacks (Model 4)

experiences more terrorist attacks, but only when China also has high FDI in that country. Substantively, a country with Chinese FDI stock value equal to $1,107 billion (two standard deviations above the average, and in the top 5 percent of the sample) tends to experience a roughly three-day increase (from 1.3 to 4.2) in the number of predicted CT-JME days in a given year as the number of terrorist attacks that target this country increases from about 9 to 225.

In Figure 5.4, we plot the marginal effect of an increase in terrorist attacks on the number of CT-JME days, over a spectrum of FDI values. This further clarifies that an increase in exposure to terrorist threats only increases the number of CT-JME days with China when China's investment in that country is high. Tellingly, this plot also shows that when a country has a low level of FDI from China, more exposure to terrorism will actually significantly *decrease* its number of Chinese CT-JMEs. The implication is that China indeed acts on its incentive to avoid military presence in regions with high terrorism but low economic interests. This, in turn, suggests that China tolerates the risk of blowback only from countries in which it is already deeply invested.

Figure 5.5 plots how the number of CT-JME days is affected by the presence of *Domestic Attacks* versus *Transnational Attacks*. A comparison between these two graphs demonstrates that, as anticipated, domestic terrorism drives the level of cooperation between the two countries. In contrast, there is no significant variation in the predicted

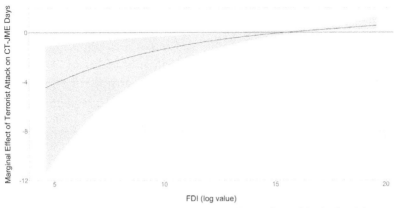

Note: shaded areas represent 95% credible intervals generated through 1000 draws of new coefficients from the posterior.

Figure 5.4 Marginal effect of an attack conditional on PRC FDI

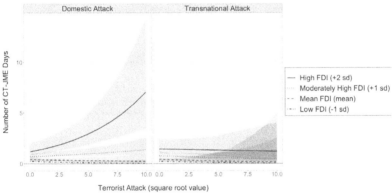

Note: shaded areas represent 95% credible intervals generated through 1000 draws of new coefficients from the posterior.

Figure 5.5 Domestic attacks and transnational attacks

number of CT-JME days associated with varying values of *Transnational Attacks*. China is steering clear of organizations with a capacity to project violence into China while cooperating in places where domestic terrorists may pose threats to Chinese investments.

Conclusion

In sum, the patterns in China's CT-JMEs reveal a policy oriented toward safeguarding existing investment while minimizing the risk of blowback. Holding CT-JMEs with foreign forces can enhance China's counterterrorism capabilities, protect its regional interests, and cultivate its reputation as a capable and responsible status quo power. However, conspicuously confronting militancy makes China a more prominent target for international terrorist organizations active in countries where China has a substantial economic or military presence.[111] As a result, despite the increasingly active role played by the PLA in China's counterterrorism foreign policy, China involves the military only when the stakes are high.

Given this strategic prioritization, we should anticipate a more substantial (but carefully targeted) presence of Chinese military in regions such as the Middle East and North Africa as China's economic interests there grow. Indeed, the PLA has already increased its assistance to African countries seeking to build their counterterrorism capacities, such as providing military assistance and arms transfers to Nigeria in its fight against Boko Haram.[112] This presents a challenge. The locations in which China is most likely to invest are increasingly fraught. At the same time, the more the Chinese do to protect their investment in these volatile host countries, particularly through visible means like CT-JMEs, the more prominent a target they become.

---

[111] Potter (2013).
[112] Duchâtel, Lafont-Rapnouil, and Gowan (2016).

6 | *Conclusion*

Forty years after Deng Xiaoping initiated the "open and reform" policy, the rise of China is no longer hypothetical. From its trade and currency policies to its handling of the coronavirus outbreak, China's moves reverberate around the globe. This is no less true when it comes to political violence and repression.

The forces that we have described in the preceding chapters – Uyghur grievances, state repression, and securitization at home and abroad – are durable. Their implications for Chinese policies, for Xinjiang, and for Central Asia will be with us for a significant period. Beijing seems to have no plan for political accommodation in Xinjiang, preferring the indefinite repression of Uyghur aspirations. But history shows that the subjugation of a population comes with mounting costs as the grievances of the oppressed grow.

At the same time, China is not likely to withdraw from the international stage and its footprint in Central Asia is expanding, increasing regional resentment and raising its profile as a target for violence.

Technological advancements will continue to complicate the picture by making information more difficult to control while simultaneously facilitating high-tech authoritarianism. As China cements its status as a developed country, explosive growth will become elusive. Without economic fires to stoke, Beijing is more likely to stoke nationalism and social stability to strengthen its grip on the polity.

This situation is one of deep contradictions that challenge easy forecasting. On the one hand, the Chinese government has stated its interests, demonstrated its capabilities, and proved its resolve in the face of Western criticism. Those facts would seem to weigh against any meaningful change in the status quo. On the other, such stasis does not erase the ever-mounting domestic grievances and international outrage. As one Chinese government official, who preferred to remain anonymous, told us, "The situation in Xinjiang is like a kettle of boiling water; once you loosen your hold on the lid, the water will splash out."

Beijing's answer to this escalating cycle of violence and repression has been social engineering and cultural genocide. Absent the political wherewithal to accommodate Uyghur grievances, the government is now attempting to erase independent Uyghur identity entirely. Scholars and political observers have so thoroughly documented this reality that it has lost some of its ability to shock the conscience. But when considered as a strategic solution to control a population, its monstrosity comes back into focus. Estimates vary, but there are perhaps ten to thirteen million Uyghurs in Xinjiang and more throughout the region. Neutralizing Uyghur identity would be a massive, brutal, and multigenerational undertaking.

The horrific grandiosity of the vision also makes it unlikely that the CCP will achieve it. The ten-year-long Cultural Revolution used massacres, torture, and book- and monument-burning in an attempt to wipe out the cultural and ideological differences within Chinese society. That effort only silenced Uyghurs and other ethnic minorities for a decade.

Adrian Zenz has estimated that China's "population optimization strategies" in Xinjiang – including forced birth control, sterilization, and interethnic marriage – could lead to a shortfall of 2.6–4.5 million Uyghur births by 2040. Other estimates have suggested a shortage of 100,000–200,000 Uyghur births each year. But even this scale and pace leaves the task of cultural erasure barely begun.

In the medium term, this implies that the grinding, repressive status quo will continue – but with the ever-present possibility for sudden and unexpected shifts and breaks. Because of the massive effort it takes to hold the status quo in place against opposition, there is always the potential for sudden inflection points. The status quo is easily mistaken for permanence.

Under mounting pressure, a release is nearly inevitable – the only question is the time and the precise point of breakage. Thus, while it is unclear what could happen, and even more unclear when it might happen, the potential for a rippling crisis is clear and foreseeable.

This is a familiar dynamic. Returning to an example from early in this volume, the pre–World War I alliance structures led to a tremendous buildup of tension. It took only a comparatively small precipitating event – the assassination of a fringe noble – to break that equilibrium and set world-changing events in motion. As historians have noted, it is too simplistic to treat the assassination of Archduke

Franz Ferdinand as the cause of World War I – it was one spark among several, and the powder keg was already there. There may be a similar explosive potential in Xinjiang, vulnerable to ignition by unforeseen weakness or turmoil in Beijing, regional conflict, foreign interference, militant violence, or some other unanticipated catalyst.

What the Response to Political Violence Reveals about China

The CCP's ferocious response to Xinjiang's modest potential for political violence teaches us a great deal about the state of Chinese politics. Much of this volume has focused on explaining the political logic behind this excessive response by exploring the CCP sensitivities and political weak spots. The evidence presented shows that Beijing's actions are driven by a sense that Uyghur unrest undermines the base of the Party's claim to legitimacy: its role as the provider of safety, security, and prosperity.

Political and media rhetoric paints China as a strident and assertive behemoth powered by its economic strength and political system; however, its actions in Xinjiang hint at a regime driven by a deep sense of insecurity. Zero tolerance policies are designed to assuage that insecurity, but they do so with unsustainable expenditures and significant opportunity costs. Money and political capital spent on surveillance and security measures in Xinjiang and Central Asia come at the expense of economic investment elsewhere, but it also undermines the capacity to pursue Chinese aspirations in the South China Sea or reunification with Taiwan. According to Scobell, Ratner, and Beckley, Beijing's greatest national security priorities lie in its eastern and coastal provinces – China's political and economic heart. Security investment in the far-flung west means resources are pulled away from those priorities.

The regime's extreme recalcitrance on the Uyghur issue is rooted in self-preservation. By suppressing Uyghur violence, Beijing is subtly painting a new portrait of its leadership in order to retain legitimacy as the economy matures into stasis. Because the Party cannot rely on unsustainable economic growth to win the consent of the governed, it seeks to build its authority by using explicit appeals to nationalism and implicit appeals to ethnonationalism. This strategy, however, comes with its own risks. Appeals to nationalism play with fire – a hotly inflamed populace may demand even harsher policies than the regime is willing or able to deliver.[1]

With Xi Jinping's rise, the country has once again shifted away from institutionalism and more toward a personalistic autocracy in which power and legitimacy are concentrated in a single autocrat's hands. This shift presents further risks. With legitimacy and power increasingly dependent on the prestige of an individual, the regime's time horizon to address a problem shortens and it becomes less resilient in the face of setbacks. Personalistic regimes typically display profound intolerance for challenges to authority and stability, and particularly for minority dissent that undermines both the legitimacy of the regime and its role as the guarantor of stability.

The implications for the Uyghur minority are profound. If the CCP gains a durable legitimacy using appeals to ethnonationalism, it will further the Party's commitment to assimilationist policies in Xinjiang rather than any form of accommodation. And if personalistic rule deepens, there will be even less tolerance for any objections to that cultural erasure. And thus, the cycle continues.

Extended Repression

Chinese authorities have fought mightily to keep the implications of minority policies tightly bottled in Xinjiang. As we have noted, this is the essence of the "two Chinas" approach – a tightly controlled Xinjiang alongside a more open East. The challenge is that both sides get a say in how this plays out. All the incentives that lead China to a containment policy lead Uyghurs to break those shackles – if a forced peace bestows legitimacy on the ruling party, the repressed will naturally seek to upend that peace.

This logic is just as true throughout the region as it is within China itself. The tighter the CCP contains Xinjiang, the more the grievances will manifest outside Xinjiang, in areas just beyond their control.

This dynamic has become increasingly central to regional relations in Central Asia. Minimizing militancy is at the very core of regional institutions such as the Shanghai Cooperation Organization (SCO); it shapes regional investment and military cooperation and

[1] Weiss (2014).

increasingly drives the adoption of Chinese models of policing and digital authoritarianism.

In this quest for domestic and political security, China is unwilling to leave any corners or edges unpoliced. But the further out the Chinese chase the unpoliced boundaries; the more toes China steps on in the process. While its regional policies may seem very aggressive, they are in fact driven by extreme levels of domestic risk aversion.

In order to minimize the long-term costs of controlling Xinjiang, Beijing has invested heavily in the technological capacity for surveillance and population control. To ensure the security and territorial integrity of the state, the surveillance infrastructure within Xinjiang is unrivaled. Outside of detention camps, the population is controlled by an intricate system of digital authoritarianism that is powered by the state's intensive physical monitoring.

Tens of thousands of checkpoints on the outskirts of Xinjiang's towns and cities monitor travelers throughout the region, and reports indicate that these checkpoints are intended primarily for Uyghurs. Travelers who are ethnic Han are directed through checkpoints while Uyghurs are ordered to get out of their vehicles, swipe their identification cards, and look into a camera lens before they are allowed to enter or exit an area. Uyghurs encounter checkpoints as they go to the bank, fill up their gas tanks, take their children to school, or visit their local mosque; they must swipe their identification cards at the store to buy knives, phones, or computers. In some areas of Xinjiang, officials "collect blood, fingerprints, voice recordings, head portraits from multiple angles, and scans of irises."[2]

Even between various checkpoints, officials have methods to track citizens' movements and activities. Areas not covered by CCTV are monitored by small surveillance drones. Those with cars in Xinjiang are required to "install a navigation system powered by BeiDou" (China's version of the Global Positioning System), allowing officials to track all vehicles from the region.[3] If an individual is deemed to be of interest, authorities may force them to download an app known as "Clean Net Guard" to monitor their phone for any suspicious activity.[4]

---

[2] Buckley and Mozur (2019).   [3] Polyakova and Meserole (2019).
[4] Buckley and Mozur (2019).

All of this collected information finds its way into databases supported by some of the country's largest tech companies.[5] Authorities in Xinjiang use an app created by the state-owned China Electronics Technology Group Corporation to take in information from several data streams to allow officers to observe the minute details of citizens' lives. Officials can see if an individual is using a suspicious amount of electricity, avoiding the front door of their home, or refraining from using their smartphone.[6] Beyond flagging these activities, these tech companies provide data management platforms to "predictively identify those suspected of harbouring extremist views and criminal intent."

Internal CCP documents revealed that the Integrated Joint Operation Platform "identified about 24,412 'suspicious' people in southern Xinjiang during one particular week." Authorities used this information to send over 15,000 of those people to detention camps and to detain over 700 people for criminal investigations. Some Chinese tech companies have gone beyond surveillance to supporting propaganda efforts. The Australian Strategic Policy Institute's International Cyber Security Center found that ByteDance, TikTok's parent company, "collaborates with public security bureaus across China, including in Xinjiang where it plays an active role in disseminating the party-state's propaganda on Xinjiang."[7]

However, while Chinese digital authoritarianism was pioneered in Xinjiang, it didn't stay there. Repression in Xinjiang has direct implications for the spread and manner of authoritarianism elsewhere – in China and around the world.

Within China, the CCP aims to blanket the entire country with advanced surveillance technology. In 2015, Beijing police claimed that the city was "100% covered" by CCTV and the National Development and Reform Commission set a goal to cover China's "public spaces and leading industries in cameras by 2020." To accomplish this goal, the "Sharp Eyes" initiative promises to link together the country's smartphones, smart TVs, and surveillance cameras, and it "has already produced smartphone apps individuals can use to monitor feeds and report suspicious activities." Beijing is making significant

---

[5] Cave et al. (2019)   [6] Buckley and Mozur (2019).   [7] Cave et al. (2019).

investments in domestic artificial intelligence (AI) startups to facilitate the technology required to analyze the countless data points provided by new surveillance systems. For example, SenseTime, one of these AI startups, aims to create a system capable of analyzing over "100,000 high-resolution video feeds simultaneously and identify and track individuals across them in real-time."[8]

As China has developed its repressive capabilities, it has begun to export its version of digital authoritarianism.[9] Chinese technology companies are the primary suppliers of surveillance technology to at least twenty-four governments, and the list of countries buying Chinese surveillance technology continues to grow.[10] Huawei surveillance technology systems equipped with facial recognition technology can now be found around the world in liberal and illiberal countries alike.[11]

China is not just exporting surveillance technology; it is exporting its entire policing model. Beijing hosts seminars "on how to conduct online censorship and surveillance for officials from other countries, such as the Philippines, Saudi Arabia, the UAE, and Thailand."[12] Others such as Tanzania, Zimbabwe, and Vietnam have emulated China's laws in drafting cybersecurity legislation.

Beyond training, China has also physically exported law enforcement officers, particularly to countries with Belt and Road Initiative (BRI) projects. Serbia, a nominal democracy that has received billions of dollars from China's state investment bank, has had Chinese police officers patrol the streets of Belgrade, "a security presence officially billed as assisting the growing number of Chinese tourists who visit the city." And while the presence of Chinese police is not common in Europe, officers can be found around various BRI projects in Africa.[13]

China's export of digital authoritarianism abroad is particularly aimed at monitoring the substantial Uyghur diasporas that now reside across Asia, Europe, and beyond. Several recent reports indicate that Beijing is creating a global registry of the Uyghur diaspora and using

---

[8] Polyakova and Meserole (2019).
[9] For more information on the activities of Chinese tech giants around the globe, visit the Australian Strategic Policy Institute's International Cyber Policy Centre's database at https://chinatechmap.aspi.org.au/#/map/.
[10] Feldstein (2020).   [11] Polyakova and Meserole (2019).
[12] Economy (2019).   [13] Stojanovic (2019).

surveillance and detention of family members who remain in China to silence dissident Uyghur voices abroad.[14]

Chinese authorities have successfully persuaded countries such as Kazakhstan to crack down on, and in some cases repatriate, Uyghur dissidents. But in other countries, particularly outside the Central Asia region, the Uyghur diaspora remains an important voice that operates mostly outside CCP control. The influence of the diaspora on the policies of their adopted countries, and China's response to this influence, will play a role in shaping an uncertain future.

Diaspora communities have historically played a central role in supporting the cause of their ethnic brethren who remain at home. This can be particularly important when populations face repression that makes organization and advocacy on their own behalf challenging. In other instances, such as the Tamil struggle in Sri Lanka or Northern Ireland, diasporas have played a central role in sustaining conflict, with their preferences at times becoming more hardline than those they are supporting.[15] This possibility is clearly on the minds of CCP planners as they risk international diplomatic relationships in their efforts to crack down on Uyghurs abroad.

The CCP leadership tends to intentionally conflate diaspora activists with the entirely separate question of foreign fighters. This foreign fighter problem, however, is potentially real and, as characterized by the vice commander of the People's Armed Police, "multicentered and dispersed."[16]

The exact number of Uyghurs who fought in Syria is uncertain, but in 2017, Syria's ambassador to China claimed that there were "around 4–5,000 Xinjiang jihadists" in the country.[17] A UN Security Council report estimated that over 3,000 Uyghurs aligned with Turkistan Islamic Party (TIP) were operating in Syria under the umbrella of the al-Qaeda affiliate Hay'at Tahrir al-Sham.

As we noted in Chapter 3, one of Beijing's greatest fears is that these battle-hardened Uyghurs will return to conduct attacks on Chinese soil. Members of the Chinese military have expressed their belief

---

[14] Feng (2018).

[15] Piazza (2018). Byman (2013: 988–989) discusses the importance of diasporas as participants in nationalist/separatist groups' political and ideological programs.

[16] Blanchard (2017).   [17] Clarke and Kan (2017).

that TIP is using its experience in Syria to amplify its cause and "gain operational experience in order to return to China and breathe new life into the insurgency back home."[18]

That particular threat from Syria, however, is likely overblown. Those who left China to fight in Afghanistan and Syria did so to aid fellow jihadis and because of their inability to operate in Xinjiang. As China tightens its control over Xinjiang and the region, the prospects of Uyghur militants going home in any significant numbers and producing strategic shifts in their battle against the state continue to fade.

The more realistic threat is the one that these foreign fighters pose to China's overseas interests and this possibility, in part, motivates China's export of digital authoritarianism. As we demonstrated in Chapter 5, attacks targeting Chinese nationals and assets abroad have risen consistently since 2014. And these attacks, such as the 2015 bombing at the Erawan Shrine in Thailand and the suicide attack on the Chinese embassy in Kyrgyzstan in 2016, were considerably more sophisticated and deadlier than those initiated by poorly equipped Uyghurs residing in Xinjiang. While the extent to which Uyghur foreign fighters were involved in these attacks remains unclear, their increasing presence in this network will spread their cause, further raising the value of Chinese targets in the broader jihadist movement.

We have demonstrated in Chapter 5 that China has cautiously calibrated its engagement in international counterterrorism cooperation to minimize the potential blowback from internationally oriented militant groups. New developments on the ground suggest that while the risk of blowback still lingers, China's strategy to keep off the jihadist radar is largely working.

According to Stewart's documentation and analysis of Islamic State propaganda and publications, China has almost entirely disappeared as a target of ire in the group's media since mid-2017.[19] She attributes this change to the group's clear desire to "preserve the useful dynamic of a non-militarized China replacing a militarized United States in the Middle East and South Asia."[20] Notably, this was happening when the global discussion of China's reeducation campaign against Uyghurs

---

[18] Clarke and Kan (2017).   [19] Stewart (2021).   [20] Stewart (2021).

was at its highest and many Muslim-majority countries were reluctant to express their support for Uyghurs – a seemingly optimal moment for Islamic State to express theirs.

While groups such as Islamic State might choose to strategically ignore the plight of Uyghurs for now, China's economic interests and increasing demand for energy have led it to build closer ties with regimes that jihadists and other terrorist groups aim to destroy.[21] This invites trouble. As we have demonstrated in the preceding chapters, several militant groups such as Balochistan Liberation Army (BLA) have repeatedly initiated attacks against Chinese assets in the name of protecting local resources or spoiling the relationship between local regimes and China.

The US withdrawal from Afghanistan adds another layer of uncertainty regarding Beijing's approach to regional relations and may have implications for political violence in Xinjiang. China's reaction to the US collapse in Afghanistan has been mixed and complex. On the one hand, the withdrawal presents a golden opportunity to reject, criticize, and delegitimize US hegemony. In a phone call with US secretary of state Blinken, Chinese foreign minister Wang Yi seemed to gloat, saying "facts have once again proved that it is difficult to gain a foothold in a country with a completely different history, culture and national conditions by mechanically copying foreign models ... and using power and military means to solve problems will only cause more problems."[22]

On the other hand, China seems reluctant to step in to provide the public goods that the United States no longer does. Wang also expressed his concern to Blinken that "the hasty US withdrawal from Afghanistan has caused a severely adverse impact on the situation" and demanded that the United States "play a constructive role in helping Afghanistan maintain stability, prevent chaos and rebuild peacefully."[23] It is unlikely, however, that the United States will take up that role.

In this power vacuum, Chinese officials and strategists have repeatedly expressed concerns about threats of militancy that may emerge from a Taliban-controlled Afghanistan. Early in 2021, during a

[21] Fishman (2011).
[22] Ministry of Foreign Affairs of PRC (2021a).
[23] Ministry of Foreign Affairs of PRC (2021a).

meeting in Tianjin with a visiting Afghan Taliban delegation led by Mullah Abdul Ghani Baradar, Wang Yi stressed Beijing's "hope [that] the Afghan Taliban will make a clean break with all terrorist organizations including the ETIM and resolutely and effectively combat them to remove obstacles, play a positive role and create enabling conditions for security, stability, development and cooperation in the region."[24]

More recently, China's deputy permanent representative to the United Nations, Geng Shuang, stated during a UN Security Council meeting:

Afghanistan must never again become a haven for terrorists. This is the bottom line that must be held firmly for any future political solution in Afghanistan. All countries should fulfill their obligations in accordance with international law and the Security Council resolutions, work with each other in combating terrorism in all its forms and manifestations, and take resolute actions to prevent terrorist organizations such as Islamic State, Al-Qaeda and ETIM from taking advantage of this chaos.[25]

Despite these efforts, Zhao Huasheng, a professor at Fudan University and director of the SCO Research Center, argues that religious and ideological affinity make it difficult for al-Qaeda and the Taliban to stop supporting "East Turkestan" forces altogether.[26]

As such, Beijing faces challenges from the nexus of diaspora politics, Uyghur foreign fighters, and the global jihadist movement that must be considered through the lens of its broader relationships in Central Asia.

Zbigniew Brzezinski, Jimmy Carter's national security advisor, dubbed Central Asia "the Eurasian Balkans."[27] Little has changed since that time. Since the collapse of the Soviet Union, Central Asia has been plagued by instability, violence, and Islamic extremism.[28] As a consequence, Chinese leaders have long been vigilant in their maintenance of this strategically important but volatile corner of their neighborhood. They have spent a great deal of effort and money to maintain the region's peace and predictability and to support secular governments through frequent high-level visits, extensive economic

---

[24] Ministry of Foreign Affairs of PRC (2021b).
[25] Geng (2021).   [26] Voice of America (2021).
[27] Brzezinski (1997).   [28] Kendzior (2013).

cooperation, and (as discussed in Chapter 5) limited military cooperation. This has, however, failed to yield an entirely satisfactory result
for Beijing. Beneath the surface of the current stability are undercur-
rents that have the potential to pull the region into crises.

To the extent that discontent (Uyghur or otherwise) in Pakistan's
tribal regions continue to fuel terrorism targeting Chinese assets
abroad, there will be the potential for tensions in the bilateral relationship between China and Pakistan that closely mirror those that
plagued the relationship between the United States and Pakistan. The
risk of regional tensions is heightened by the reality that if attacks
escalate, particularly if they project into China itself, there will be
a temptation to place the blame on the neighboring countries from
which terrorist organizations operate, whether it be Pakistan, Afghanistan, or elsewhere. Even if Chinese policymakers view such moves
as strategically unwise, they may prove necessary in order to appease
mounting nationalist sentiments domestically and deflect critiques of
the state.

International Headwinds

China faces serious challenges as it attempts to pursue its preferred
policies in Xinjiang while advancing its position on the larger, global
stage. Officially, 2020 should have marked an end to "the period of
important strategic opportunities" for China – a formulation of the
Chinese approach to the first two decades of the twenty-first century,
which former president Jiang Zemin introduced in his last report to
the Party Congress in 2002.

As we have noted, with the United States occupied by the war on
terror, internationalizing the Uyghur violence issue was an important
strategy to facilitate elements of China's rise during this period. The
tides, however, are shifting. According to some Chinese strategists,
Jiang's conceptual period has been outdated since the United States
executed its strategic pivot to build alliances in the Asia-Pacific region.
Accordingly, strategists believe China will inevitably face the more
complicated challenges that come with economic and ideological
competition from major countries.[29] Repression in Xinjiang and the

---

[29] Cui Liru (2018).

distasteful policies that emerge from it are likely to figure prominently in peer competition with the United States.

While counterterrorism cooperation between China and the United States (and, by extension, the West in general) has never been able to transcend the divergent legal structures and ideological values of the two countries, general agreement on the issue of terrorism has served as an important de-escalatory device on several occasions, at least rhetorically. This is changing. Beijing's increasingly harsh policies in Xinjiang have made Washington unwilling to cooperate with China to combat terror as China defines it.

The divide that has opened in the relationship since the post-9/11 halcyon days is reflected clearly in the two side's official media notes after the second US–China Diplomatic and Security Dialogue – the framework launched by Trump and Xi at Mar-a-Lago in 2017. The Chinese take, which was highlighted in the opening paragraph of the *Xinhua* report, focused on counterterrorism cooperation. The US readout instead highlighted "concerns about China's lack of adherence to its international obligations and commitments on human rights and religious freedom [in Xinjiang]." The Chinese note, perhaps anticipating the US criticism, made it clear that "what happens inside Xinjiang is China's domestic affairs, and foreign nations have no rights to meddle."

The nearly unanimous support in 2019 and 2020 for the Uyghur Human Rights Policy Act in both houses of the US Congress is a further indication that relations are deteriorating over the issue. To Beijing, the Uyghur bill sent two worrying signals. First, despite the wide partisan divide in Washington, confronting Beijing has become one of the few areas of consensus. Second, the overwhelming vote count suggested that this bipartisan consensus toward China is particularly strong when it comes to human rights. The final vote on the Uyghur bill came just six months after Congress unanimously approved the Hong Kong Human Rights and Democracy Act.

This presents a significant problem for Beijing. Unlike trade disputes, or even territorial disputes in the South China Sea and elsewhere, the Party sees no room for negotiation on human rights. As we have noted, Beijing has consistently perceived criticism of human rights as indirect attacks on its political system and the Party's ruling legitimacy, both of which are sacrosanct "core interests." Xi Jinping made it clear on the ninety-fifth birthday of the Party that "any foreign country should not expect us to bargain over our core interests."

Human rights violations are the glue that holds together an emerging Western consensus that Beijing should be confronted more forcefully across a range of policy dimensions. As the divide between China and the United States grows, other countries are increasingly required to pick a side. Human rights issues weigh in favor of the United States, particularly in Europe.

In sum, the violence and repression in Xinjiang is likely to continue playing a role on the international stage, despite the political shift in focus from the war on terror to major-power competition. However, in contrast to the past where Uyghur violence could help China align itself with the broader international community, the issue today is likely to disadvantage Beijing as the Western world shifts its gaze from Uyghur militancy to the Chinese state's repressive tactics.

To some extent, Xinjiang has already become a potent symbol for those opposed to Beijing, even when their complaints are distant from the situation in Xinjiang. When a group of political activists marched on the Chinese Liaison Office in Hong Kong on May 22, 2020, their banners warned that the new Hong Kong national security law would turn Hong Kong into Xinjiang. Across the globe, the East Turkestan "sky flag" is increasingly popping up at protests of all things Chinese – not just those directly related to the plight of Uyghurs. We are increasingly moving to a world where the Uyghur blue and white is supplanting the iconic Tibetan snow lion as the symbol of opposition to CCP policies writ large. In short, repression in Xinjiang is rapidly becoming a major impediment to China's bid for international status.

The United States continues to lead the international community's response to the human rights situation in Xinjiang. In October 2019, the Trump administration blocked eight Chinese companies and "a number" of police departments from purchasing American-made technology. The administration also imposed visa restrictions on a number of Chinese officials "believed to be involved in the detention or abuse of Muslim ethnic minorities."[30]

As a rising state under unipolarity, China has long avoided openly challenging the US hegemony with traditional balancing strategies such as alliances or arms races. Instead, it has relied primarily on

---

[30] Mozur and Wong (2019).

what Schweller and Pu refer to as a de-legitimation strategy, such as denouncing US unilateralism and creating alternative international institutions. Xinjiang, and the widespread human rights violations unfolding there, challenge China's own legitimacy and therefore undercut that approach.[31]

The Uyghur Human Rights Policy Act requires the US president to provide Congress a periodic report identifying foreign individuals and entities responsible for human rights abuses in Xinjiang and to then impose property-blocking and visa-blocking sanctions on them.[32] Following this requirement, the Trump administration imposed sanctions on a number of Chinese officials, including Chen Quanguo, a member of the Politburo and Party secretary of Xinjiang. The administration also blocked another eleven Chinese entities accused of being complicit in human rights violations.[33] As is the case with most sanctions on high-level Chinese policymakers, it is unlikely that this will have any impact beyond messaging, as none of the officials sanctioned hold meaningful assets outside China.[34] The message, however, is unmistakable.

The Uyghur Forced Labor Prevention Act may result in much more biting economic repercussions. The legislation directs "the U.S. Customs and Border Patrol to presume that any goods produced in the Uyghur region are the product of forced labor."[35] Among other things, this action will have an immediate impact on the Chinese textile industry. The United States imports about $50 billion worth of textiles and clothing from China each year, and Xinjiang accounts for 85 percent of Chinese cotton production.[36]

Aside from the United States, European countries and the United Nations have been the main international actors opposed to the human rights situation in Xinjiang. However, their policy responses have been more muted, limited to individual denunciations of China's behavior and joint statements. On July 22, 2019, the UN's Human Rights Council published a joint statement demanding that China stop detentions and human rights violations against Uyghurs in the

---

[31] Schweller and Pu (2011).
[32] Uyghur Human Rights Policy Act of 2020.
[33] Swanson and Wong (2020). [34] Verma and Wong (2020).
[35] Turkel (2020). [36] Palmer (2020).

Xinjiang region.[37] British UN Ambassador Karen Pierce delivered the statement, which was issued on behalf of twenty-three countries, including Canada, France, Germany, Japan, New Zealand, Norway, Sweden, the United Kingdom, and the United States.[38]

The European Union as a whole has pressured China to respect religious freedom and Uyghurs' rights in Xinjiang.[39] Germany and the United Kingdom have continued to press for China to give UN observers "immediate and unfettered access" to Xinjiang detention centers.[40] France has also joined in these calls, demanding that detention centers be closed and urging an increase in human rights observers in the region.[41] Sweden has gone a step farther – in 2019, Sweden's Migration Agency identified Uyghurs as a collectively persecuted group, freeing Uyghur migrants "from the burden of trying to prove persecution as an individual."[42]

Other Western countries have taken similar diplomatic actions. Canada faces public pressure to repudiate forced labor camps in Xinjiang that manufacture products such as cotton and clothing.[43] New Zealand's and Australia's relations with China have become increasingly tense, particularly in response to China's detention of New Zealander and Australian Uyghur citizens in Xinjiang.[44]

However, despite the West's emerging consensus on opposition to China's human rights abuses in Xinjiang, many other countries have supported China's actions or remained silent. This trend is particularly notably among a group of powerful Muslim majority countries. Over three dozen countries, including Pakistan and Saudi Arabia, signed a letter in response to the UN Human Rights Council's joint statement on China's detention centers in Xinjiang. In it, they lauded China for its counterterrorism efforts and "remarkable achievements" on human rights.[45]

Since then, Turkey has been the only Muslim-majority country to voice concern. Its foreign minister called on China to ensure "the full protection of the cultural identities" of the Uyghurs and other

---

[37] Garside and Graham-Harrison (2019).
[38] Charbonneau (2019).   [39] Maizland (2020).
[40] Made (2019).   [41] Regan (2020).   [42] Hayes (2020).
[43] Chase (2020).   [44] Hayes (2020).   [45] Maizland (2020).

Muslims during a UN Human Rights Council session, but despite its longstanding support of the ethnically Turkic Uyghur minority, Turkey's opposition has dimmed in the face of Chinese pressure.[46]

Turkey's muted response – and the silence of dozens of other Muslim countries – reflects the extent to which Chinese investment and financial power have succeeded in buying acquiescence.[47] According to an article from the Australian Institute for International Affairs, "Beijing is the top trading partner of 20 out of 57 members of the Organization of Islamic Cooperation and has invested heavily in Saudi Arabia and Indonesia, two of the self-declared leaders of the Islamic world."[48] Acquiescence from these states is crucial for China as its prior alignment with the US War on Terror recedes into the past. The cover provided by majority Muslim states serves a similar function by allowing China to reframe its treatment of Muslims.

The actions of the United States and the broader international community have thus far had little or no impact on China's human rights abuses in Xinjiang. As we have noted, this is unsurprising given the extent to which these policies reflect the self-perceived core interests of the CCP. China's UN representative, Zhang Jun, has defended China's actions in the region, stating, "Xinjiang's preventive measures of counter-terrorism and de-radicalization are based on law and consistent with the will of the people."[49] Zhang Jun has painted criticism of China's actions as a political attack orchestrated by the United States.[50] State news outlets claimed that the passage of the Uyghur Human Rights Policy Act by the House of Representatives in 2019 revealed the true intentions of the "hegemonic power" – to "sow discord among different ethnic groups in China, undermine prosperity and stability in Xinjiang, and contain China's growth."[51]

Beijing's posture has led to calls in the United States for additional sanctions or other interventions. This may be the right thing to do, but it is unlikely that it will work. The story that we have spelled out about the centrality of Xinjiang to Beijing's conception of its ruling legitimacy and state stability explains why, for them, this boils down to an issue of regime survival. Given Chinese emergence as a great

---

[46] Maizland (2020). [47] Storey (2019). [48] Storey (2019).
[49] Tiezzi (2019). [50] Tiezzi (2019). [51] Xinhua (2019).

power, it is increasingly unrealistic to believe that foreign governments will be able to forcefully shape Chinese domestic and regional policy on an issue of such high salience – it is much more likely that the United States and the world will only be in a position to react, respond, and raise costs.

One of the first areas to keep an eye on will be the evolving BRI. This is a bold strategic move aimed at establishing China as the preeminent Asian power, but Central Asia has long been the graveyard of empires, even China. Were China in a position to challenge the United States on the open seas, it would not be throwing in with the likes of Pakistan and Kazakhstan and incurring the risks to domestic stability that come with provoking the militant organizations active in this region.

China's growing influence in Central Asia, and its rise in general terms, should also make US policymakers think carefully about the larger regional implications of the United States' withdrawal from Afghanistan. For many years, the US military presence in Afghanistan and Pakistan has been seen by Chinese leaders as a double-edged sword. Although the deployment of US forces, especially airpower, along China's borders unnerved Beijing, these forces also have undeniably and effectively helped Beijing manage the threat of political violence, which still remains China's top concern on its western border.[52] As a consequence, China explicitly advised the United States against any abrupt troop withdrawal from Afghanistan and called for collective international efforts to help initiate a peace process between the nation's warring parties.[53]

The full US withdrawal from Afghanistan undoubtedly clears the way for China to increase its influence in the region, but it also leaves China with many of the same responsibilities that the United States came to find burdensome. China views Afghanistan as the bridge to the Middle East and the last piece of the puzzle for its BRI but also as one of its great vulnerabilities.[54]

As a matter of policy, China has slowly advanced its influence westward of Afghanistan. Iran is now an important strategic partner, while Iraq benefits from Chinese investments in its oil industry. However, with each country brought into the Chinese security

---

[52] Scobell, Ratner, and Beckley (2014).
[53] Gul (2018).   [54] Marano (2019).

sphere, the fundamental problem – an uncontrolled periphery – is simply pushed farther to the west. At some point, expansion will cause tension with countries that China is unable to cajole or compel. At a minimum, China's push to secure its strategic investments through the advancement of its population-control policies will force fundamental changes to the nature of authoritarianism across Central Asia as these countries choose to either bandwagon or balance. At a maximum, these efforts present an additional arena in which emerging Chinese power can come into direct competition with Western interests.

What China Teaches Us about Repression and Political Violence

The story of political violence and repression in China is specific and nuanced, but it still holds important lessons for our broader understanding of autocratic behavior. It turns out that while China's population, economy, and governance usually make it a global outlier, the country's experiences with (and behaviors toward) political violence mirror much of what scholars have learned from around the globe. The Chinese experience provides a window into the political calculations that drive these broader findings, particularly in institutionalized autocracies.

China is arguably the case-in-point for Wilson and Piazza's argument that party-based autocracies are well positioned to coercively curb militancy.[55] Reflecting this capability, overall violence in China has remained low (Chapter 2). However, the periodic surges in violence that China has suffered are consistent with another truism in the literature – failure to provide the viable outlet for grievances allows the potential for violence to fester and grow.[56]

The literature consistently finds that repression is not an effective long-term tactic to address the grievances that produce political violence.[57] But, as the Chinese case makes very clear, a durable resolution is not always the priority for decision-makers in autocracies. Instead, if violence can be simply suppressed at acceptable political and economic costs, it is easier to prioritize regime security and political

[55] Wilson and Piazza (2013).   [56] Chenoweth (2013).   [57] Piazza (2017).

advancement. In China and elsewhere, the calculus is all about generating the legitimacy and stability required to ensure political survival and further a state vision of absolute political control.

Our analysis suggests an additional insight largely missing from existing findings – repression can actually advance legitimacy and regime popularity under some circumstances. This may hold lessons for other contexts around the world. In the case of Xinjiang, because the violence is perpetrated by a marginalized minority, authorities are incentivized to embrace a zero-tolerance approach to appeal to the sentiments of the majority – the group from which they derive authority. Minority repression in the name of stability is even more attractive when other sources of legitimacy (such as high economic growth) are diminishing.

Even leaders with an electoral incentive to act tough will increase repressive tactics even in the face of associated political costs.[58] Russia's Second Chechen War and Rodrigo Duterte's brutal crackdown on drugs in the Philippines provide two notable examples.[59] Viewed through this lens, the strategic logic that guides Chinese policies in Xinjiang seems less like an outlier and more like an emerging trend.

The implication is that the domains of repression and political violence are yet another dimension on which single-party autocracies, due to their institutionalization and reliance on mass opinion, behave more like democracies than personalistic dictatorships.[60]

The Chinese case also sheds light on the ways in which international pressure can – and cannot – shape the repressive behavior of autocracies. The broader deterioration of China's international relationships, particularly in the West, seems to have weakened the West's few levers of influence over policies in Xinjiang and Central Asia. In recent years, China has been more responsive to the sensitivities and policy preferences of its neighbors on these issues than it has to the preferences of the United States and other Western countries – despite the vast disparity in diplomatic, military, and economic strength.

---

[58] Dragu and Polborn (2014). See also Dragu (2017).

[59] An alternative explanation for these two cases could be that new leaders (Putin in Russia in 2000 and Duterte in the Philippines in 2016) are eager to establish a reputation for resolve and thus more likely to opt for harsh repression against domestic dissents (Licht and Allen 2018). However, this argument can hardly explain China's upgraded repression in 2017 as President Xi had been in office more than four years by then.

[60] See, for example, Weeks (2014).

It is reasonable to conclude that the hostile diplomatic conditions between China and the West have weakened the international community's power to restrain China. This may be inevitable given the extent to which China's bold use of repression has driven the diplomatic rift, but it sends a crucial message to those in the West: The ability to shape Chinese policy on perceived core interests is now minimal. A similar dynamic is likely to develop in other autocratic states that have the military and economic capacity to hold their own in the international system.

This pushes us to think harder about the effectiveness of international interventions to prevent state repression and whether they might be improved. There is consensus among scholars that forceful interventions such as sanctions can worsen repression.[61] This is certainly the case in China, where authorities have bristled and brushed off sanctions, boycotts, and other economic inducements. These are rapidly painted as disingenuous impositions on sovereignty; reciprocal measures are employed and repression proceeds apace. If Chinese policy is driven by a fixation on ruling legitimacy and regime stability, it may be that policies that change the equation on these dimensions would be more productive.

In sum, while the long-term inefficacy of repression in dealing with political violence seems to be clear, China's experience sheds important light on why authorities still opt for it. For wealthy and powerful autocracies, even the draconian levels of repression witnessed in Xinjiang are "affordable" when weighed against the potential consequences of political change.

Where to from Here?

CCP policies in Xinjiang are increasingly driven by short-term interests rather than long-term strategy. The coercive capacities of the Chinese state can suppress violence and unrest in the region long enough to secure immediate Party priorities and to pave individual officials' paths to promotion and power. There is, however, no obvious offramp toward longer-term de-escalation. As such, the situation in Xinjiang defies easy resolution. It is challenging to envision a future in which China loosens its grip on the region, Uyghurs acquiesce quietly

---

[61] Wood (2008); Escribà-Folch (2012).

to repression, or regional actors stand down in the face of what amounts to, at a minimum, cultural genocide.

The implication is that Beijing has painted itself into a corner. The Party faces a series of dilemmas of its own creation. It cannot reduce repression without opening the door to violence. It cannot address grievances among the Uyghur minority without risking backlash from an increasingly nationalist Han majority. It cannot invest in long-term legitimacy without risking short-term stability. It cannot engage internationally on counterterrorism without risking critique of its human rights practices and inviting terrorist blowback.

A prior iteration of the CCP, though responsible for many of the sins that led to this point, might have been better positioned to incur the costs required to work its way out of these dilemmas. It has become cliched to note that Xi Jinping is the most powerful Chinese leader since Mao, but what often goes underappreciated is the extent to which such personalistic power comes with an underlying weakness. Compromise becomes hard and middle paths narrow. When power is based in an individual, particularly one who has staked a reputation on strength, it is much harder to change direction. Xi has publicly and privately tied his own hands with statements and policies on the strife in Xinjiang. He has already overruled voices in the Party who see peril in the present course of action. For all his strength, changing course on Uyghur rights and counterterrorism policy seems out of reach as it would come at enormous cost to his personal prestige and would weaken the grip of the Party on other facets of Chinese life. Consequently, and most significantly, the immediate future seems bleak for individual Uyghurs in Xinjiang.

Appendices
Appendix to Chapter 2

Data on Uyghur Political Violence: 1990–2014

For an incident to be included in our data on political violence:

1. It must be Uyghur-initiated;
2. It must occur in China;
3. It must be premeditated;
4. It must be violent;
5. It must be motivated by political, religious, or social concerns; and
6. It must have been executed rather than merely planned.

It is worth noting that criteria (3), (4), and (6) exclude some incidents documented by other scholars. Specifically, criterion (4) leads us to drop nonviolent protests, demonstrations, and strikes, such as two student protests in March 2003 that happened in Khorgos and Manas and the Korla taxi drivers' strike that lasted three days in April 2005.[1] (In contrast, many official Chinese accounts seek to draw an equivalency between civil unrest and terrorist violence.)

Criteria (3) and (6) together exclude three types of incidents that are widely included in other assessments. First, spontaneous violence is excluded. An example of this is an incident on April 5, 2003, in which an assistant in a family planning office was killed by the husband of a pregnant woman being examined.[2] Second, acts of collective, spontaneous political violence, such as riots, demonstrations, or revolts, are also dropped. The most notable among these are the Ghulja riot on February 5, 1997, and the Urumqi riot on July 5, 2009. Third, we exclude both plots that are not physically carried out and preemptive violence initiated by the police. Examples include the gun battle that occurred on August 7, 2001, in Quca, where "police surprised a house

---

[1] Bovingdon (2010).   [2] Bovingdon (2010).

full of suspected separatists; four died in the gun battle, including the chief, Chen Ping; [and] a cache of weapons was reportedly found,"[3] and the six stings on weapon-production facilities conducted by the government between 1990 and 2005.[4] Regarding plots not carried out, we require that the attackers must be "out the door" to execute the attack, meaning that it is underway and no longer in the planning/ waiting phase. Notably, attacks that were physically carried out but failed to achieve their desired objective still meet this criterion and therefore are included in our dataset. An example of this is the failed bombing on September 5, 1993, in Yengisar County. An explosive device was set at the front door of the apartment of the director of the County Public Security Bureau, but it was detected and removed before it exploded.

Alternative Models for Assessing the Timing of Violence

To assess the possibility that political violence is partially responsive to audiences abroad, we employ negative binomial models to assess the relationship between Uyghur violence and the changing international conditions facing Beijing. To establish robustness of our findings, we reassess this relationship with vector autoregressive (VAR) models.

We rely on the same machine-coded events data from the Integrated Crisis Early Warning System (ICEWS) data to measure the international diplomatic environment facing China. We recode and rescale this score to range from 0 to 10 with a higher value indicating a more hostile environment for China and a lower value indicating a more cooperative one. Figure A.2.1 plots these two time-series. The spike of the external intensity score in May 1999 marks the period when the Chinese embassy in Belgrade was bombed by North Atlantic Treaty Organization forces.

One important prerequisite for VAR models is that the time-series data need to be stationary.[5] Figure A.2.2 plots the autocorrelation functions (ACF) of each series. Notably, both graphs show few significant lags that exceed the confidence intervals of the ACF (black dashed line), which indicates that both are stationary. We further

---

[3] Bovingdon (2010).   [4] Cao et al. (2018).   [5] Box-Steffensmeier et al. (2014).

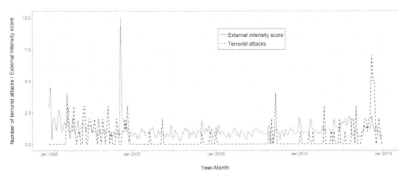

Figure A.2.1 Uyghur violence and China's external environment

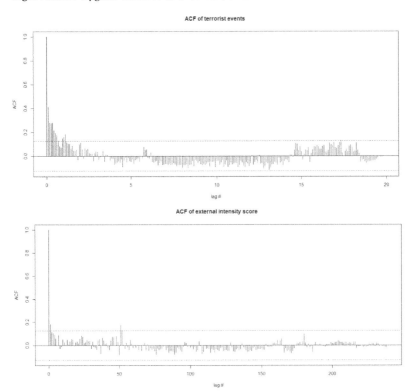

Figure A.2.2 ACF plots of violence and external intensity score

conduct Dickey-Fuller tests, which further confirm the stationarity of these two time-series.

Following the norm in VAR analyses, we rely on three different information criteria (IC) to choose the appropriate lag length (K) with

Table A.2.1 *Granger causality test based on the 1-lag VAR model*

Hypothesized exogenous cause	*F*-statistics	*P*-value
International condition	5.459	0.020**
Number of terrorist attacks	0.147	0.702

Note: ** p<0.05, * p<0.1

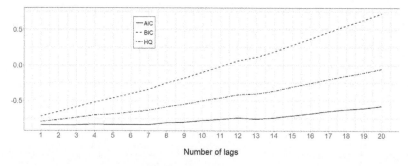

Figure A.2.3 IC for VAR model selection

smaller IC values indicating better fit. These are plotted in Figure A.2.3.[6] All three IC suggest that a single lag should be included in the model. Thus, the results we present here are obtained from a 2-variable-1-lag VAR model.

Table A.2.1 presents the Granger causality test of the relationship between these two variables. The results demonstrate that changes in the international environment facing China statistically forecasts the number of terrorist attacks initiated by Uyghurs, but not vice versa. This suggests that Uyghur violence is indeed sensitive to the changes in the international context.

Figure A.2.4 plots the impulse response function (IRF).[7] The plot shows that adverse international conditions are associated with an uptick in violence above the baseline average that lasts about three months.[8] This pattern is consistent with the findings we present in

---

[6] Box-Steffensmeier et al. (2014).

[7] In all of the IRF analyses, we use the orthogonalized unit shock, which is equal to one standard deviation of the residuals in the VAR equation that corresponds to the shock variable.

[8] We recode the *International Condition* variable so that a higher value indicates a more hostile foreign diplomatic condition.

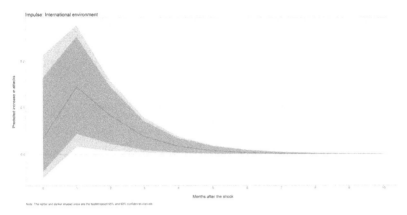

Figure A.2.4 The relationship between violence and international conditions

Chapter 2, suggesting that perpetrators might indeed seek to leverage external pressures. In other words, they are more likely to initiate violence when the Chinese government is already facing international headwinds.

Robustness

While VAR models can handle the potential endogeneity between two variables, they do nothing to address any omitted variable bias that might exist. To address concerns about bias due to missing confounders, we run an additional VAR model with two additional endogenous variables and one exogeneous variable.

To account for the possibility that perpetrator's decision is also shaped by a changing domestic environment, we add *China's Domestic Environment*, which is measured as the monthly average of the Intensity Score of all domestic events from the ICEWS dataset in which the government, military, or political elites are on the target side.

It is also possible that some Uyghur violent incidents are motivated by high-profile terrorist attacks that occurred elsewhere in the world. We thus include into the model another endogenous variable, *Global Terrorist Attacks,* which is the monthly sum of terrorist attacks around the world drawn from the Global Terrorism Database.

Finally, we add to the model an exogenous dummy variable, *Sensitive Period*, which is coded 1 if the month is considered a politically sensitive month in China. We identify these periods as: (1) a month

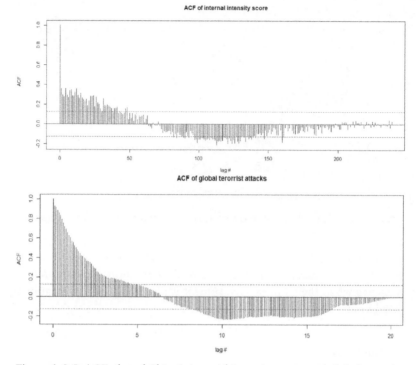

Figure A.2.5 ACF plot of China's internal intensity score and global terrorist attacks

in which annual sessions of National People's Congress (NPC) and National Committee of the People's Political Consultative Conference (CPPCC) is held (*liang hui*) and (2) a month in which the National Congress of the Chinese Communist Party is held.

Figure A.2.5 plots the ACF of these two additional endogenous variables, which suggests that they are not stationary (since later lags exceed the confidence interval). We therefore calculate the first difference of these two variables. Both the graphical check (Figure A.2.6) and the Dickey-Fuller test suggests that the first-differenced variables are stationary.

Again, we rely on three different IC to choose the appropriate lag length (K), which is plotted in Figure A.2.7. While both Bayesian information criterion and Hannan–Quinn information criterion suggest that 1 lag should be used, Akaike information criterion supports including 3 lags.

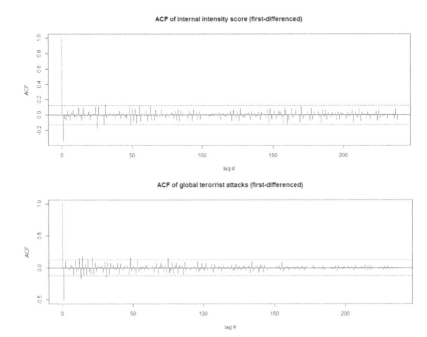

Figure A.2.6 ACF plot of first-differenced variables

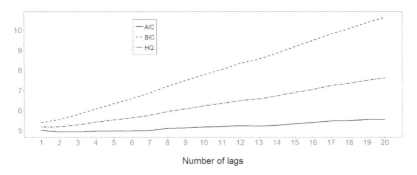

Figure A.2.7 IC for VAR model selection

We then fit models with 1- and 3-unit lags, respectively, and conduct diagnostic analyses of the residuals of each model. The test for serial correlation for the residuals (Table A.2.2) from the 3-lag model is statistically significant at the 0.05 level (rejecting the null hypothesis that there is no serial correlation). Thus, we finalize the model with 1 lag.

Table A.2.2 *Serial correlation test for residuals*

	The portmanteau test (10 lags in the residuals)	
	Chi-square statistic	*P*-value
1-lag model	133.9	0.078
3-lag model	174.17	0.044**

Note: ** <0.05, * <0.1

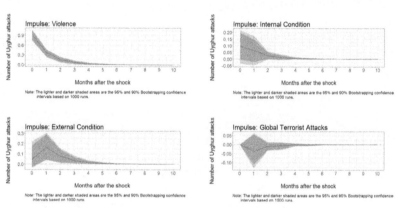

Figure A.2.8 Response to violence

Figure A.2.8 shows four IRF plots generated from this new VAR model. The result is consistent with the prior findings. Only shocks to *violence* itself and the *international environment* tend to have a significant and positive effect on future attacks, while the impulse from violence to both *domestic environment* and *global terrorist attacks* are not significant.

Appendix to Chapter 3

Summary Statistics and Nonparametric Modeling

Table A.3.1 provides summary statistics for all variables used in our models.

Table A.3.1 *Summary statistics*

Variables	N	Mean	St. dev.	Min	Max
Dependent variable					
Duration (days)	137	320.19	119.51	1	365
Key independent variables					
Growth (%)	137	9.08	2.14	3.93	14.28
CCI	137	99.71	2.10	97.03	104.17
Li-Index (%)	137	8.23	3.44	4.19	14.44
Majority Frequency (%)	137	49.57	12.61	26.67	77.78
Majority Frequency: G20 (%)	137	39.73	10.14	23.08	71.43
Majority Frequency: Security Council Members (%)	137	37.28	10.60	20.00	70.00
US–China Distance	137	3.56	0.48	2.69	4.34
Natural Disaster (days)	137	85.62	35.91	12	128
External Condition	117	6.85	1.91	1.00	10.00
Internal Condition	117	5.59	2.55	1.00	10.00
Control Variables					
Target Civilian	137	0.42	0.49	0	1
Urban	137	0.36	0.48	0	1
Sensitive Period	137	0.18	0.38	0	1
Casualty	122	11.01	23.50	0.00	172.00
Bombing	137	0.42	0.50	0	1
Internet Penetration (%)	137	18.08	21.33	0.00	47.55
China Ideal Point	137	−0.85	0.33	−1.60	−0.16
Global Terrorist Incidents (Logged)	137	8.34	0.92	6.75	9.61

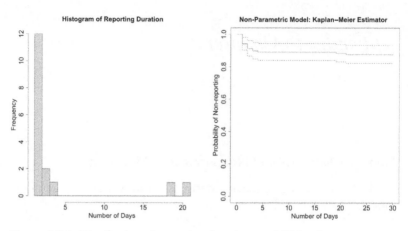

Figure A.3.1 Distribution of reporting durations and KM estimator

The left-hand side of Figure A.3.1 shows the distribution of the reporting duration of uncensored observations, and the graph on the right side plots the nonparametric Kaplan–Meier (KM) estimator of the survival function. The average length of the wait-to-report periods for those that are reported is 3.88 days. As the histogram of reporting duration shows, the length of the durations cluster on short periods. Indeed, more than half of those reported attacks (seven out of sixteen) are reported only one day after their occurrences, while an attempted hijacking of the CZ 6901 from Urumqi to Beijing on March 7, 2008, took twenty-one days to be mentioned in the *People's Daily*, which is the longest of all reported incidents.

The nonparametric KM plot reveals the same pattern in the change of the estimated probability of survival (nonreporting) over time. The right-hand-side KM plot indicates that the probability of being not reported decreases over time or the probability of being reported increases over time. However, most of the variations in the probability of being not reported (or reported) happen within about seven days after the occurrence of the event; the estimated survival curve tends to be relatively stable after seven days. In other words, if an event is not reported within seven days after the occurrence, there is a great chance that it will never be reported. In addition, the KM plot also indicates that any incident's probability of being reported is relatively low, smaller than 20 percent on average. Our main interest here is to investigate what factors may lead to the immediate reporting of these attacks, given such a low average probability of their being reported.

Table A.3.2 *Schoenfeld residuals test for Models 1–13*

	Chi-square statistic	df	P-value
Model 1	3.29	3	0.35
Model 2	4.82	5	0.44
Model 3	11.12	9	0.27
Model 4	7.37	9	0.60
Model 5	8.65	9	0.47
Model 6	11.93	9	0.22
Model 7	10.88	9	0.28
Model 8	11.20	11	0.43
Model 9	12.17	9	0.20
Model 10	8.73	10	0.56
Model 11	13.18	10	0.21
Model 12	15.15	10	0.13
Model 13	14.17	10	0.17

Note: ** <0.05, * <0.1

Tests of Proportional Hazards Assumption

Cox models require a proportional hazards assumption. The proportional hazards assumption holds if the ratio of the hazards for individuals i and j are independent of t and are constant for all t:

$$\frac{h_i(t)}{h_j(t)} = e^{\beta(x_i - x_j)}$$

To test nonproportionality, we rely on scaled Schoenfeld residuals, gained from each Cox model (Models 1–7 in Table 3.1 in the text and Models 8–13 in Table A.3.3 in this appendix). This is equivalent to testing that the log hazard ratio function is constant over time.

Table A.3.2 presents the global chi-squared tests of the proportional hazards assumption for each Cox model reported in the text. Given that all these p-values are greater than 0.05, we cannot reject the null hypothesis that there is no significant relationship between residuals and time (the Schoenfeld residuals are independent of time). Therefore, the proportional hazards assumption is satisfied.

Results from Models 4–7

Figure A.3.2 demonstrates how the relative risk of coverage varies at different combinations of *Li-Index* and *Majority Frequency* (non-centered) based on Model 4.[1] The left-hand panel shows that when *Li-Index* is high (one standard error above the mean), the probability that an incident be reported by *People's Daily* becomes significantly higher than the sample mean probability only when *Majority Frequency* is also high. Specifically, when *Li-Index* is high and *Majority Frequency* is lower than its mean (49.57 percent), the probability of being reported is not significantly different from the sample mean probability. However, this ratio becomes 3.92 times and then 11.59 times higher than the sample mean as the *Majority Frequency* increases to 55 percent and 60 percent respectively.

In contrast, the right-hand panel in demonstrates that when internal conditions are not favorable, the probability of coverage is indistinguishable from the sample mean probability regardless of the proportion of UN votes in which China is a majority.

In Figure A.3.3, we plot the variation in the probability of nonreporting by the twenty-first day (three weeks) after a terrorist attack across different values of the Consumer Confidence Index when *Majority Frequency* is high and low (one standard error above and below the mean). Again, the graph indicates that prompt reporting is likely only when both domestic and international conditions are favorable to the government. When *Majority Frequency* is high, the probability of nonreporting by the twenty-first day after an attack is nearly 1 when the Consumer Confidence Index (*CCI*) is below its mean value (about 99.7). This decreases to 0.86 (meaning coverage is more likely) at the mean value for *CCI*. The probability of nonreporting plunges to 0.02 at one standard deviation above the mean (about 101.8). However, if the Chinese government is internationally isolated (i.e., *Majority Frequency* is low), there is essentially no change in the probability of nonreporting regardless of the state of the economy.

---

[1] Figures A.3.2 and A.3.3 are based on models of the original values of the interaction variables (i.e., not the centered values employed in Table 3.1 and Figure 3.2 in chapter 3) to ease interpretation. In the cases of Figures A.3.2 and A.3.3, centered values lead to negative ranges that can lead to confusion. The substantive interpretation is, however, unchanged.

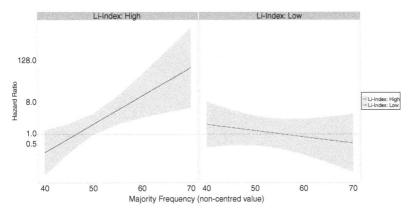

Figure A.3.2 Relative risk of coverage (Model 4)

Figure A.3.4 plots the four-case simulations for Models 6 and 7, which shows almost identical patterns to those we presented in Chapter 3.

Results from Models 8–13

Table A.3.3 presents the results from six additional model specifications. In each, the coefficients for the interaction term remain significant and in the anticipated direction.

In Figure A.3.5 we repeat the four-case survival curve comparison. These plots reveal almost identical patterns, with the probability of nonreporting sharply dropping only when both domestic and international political conditions are favorable. The plot based on post-2000 subsample (Model 13) produces predicted probabilities that are relatively lower than those using full samples, which suggests that the 9/11 was indeed a turning point after which China became more willing to internationalize its domestic terrorist incidents. However, even in this period, official acknowledgments were still more likely when both domestic and international conditions are favorable.

In Table A.3.4, we present four additional models that replicate Model 10, 11, 12, and 13 without controlling for GDP growth rate. The results are again consistent with those reported.

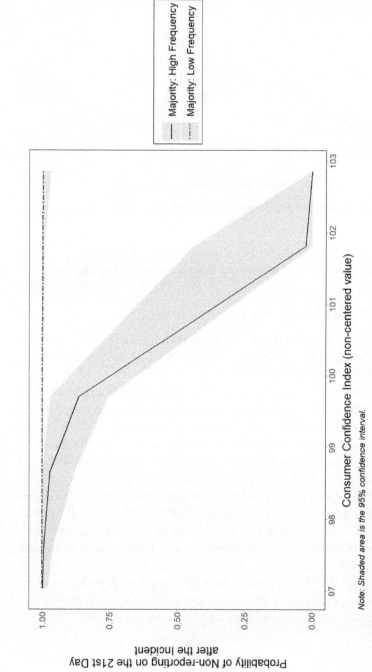

Majority: High Frequency
Majority: Low Frequency

Consumer Confidence Index (non-centered value)

Note: Shaded area is the 95% confidence interval.

Probability of Non-reporting on the 21st Day after the Incident

Figure A.3.3 Probability of nonreporting by the seventh day after a terrorist attack (Model 5)

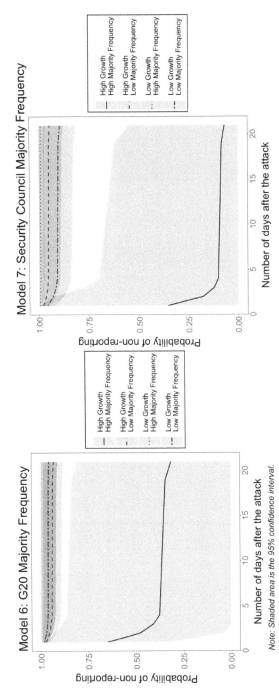

Figure A.3.4 Probability of nonreporting (Models 6 and 7)

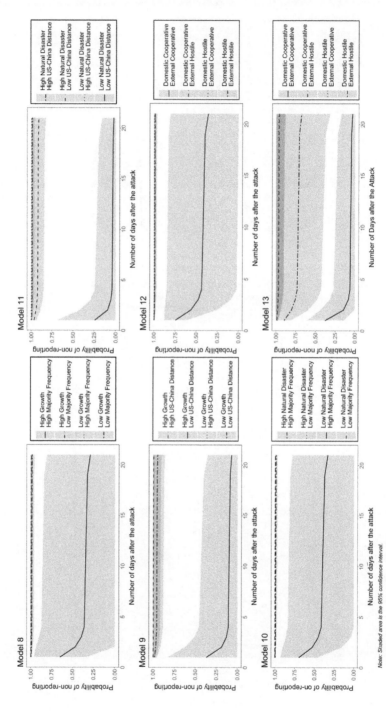

Figure A.3.5 Case simulations with alternative specifications

Table A.3.3 *Alternative model specifications*

		Cox proportional hazards models				Post-2000 sample
	(8)	(9)	(10)	(11)	(12)	(13)
Growth	0.486 (0.353)	0.177 (0.154)				
Majority Frequency	0.060 (0.049)		0.425*** (0.129)			
US–China Distance		−3.328*** (1.080)		−5.053*** (1.431)		
Natural Disaster			−0.005 (0.030)	−0.011 (0.012)		
Growth × Majority Frequency	0.045** (0.020)					
Growth × US–China Distance		−1.543*** (0.503)				
Natural Disaster × Majority Frequency			−0.010*** (0.003)			
Natural Disaster × US–China Distance				0.085*** (0.021)		
Internal Condition					0.391* (0.210)	0.356 (0.220)
External Condition					0.377* (0.197)	0.328* (0.199)
Internal Condition × External Condition					0.193*** (0.065)	0.167** (0.068)

Table A.3.3 *(cont.)*

	Cox proportional hazards models					
	(8)	(9)	(10)	(11)	(12)	Post-2000 sample (13)
Growth (noncentered)			1.219**	0.503***	0.472*	0.239
			(0.326)	(0.184)	(0.244)	(0.272)
Internet Penetration	0.063	0.036**	0.258***	0.061***	0.136***	0.086**
	(0.055)	(0.015)	(0.068)	(0.019)	(0.028)	(0.041)
Sensitive Period	1.045*	1.425***	-2.380**	1.213**	0.787	0.525
	(0.560)	(0.545)	(0.990)	(0.541)	(0.547)	(0.525)
Casualty	0.022***	0.020***	0.038***	0.022***	0.024***	0.025***
	(0.007)	(0.006)	(0.010)	(0.006)	(0.007)	(0.007)
Urban	0.166	0.067	0.289	0.178	0.118	0.175
	(0.493)	(0.538)	(0.488)	(0.536)	(0.483)	(0.489)
Target Civilian	-0.791	-0.792	-1.006*	-0.972*	-0.359	-0.395
	(0.555)	(0.579)	(0.577)	(0.571)	(0.517)	(0.517)
Bombing	0.573	0.461	-0.113	0.510	0.207	0.209
	(0.446)	(0.496)	(0.521)	(0.481)	(0.417)	(0.403)
China Ideal Point	4.303					
	(3.944)					
Global Terrorist Incidents	0.615					
	(1.151)					
Observations	122	122	122	122	103	57
Max. possible R^2	0.734	0.734	0.734	0.734	0.779	0.904
Log likelihood	-57.584	-61.099	-54.863	-60.287	-54.122	-53.495
LR test	46.425***	39.394***	51.867***	41.018***	47.249***	26.485***

Note: Table entries are coefficients obtained from Cox proportional hazards models. Robust standard errors clustered on incidents are in the parentheses. *p<0.1; **p<0.05; ***p<0.01

Table A.3.4 *Alternative model specifications without GDP growth as a control*

	Cox proportional hazards models			
	(A1)	(A2)	(A3)	(A4)
Natural Disaster	−0.032	−0.020		
	(0.028)	(0.016)		
Majority Frequency	0.142***			
	(0.031)			
US–China Distance		−3.549***		
		(0.982)		
Internal Condition			0.432**	0.363
			(0.203)	(0.222)
External Condition			0.446**	0.348*
			(0.197)	(0.199)
Natural Disaster × Majority Frequency	−0.003***			
	(0.001)			
Natural Disaster × US–China Distance		0.060***		
		(0.023)		

Table A.3.4 (cont.)

	Cox proportional hazards models			
	(A1)	(A2)	(A3)	(A4)
Internal Condition × External Condition			0.200**	0.163**
			(0.069)	(0.070)
Internet Penetration	0.096***	0.052**	0.123***	0.073*
	(0.035)	(0.023)	(0.028)	(0.040)
Sensitive Period	−0.456	0.959*	0.884*	0.549
	(0.675)	(0.526)	(0.525)	(0.509)
Casualty	0.029***	0.020***	0.022**	0.024***
	(0.007)	(0.006)	(0.007)	(0.007)
Urban	0.745	0.426	0.108	0.205
	(0.565)	(0.549)	(0.506)	(0.514)
Target Civilian	−1.144*	−0.900	−0.244	−0.347
	(0.640)	(0.600)	(0.484)	(0.491)
Bombing	0.224	0.400	0.189	0.228
	(0.463)	(0.476)	(0.411)	(0.385)
Observations	122	122	103	57
Max. possible R²	0.734	0.734	0.779	0.904
Log likelihood	−58.784	−62.140	−54.853	−53.660
LR test	44.024***	37.313***	45.788***	26.155***

Note: Table entries are coefficients obtained from Cox proportional hazards models. Robust standard errors clustered on incidents are in the parentheses. *p <0.1; **p<0.05; ***p<0.01

Logit Models

Table A.3.5 shows the results from basic logistic models using GDP growth rate and UN voting majority as measures of domestic and international environments, in which the dependent variable is simply whether each incident was acknowledged or not acknowledged. In all of these models, the interaction term remains significant and in the anticipated direction.

Figure A.3.6 plots how the predicted probability of being reported varies over the GDP growth rate when *Majority Frequency* is held at low and high values (one standard deviation below and above the mean), based on Model A8. When *Majority Frequency* is high, the probability of timely official coverage increases from 0.25 to 0.44, and then to 0.72 as the GDP growth rate increases from 8 percent to 9 percent, and then to 10 percent. In contrast, when *Majority Frequency* is low, this probability remains low even when domestic conditions are favorable.

Table A.3.5 *Logit regression*

	Logit models			
	(A5)	(A6)	(A7)	(A8)
Growth	–0.509	0.337	–0.557	0.250
	(0.333)	(0.348)	(0.514)	(0.600)
Majority Frequency	0.094***	0.072**	0.182***	0.156***
	(0.030)	(0.033)	(0.057)	(0.059)
Growth × Majority Frequency	0.040*	0.043**	0.087**	0.079**
	(0.021)	(0.020)	(0.041)	(0.037)
Internet Penetration		0.104***		0.095***
		(0.016)		(0.022)
Sensitive Period		1.449**		1.596*
		(0.687)		(0.836)
Casualty			0.069***	0.076***
			(0.021)	(0.024)
Urban			1.300*	0.778
			(0.719)	(0.753)
Target Civilian			–1.771*	–2.181**
			(0.932)	(0.931)
Bombing			–0.680	–0.669
			(1.011)	(0.996)

Table A.3.5 (*cont.*)

	Logit models			
	(A5)	(A6)	(A7)	(A8)
Constant	-2.633***	-5.783***	-3.797***	-6.447***
	(0.432)	(0.601)	(0.947)	(1.086)
Observations	137	137	122	122
Log likelihood	-43.270	-34.925	-27.139	-22.743
Akaike Inf. Crit.	94.540	81.850	70.279	65.486

Note: Table entries are coefficients obtained from Logit models. Robust standard errors clustered on incidents are in the parentheses. *p <0.1; **p<0.05; ***p<0.01

Robustness Checks: Ethnic Violence in China Database

To assess the implications of the distinction between Ethnic Violence in China (EVC) data and our data for our findings, we added the necessary covariates to the EVC data and conducted robustness checks using EVC data (1990–2005) plus our post-2005 data. The *Casualty* variable is dropped in the full EVC model because the EVC dataset does not have information on the number of casualties at the event level. The results are reported in Table A.3.6, which shows that models using EVC data yield almost identical results.

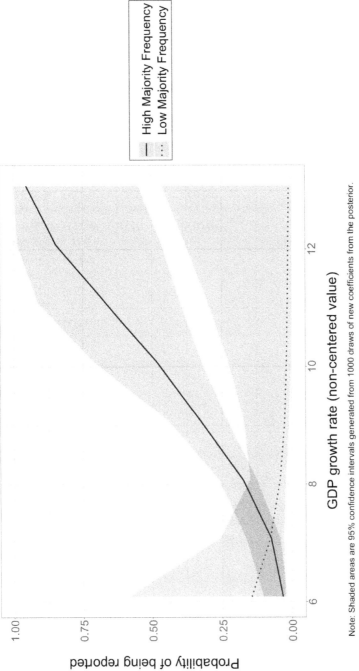

High Majority Frequency
Low Majority Frequency

Probability of being reported

GDP growth rate (non-centered value)

Note: Shaded areas are 95% confidence intervals generated from 1000 draws of new coefficients from the posterior.

Figure A.3.6 Predicted probability of being reported by the *People's Daily*

Table A.3.6 *Robustness checks with EVC data*

	Cox proportional hazards Models			
	(1)	(2)	(3)	(4)
	Our data	Our data + EVC data	Our data	Our data + EVC data
Growth	−0.454	−0.606**	0.150	0.076
	(0.291)	(0.295)	(0.362)	(0.399)
Majority Frequency	0.074***	0.085***	0.108***	0.098**
	(0.018)	(0.021)	(0.034)	(0.040)
Growth × Majority Frequency	0.030**	0.036***	0.048**	0.058**
	(0.014)	(0.013)	(0.021)	(0.023)
Internet Penetration			0.071***	0.087***
			(0.012)	(0.019)
Sensitive Period			0.731	1.037*
			(0.521)	(0.546)
Casualty			0.023***	
			(0.007)	
Urban			0.357	0.399
			(0.485)	(0.475)
Target Civilian			−0.897	−0.213
			(0.547)	(0.462)
Bombing			0.317	0.531
			(0.470)	(0.484)
Observations	137	149	122	129
Max. possible R^2	0.702	0.678	0.734	0.719
Log likelihood	−75.530	−75.405	−58.289	−65.440
LR test	14.675***	17.910***	45.015***	32.710***

Note: Table entries are coefficients obtained from Cox proportional hazards models. Robust standard errors clustered on incidents are in the parentheses. *p <0.1; **p<0.05; ***p<0.01

Appendix to Chapter 4

Security Expenditure Data

While China's *Statistical Yearbook* provides provincial-level data dating back only to 1995, in 2005 the Statistical Bureau of the Xinjiang Uyghur Autonomous Region (XUAR) published its own yearbook, *Fifty Years of Xinjiang*, which has local government public expenditure data that go back to 1950. However, this resource does not report a stand-alone category for security expenditures; rather, it reports a category labeled "Expenditures for Government Administration and Public Security System, Procuratorial System, Court System, and Judicial System" (PPCJ).

In order to tease out security-related expenditures, we first calculate the ratio between government administration expenditures and expenditures for the PPCJ for each year in the 1995–2006 period, during which these two categories are reported separately in the *China Statistical Yearbooks*. The ratio is fairly stable and averages around 2. We then obtain the estimated PPCJ expenditures for the 1950–1994 period by multiplying the raw numbers (government administration + PPCJ) by 0.33.

$$\frac{PPCJ}{Government\ Administraion + PPCJ} = \frac{PPCJ}{1.99 * PPCJ + PPCJ} \approx 0.33$$

With these estimated PPCJ expenditures in hand, we then calculate the ratio between the PAP expenditures and the PPCJ expenditures for the 1997–2006 period (when these two categories are reported separately), which averages 0.03. As a final step, we calculate the estimated public security–related expenditures for the whole pre-1997 period by multiplying the PPCJ expenditures by 1.03 to include estimated PAP expenditures. We further rely on local population data from *Fifty Years of Xinjiang* to construct the public security expenditures per capita (PSEpc) to better reflect the intensity of securitization. Finally, since our own violence data cover only the 1990–2014 period, we adapt Bovingdon's data – the best available historical data on political violence in Xinjiang – for the 1950–1989 period and the Global Terrorism Database (GTD) data for the 2015–2017 period.[1]

The Model

We assessed the stationarity of these two variables following the same procedure outlined in the appendix to Chapter 2. While Dickey–Fuller tests indicate that neither PSEpc nor the number of violent incidents is stationary in its original form, the same set of tests shows that the annual growth rate of PSEpc and the first difference of the number of violent incidents (the annual change in the number of events) are stationary. These are plotted in Figure A.4.1 and used in the models.

The reduced form vector autoregressive (VAR) model of order K is:

$$
\begin{cases}
y_{1,t} = \alpha_1 + \sum_{k=1}^{K} \delta_k y_{1,t-k} + \sum_{k=1}^{K} \beta_k y_{2,t-k} + \varepsilon_{1,t} \\
y_{2,t} = \alpha_2 + \sum_{k=1}^{K} \gamma_k y_{2,t-k} + \sum_{k=1}^{K} \eta_k y_{2,t-k} + \varepsilon_{2,t}
\end{cases}
$$

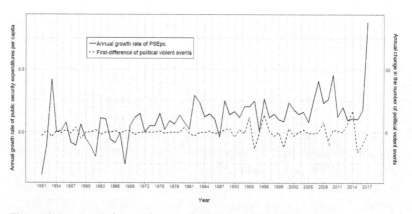

Figure A.4.1 Annual growth rate of PSEpc and first difference of political violence

[1] Bovingdon (2010).

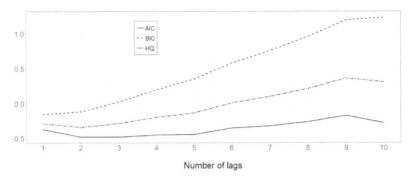

Figure A.4.2 IC for VAR model selection

Table A.4.1 *Serial correlation test for residuals*

	Edgerton–Shukur F test (5 lags in the residuals)	
	F-statistics	*P*-value
1-lag model	2.22	0.004956***
2-lag model	1.8021	0.03057
3-lag model	0.75938	0.7537

Note: *** $p<0.01$; ** $p<0.05$; * $p<0.1$

where y_1 and y_2 represent the annual growth rate of PSEpc and the annual change in the number of PVEs, respectively.

We rely again on three different information criteria (IC) to choose the appropriate lag length (K), with smaller IC values indicating better fit; these are plotted in Figure A.4.2.[2] As is usually the case in finite samples, these criteria do not agree with each other. While Akaike information criterion supports including three lags (the lowest Akaike information criterion value) in the model, Bayesian information criterion and Hannan–Quinn information criterion indicate two lags and one lag, respectively.

In response, we fit models with one, two, and three lags and conducted diagnostic analyses of the residuals of each model. Tests for serial correlation for the residuals (Table A.4.1) from the one- and two-lag models are statistically significant at the 0.05 level at several lags (rejecting the null hypothesis that there is no serial correlation),

---

[2] Box-Steffensmeier et al. (2014).

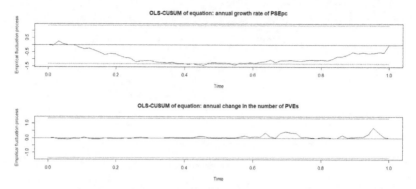

Figure A.4.3 Stability test for 1-lag model

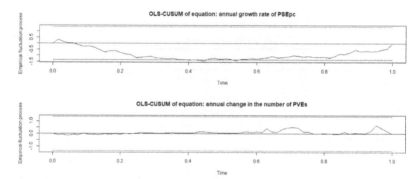

Figure A.4.4 Stability test for 2-lag model

and these two models also fail the stability test (Figures A.4.3, A.4.4, and A.4.5). We therefore finalize the model with three lags.

The Granger causality test results in Table A.4.2 demonstrate that the annual change in the number of political violent events (PVEs) forecasts the annual growth rate of PSEpc but not vice versa. In other words, the changes in securitization measures in a given period do depend on changes in violence intensities in previous periods.

The pattern revealed in Figure A.4.6 – the impact of a shock in violence on subsequent violence – is largely consistent with conventional wisdom. It shows a strong immediate response but quickly becomes significantly negative one year after the shock and remains so in the second year.[3] A careful examination of the magnitude of

---

[3] This pattern is consistent with what we uncover in Chapter 2 by using monthly data.

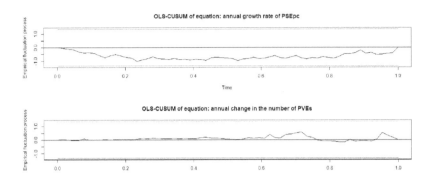

Figure A.4.5 Stability test for 3-lag model

Table A.4.2 *Granger causality test*

Hypothesized exogenous cause	*F*-statistics	*P*-value
Annual growth rate of PSEpc	0.521	0.669
Annual change in the number of PVEs	4.751	0.004**

Note: *** p<0.01; ** p<0.05; * p<0.1

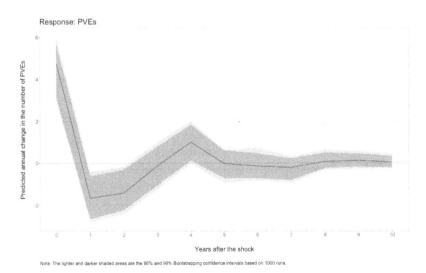

Figure A.4.6 Response of violence to prior violence

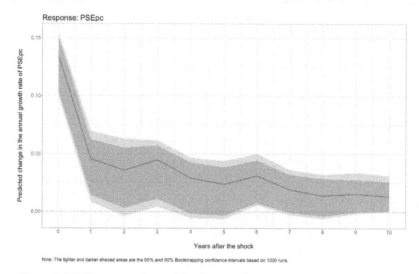

Figure A.4.7 Response of securitization to prior securitization

each significant response (+4.8 at *time 0*, –1.7 at *time 1*, –1.4 at *time 2*, and +1 at *time 4*) indicates that declines do not fully cancel out the increases, which suggests that the increased violence of campaigns can be durable. The oscillation between positive and negative is indicative of the cat and mouse game between violence and repression as these campaigns unfold.

Figure A.4.7 shows the response of securitization to prior securitization. Two interesting insights emerge. First, similar to the violence self-response plot in Figure A.4.6, the initial strong response from the annual growth rate of PSEpc to its own shock dies out quickly, which implies that the high costs associated with massive securitization efforts, both material and political, are hard for the government to sustain. This is consistent with the fact that strike-hard campaigns in Xinjiang usually last for only one year. Even those that persist, as has been the case since 2014, evolve in ways that would produce the pattern observed in Figure A.4.7. Second, while the magnitude of the response quickly diminishes over time (from about 13.3 percent at *time 0* to 3.2 percent at *time 6*), it remains positive. These consecutive positive responses suggest a persistent upward trend in the level of PSEpc.

Robustness Checks

Results from a model with three exogenous dummy variables (coded 1 for 1995, 1997, and 2007, and 0 otherwise) are presented in Figure A.4.8. The left panel plots the response from the annual growth rate of PSEpc to a one-unit increase in the annual change in the number of PVEs, while the right panel shows the violence response to the securitization impulse. The patterns of these plots remain similar to those presented in Chapter 4.

In the third VAR model, we add another endogenous variable, the annual growth rate of XUAR expenditures on education, to the model. Thus, the reduced form of the model becomes

$$
\begin{cases}
y_{1,t} = \alpha_1 + \sum_{k=1}^{K} \delta_{ky1,t-k} + \sum_{k=1}^{K} \beta_{ky2,t-k} + \sum_{k=1}^{K} \beta_{ky3,t-k} + \varepsilon_{1,t} \\
y_{2,t} = \alpha_2 + \sum_{k=1}^{K} \gamma_{ky2,t-k} + \sum_{k=1}^{K} \eta_{ky1,t-k} + \sum_{k=1}^{K} \beta_{ky3,t-k} + \varepsilon_{2,t} \\
y_{3,t} = \alpha_3 + \sum_{k=1}^{K} \gamma_{ky3,t-k} + \sum_{k=1}^{K} \eta_{ky2,t-k} + \sum_{k=1}^{K} \beta_{ky1,t-k} + \varepsilon_{3,t}
\end{cases}
$$

where y_1 and y_2 still represent the annual growth rate of PSEpc and the annual change in the number of PVEs, respectively, while y_3 represents the annual growth rate of XUAR expenditures on education.

Figure A.4.9 plots the response from the annual growth rate of PSEpc (left panel) and the response from the annual growth rate of education expenditures (right panel) to a one-unit increase in the annual change in the number of PVEs. The response from PSEpc is almost identical to the one generated by the original model. While the pattern of the response from the annual growth rate of education expenditures is quite similar to the PSEpc, only the decrease in the seventh year after the shock is significant, suggesting that the impact of violence on education expenditures is tenuous.

In Figure A.4.10, we plot the response of violence to a one-unit increase in the annual growth rate of PSEpc (left panel) and the annual growth rate of XUAR education expenditures (right panel). In contrast to the original results reported in Chapter 4, an increase in securitization measures does have a significant negative effect on violence in this model, though this negative impact appears only in the sixth year after the shock. Education expenditures, however, do not have any significant impact on the violence.

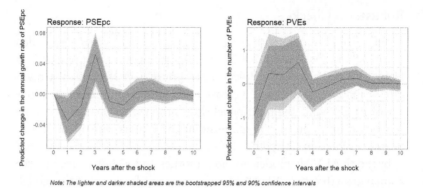

Figure A.4.8 Impulse response plot of the relationship between securitization and violence

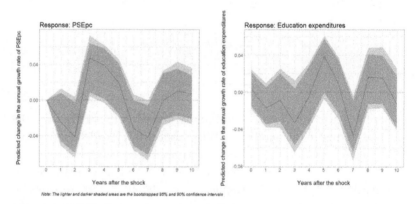

Figure A.4.9 Impact of violence on security and education expenditures

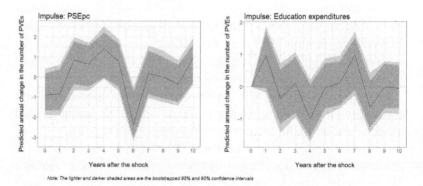

Figure A.4.10 Impact of securitization and education on violence

Table A.4.3 presents the results from the intervention model (an ARIMA model with three exogenous interventions), and Figure A.4.11 plots the forecasting pattern of Uyghur-initiated violence based on this simple model.

Table A.4.3 *Intervention model results*

	Estimate	Std. error	z value	Pr(>|z|)
ar1	0.789	0.173	4.546	0.000***
ma1	-0.429	0.182	-2.359	0.018**
ma2	-0.122	0.103	-1.189	0.234
Intercept	0.415	0.115	3.601	0.000***
SH1	0.422	0.402	1.049	0.294
SH2	-0.196	0.458	-0.430	0.668
SH3	0.650	0.651	0.998	0.318

Note: ***<0.01; ** <0.05; * <0.1

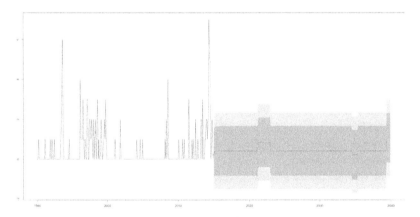

Figure A.4.11 Forecast from regression with ARIMA (1, 0, 2) errors

Appendix to Chapter 5

Summary Statistics

Table A.5.1 provides the summary statistics of all variables used in the subsequent statistical models.

Statistical Results

Table A.5.2 presents results from a series of statistical models. Because our main dependent variable is a count and overdispersion is present, which is primarily caused by an excessive number of observations

Table A.5.1 *Summary statistics*

Statistic	N	Mean	St. dev.	Min	Max
CT-JME Days	2,350	0.648	3.364	0	68
Terror Attack (square root value)	2,350	2.457	5.851	0	63
PRC FDI	2,195	13.177	2.673	4.605	20.222
Domestic Attack (square root value)	2,350	1.035	3.223	0.000	33.985
Transnational Attack (square root value)	2,350	0.906	2.438	0.000	34.857
PRC Arms Transfer	2,350	2.405	5.997	0	22
Regime Type	2,034	3.873	6.321	−10.000	10.000
GDP per capita (logged value)	2,350	24.212	2.242	16.994	30.562
US Defense Pact	2,350	0.266	0.442	0	1
SCO	2,350	0.030	0.170	0	1
Extradition	2,350	0.144	0.351	0	1
Distance	2,350	8.962	0.515	6.696	9.868
OBOR	2,350	0.106	0.307	0	1

Table A.5.2 *Models of CT-JMEs*

	ZINB models					
	(1)	(2)	(3)	(4)	(5)	(6)
Count Part						
Terror Attack	0.027***		−0.222***	−0.245***		
	(0.004)		(0.068)	(0.069)		
PRC FDI	0.017	−0.058***	−0.115***	−0.021	−0.099***	
	(0.028)	(0.017)	(0.031)	(0.022)	(0.028)	
Terror Attack × PRC FDI			0.015***	0.016***		
			(0.004)	(0.004)		
Domestic Attack					−0.403*	−0.511**
					(0.215)	(0.232)
Transnational Attack					−0.081	−0.108
					(0.358)	(0.555)
Domestic Attack × PRC FDI					0.027**	0.034**
					(0.012)	(0.013)
Transnational Attack × PRC FDI					0.003	0.003
					(0.021)	(0.032)
GDP per capita				0.056**		0.070***
				(0.026)		(0.024)
PRC Arms Transfer				0.005		0.008*
				(0.004)		(0.004)
Regime Type				−0.006		−0.006
				(0.008)		(0.007)

Table A.5.2 (cont.)

	ZINB models					
	(1)	(2)	(3)	(4)	(5)	(6)
US Defense Pact				-0.006		-0.014
				(0.136)		(0.134)
SCO				-0.201		-0.204
				(0.138)		(0.156)
Extradition				0.072		0.058
				(0.087)		(0.110)
Distance				0.199		0.241**
				(0.137)		(0.118)
OBOR				-0.029		-0.093
				(0.247)		(0.267)
Constant	1.872***	1.727***	2.710***	0.577	2.280***	-0.239
	(0.050)	(0.335)	(0.236)	(0.983)	(0.256)	(0.838)
Zero-Inflation Part						
Terror Attack	-0.063**		0.318*	0.283		
	(0.026)		(0.189)	(0.190)		
PRC FDI		-0.710***	-0.636***	-0.459***	-0.672***	-0.475***
		(0.098)	(0.097)	(0.133)	(0.102)	(0.135)
Terror Attack × PRC FDI			-0.023**	-0.021*		
			(0.012)	(0.011)		
Domestic Attack					0.263	0.258
					(0.451)	(0.375)
Transnational Attack					0.568	0.376
					(0.516)	(0.474)

	(1)	(2)	(3)	(4)	(5)	(6)
Domestic Attack × PRC FDI					-0.022	-0.021
					(0.029)	(0.023)
Transnational Attack × PRC FDI					-0.033	-0.024
					(0.030)	(0.028)
GDP per capita				-0.350***		-0.363***
				(0.129)		(0.135)
PRC Arms Transfer				-0.033		-0.039
				(0.023)		(0.024)
Regime Type				-0.041		-0.043
				(0.033)		(0.033)
US Defense Pact				0.303		0.353
				(0.563)		(0.579)
SCO				-5.470***		-5.409***
				(1.177)		(1.210)
Extradition				0.798*		0.683
				(0.474)		(0.494)
Distance				1.154***		1.111***
				(0.267)		(0.267)
OBOR				-1.799***		-1.847***
				(0.458)		(0.456)
Constant	3.767***	11.987***	11.019***	8.884**	11.402***	9.744**
	(0.516)	(1.392)	(1.377)	(3.927)	(1.450)	(4.286)
Observations	2,350	2,195	2,195	1,956	2,195	1,956
Log likelihood	-864.658	-793.398	-758.846	-617.208	-765.176	-617.773

Note: Year fixed effects are used in all models. Robust standard errors clustered on countries are in the parentheses. * $p<0.1$; ** $p<0.05$; *** $p<0.01$

with a count of 0 (country-years that do not have CT-JMEs [counterterrorism joint military exercises]), we perform our analysis using Zero-Inflated Negative Binomial (ZINB) models.[1]

We begin with simple models that exclude the control variables.[2] Models 1 and 2 are two parsimonious models that examine the binary relationship between *Terror Attack* and *PRC FDI* and the number of days on CT-JME with China respectively. Model 3 is another parsimonious model that includes only the two key independent variables and their interaction term. Model 4 is the full model that adds all control variables. Models 5 and 6 probe the different effects of *Domestic Attack* and *Transnational Attack* without and with control variables respectively.

The results are largely consistent with our expectations. Model 1 shows that the coefficient of *Terror Attack* is positive and significant in the count portion of the model but negative and significant in the zero-inflation portion. This indicates that as a country's exposure to terrorist threat increases, it will be significantly less likely to belong to the certain-zero group (countries that would never participate in CT-JMEs with China) and tend to spend more days on CT-JMEs. Similarly, the negative and significant coefficient of *PRC FDI* in the zero-inflation portion of Model 2 indicates that a country is less likely to belong to the certain-zero group if it is an important destination for China's outgoing FDI (higher values in *PRC FDI*). However, although the coefficient of *PRC FDI* in the count model part is also positive, it is not statistically significant, suggesting that among countries who are on the radar of China's potential CT-JME partners, FDI alone is not a significant determinant. It is worth noting that this finding does not undermine our predictions. We argue that FDI should act as a conditioning factor, which will only affect China's CT-JME participation pattern when combined with a potential partner's exposure to terrorist threats.

Once the interaction term between *Terror Attack* and *PRC FDI* is added, Models 3 and 4 indicate that the impact of a country's exposure to terrorism on the number of days spent on CT-JMEs with China is

---

[1] Year-fixed effects are used in all models, and robust standard errors clustered on country are reported.

[2] Achen (2005).

significantly conditional on China's FDI level in that country.[3] Further, Models 5 and 6 demonstrate that this interaction effect is significant only for *Domestic Attack*.

Robustness Checks

To establish the robustness of these findings, we perform additional analysis with alternative models, different samples, and different dependent variables.

To begin with, a ZINB model might be inappropriate if Chinese decision-making is strictly sequential. We therefore fit a hurdle model (Model A1) to account for this possible misspecification.[4] Similar to zero-inflated count models, the hurdle model is also a two-component model that augments the count component with a zero component. The subtle difference between them is that ZINB models allow zeros in the count component (e.g., China can choose to *not* hold CT-JMEs with potential partners), while the hurdle model only models positive values in the count component.[5] In other words, if the Chinese decision-making is to first decide whether or not they want to hold a CT-JME with a country, and then they must decide how many days they want to spend with this partner if the answer to the first stage question is yes, then a hurdle model is more appropriate.

Next, to further account for possible aggregation bias, we run an additional ZINB model with a sample of countries that had experienced at least one terrorist attack in the 2003–2016 period. In another model, we drop potential confounding outliers in the sample in terms of the number of terrorist attacks and China's FDI level. Specifically, we exclude the United States (outliers in *PRC FDI*) in Model A2 and Afghanistan, Iraq, Pakistan, and Syria (outliers in *Terror Attack*) in Model A3.

Last but not least, while the number of CT-JME days is the most straightforward proxy for the degree of cooperation, it is not flawless.

---

[3] Drop in observations is due to missing values in *PRC FDI* and *Polity IV* scores.
[4] Similar to ZINB, we fit the count component with negative binomial distribution and the zero component with binomial distribution.
[5] For more details on the difference between zero-inflated count models and hurdle models, see Dalrymple, Hudson, and Ford (2003) and Zeileis, Kleiber, and Jackman (2008).

Since multinational joint military exercises usually involve more participants, and therefore more complex maneuvers, they last longer.[6] In other words, a longer duration in a multinational exercise may not reflect higher intensity of the exercise or China's preference in participants but rather in managing and organizing the event. To account for this potential measurement error, we create another measure of intensity for country i in year j:

$$\sum_k \frac{D_k}{P_k}$$

where D is the total number of days a country spent with China on one CT-JME and P is the total number of participants in that CT-JME, while k represents the total number of CT-JMEs with China in a given year. This gives us a continuous measure that accounts for three components of CT-JMEs: the total number of days, the total number of CT-JMEs, and the total number of participants. The variable ranges from 0 to 68 with larger values indicating higher levels of intensity. We fit a simple OLS model (Model A4) with this alternative measure of the intensity of CT-JMEs.

Results from these additional models are reported Table A.5.3. The coefficients of key independent variables and the interactions terms are consistent.

---

[6] This issue cannot be addressed by simply adding a control variable in statistical models. The unit of analysis in our models is country-year. Some countries participated in more than one CT-JME with China, including both bilateral and multinational, in a given year.

Table A.5.3 *Robustness checks of China's CT-JME partner selection*

| | | | Robustness checks | |
| | (A1) | (A2) | (A3) | (A4) |
	Hurdle model	Subsample 1	Subsample 2	Continuous DV
Count Part				
Terror Attack	-0.251***	-0.252***	-0.204**	-0.811***
	(0.070)	(0.069)	(0.080)	(0.242)
PRC FDI	-0.113***	-0.121***	-0.096***	-0.043
	(0.030)	(0.036)	(0.033)	(0.031)
Terror Attack × PRC FDI	0.016***	0.016***	0.013***	0.059***
	(0.004)	(0.004)	(0.005)	(0.017)
GDP per capita	0.060**	0.060**	0.052	0.028
	(0.026)	(0.026)	(0.042)	(0.045)
PRC Arms Transfer	0.004	0.005	0.003	0.014
	(0.004)	(0.005)	(0.006)	(0.015)
Regime Type	-0.007	-0.005	-0.005	-0.004
	(0.008)	(0.009)	(0.010)	(0.011)
US Defense Pact	-0.006	-0.005	0.042	0.092
	(0.132)	(0.141)	(0.196)	(0.305)
SCO	-0.160	-0.201	-0.146	1.196**
	(0.127)	(0.167)	(0.157)	(0.529)
Extradition	0.072	0.072	0.085	0.326
	(0.093)	(0.085)	(0.086)	(0.284)

Table A.5.3 (*cont.*)

	Robustness checks			
	(A1) Hurdle model	(A2) Subsample 1	(A3) Subsample 2	(A4) Continuous DV
Distance	0.187	0.196	0.198	−0.170
	(0.130)	(0.146)	(0.125)	(0.139)
OBOR	0.003	−0.015	0.053	0.558**
	(0.232)	(0.239)	(0.285)	(0.269)
Constant	0.530	0.597	0.378	1.456
	(0.908)	(1.054)	(0.979)	(1.996)
Zero–Inflation Part				
Terror Attack	−0.263	0.374*	−0.029	
	(0.186)	(0.191)	(0.201)	
PRC FDI	0.439***	−0.458***	−0.460***	
	(0.124)	(0.154)	(0.135)	
Terror Attack × PRC FDI	0.019*	−0.026**	−0.002	
	(0.011)	(0.011)	(0.013)	
GDP per capita	0.309**	−0.271*	−0.380***	
	(0.122)	(0.144)	(0.118)	
PRC Arms Transfer	0.033	−0.028	−0.016	
	(0.022)	(0.024)	(0.020)	
Regime Type	0.035	−0.036	−0.055*	
	(0.033)	(0.037)	(0.030)	
US Defense Pact	−0.162	0.236	0.743*	
	(0.591)	(0.571)	(0.449)	

	(1)	(2)	(3)	(4)
SCO	4.942***	−5.277***	−5.477***	
	(0.756)	(1.276)	(1.120)	
Extradition	−0.825*	0.972*	0.976*	
	(0.440)	(0.502)	(0.499)	
Distance	−1.144***	1.429***	1.122***	
	(0.260)	(0.404)	(0.250)	
OBOR	1.688***	−1.606***	−1.786***	
	(0.432)	(0.478)	(0.475)	
Constant	−7.513**	4.359	9.715**	
	(3.632)	(4.965)	(4.092)	
Observations	1,956	1,713	1,905	1,956

1. Year fixed effects are used in all models. Robust standard errors clustered on countries are in the parentheses.
2. Subsample 1: Only include countries that experienced at least one terror attack in the 2003–2016 period.
3. Subsample 2: Exclude Afghanistan, Iraq, and Syria (outliers in Terror Attack); United States (outlier in PRC FDI); Pakistan (outlier in both Terror Attack and PRC FDI).
4. * p <0.1; ** p<0.05; *** p<0.01

Bibliography

Abedine, Saad. 2009. "Al Qaeda Tells China's Uyghurs to Prepare for Holy War." *CNN*, October 9. www.cnn.com/2009/WORLD/asiapcf/10/08/china.uyghur.threat/index.html.

Abuza, Zachary. 2017. "The Uighurs and China's Regional Counter-Terrorism Efforts." *Terrorism Monitor* 15 (16): 8–12.

Achen, Christopher H. 2005. "Let's Put Garbage-Can Regressions and Garbage-Can Probits Where They Belong." *Conflict Management and Peace Science* 22 (4): 327–339.

Allen, Kenneth W., John Chen, and Phillip Charles Saunders. 2017. *Chinese Military Diplomacy, 2003–2016: Trends and Implications*. Washington, DC: National Defense University Press.

Amnesty International. 2020. "China: Uyghur Jailed for 15 Years in Secret Trial: Ekpar Asat." May 13. www.amnesty.org/en/documents/asa17/2314/2020/en/.

Anand, Dibyesh. 2019. "Colonization with Chinese Characteristics: Politics of (In)Security in Xinjiang and Tibet." *Central Asian Survey* 38 (1): 129–147.

Atkinson, Scott E., Todd Sandler, and John Tschirhart. 1987. "Terrorism in a Bargaining Framework." *The Journal of Law and Economics* 30 (1): 1–21.

Azman, Nur Aziemah. 2020. "'Divine Retribution': The Islamic State's COVID-19 Propaganda." *The Diplomat*, March 24. https://thediplomat.com/2020/03/divine-retribution-the-islamic-states-covid-19-propaganda/.

Bailey, Michael A., Anton Strezhnev, and Erik Voeten. 2017. "Estimating Dynamic State Preferences from United Nations Voting Data." *Journal of Conflict Resolution* 61 (2): 430–456.

Bandurski, David. 2012. "Preserving Stability." *China Media Project*, September 14. http://chinamediaproject.org/2012/09/14/preserving-stability/.

Barbour, Brandon, and Reece Jones. 2013. "Criminals, Terrorists, and Outside Agitators: Representational Tropes of the 'Other' in the 5 July Xinjiang, China Riots." *Geopolitics* 18 (1): 95–114.

Baum, Matthew A., and Philip B. K. Potter. 2015. *War and Democratic Constraint: How the Public Influences Foreign Policy*. Princeton: Princeton University Press.

BBC News. 2010. "China Bans English Words in Media." December 21. www.bbc.com/news/world-asia-pacific-12050067.

BBC News. 2013. "What Does Xi Jinping's China Dream Mean?" June 6. www.bbc.com/news/world-asia-china-22726375.

BBC News. 2014. "The CCP Held the Second Xinjiang Work Forum [中共 举行第二次新疆工作座谈会]." May 29. www.bbc.com/zhongwen/simp/ china/2014/05/140529_china_xinjiang_education.

BBC News. 2019. "Sakharov Prize: Jailed Uighur Academic Ilham Tohti Wins Award." October 24. www.bbc.com/news/world-asia-china-50166713.

BBC News. 2020a. "Li Wenliang: Coronavirus Death of Wuhan Doctor Sparks Anger." February 7. www.bbc.com/news/world-asia-china-51409801.

BBC News. 2020b. "Coronavirus: Senior Chinese Officials 'Removed' as Death Toll Hits 1,000." February 11. www.bbc.com/news/world-asia-china-51453848.

Becquelin, Nicolas. 2000. "Xinjiang in the Nineties." *The China Journal* 44: 65–90.

Beech, Hannah. 2016. "China Campaigns against 'Western Values,' but Does Beijing Really Think They're That Bad?" *Time*, April 29. https:// time.com/4312082/china-textbooks-western-values-foreign-ngo/.

Bennhold, Katrin, and Elisabeth Rosenthal. 2008. "Olympic Torch Relay through Paris Turns into Melee." *The New York Times*, April 7. www .nytimes.com/2008/04/07/world/europe/07iht-torch.4.11743769.html.

Benson, Linda. 1988. "Osman Batur: The Kazak's Golden Legend." In *The Kazaks of China*, edited by L. Benson and I. Svanberg, 141–189. Uppsala: Uppsala University.

Betts, Richard. 1998. "The New Threat of Mass Destruction." *Foreign Affairs*, January–February. www.foreignaffairs.com/articles/1998-01-01/ new-threat-mass-destruction.

Blackwill, Robert D., and Jeffrey W. Legro. 1989. "Constraining Ground Force Exercises of NATO and the Warsaw Pact." *International Security* 14 (3): 68–98.

Blair, Christopher W., Erica Chenoweth, Michael C. Horowitz, Evan Perkoski, and Philip B. K. Potter. 2022. "Honor among Thieves: Under-standing Rhetorical and Material Cooperation among Violent Nonstate Actors." *International Organization* 76 (1): 164–203.

Blanchard, Ben. 2008. "China Tries to Shift Focus Away from School Collapses." Reuters, May 26. www.reuters.com/article/us-quake-schools/china-tries-to-shift-focus-away-from-school-collapses-idUS-PEK16279720080526.

Blanchard, Ben. 2014. "Three Get Death for China Train Station Attack." Reuters, September 12. www.reuters.com/article/us-china-xinjiang/three-get-death-for-china-train-station-attack-idUSKBN0H70A220140912.

Blanchard, Ben. 2017. "Syria Says up to 5,000 Chinese Uighurs Fighting in Militant Groups." Reuters, May 11. www.reuters.com/article/uk-mideast-crisis-syria-china/syria-says-up-to-5000-chinese-uighurs-fighting-in-militant-groups-idUSKBN1840UP.

Blasko, Dennis J. 2010. "People's Liberation Army and People's Armed Police Ground Exercises with Foreign Forces, 2002–2009." In *The PLA at Home and Abroad: Assessing the Operational Capabilities of China's Military*, edited by Roy Kamphausen, Andrew Scobell, and David Lai, 337–428. Carlisle, PA: Strategic Studies Institute, US Army War College.

Blasko, Dennis J. 2015. "Chinese Special Operations Forces: Not Like 'Back at Bragg.'" War on the Rocks, January 1. https://warontherocks.com/2015/01/chinese-special-operations-forces-not-like-back-at-bragg/.

Blumenthal, Daniel. 2019. "The Unpredictable Rise of China." *The Atlantic*. February 3. www.theatlantic.com/ideas/archive/2019/02/how-americans-misunderstand-chinas-ambitions/581869/.

Boschee, Elizabeth, Jennifer Lautenschlager, Sean O'Brien, Steve Shellman, James Starz, and Michael Ward. 2018. "ICEWS Coded Event Data." Harvard Dataverse, V22.

Botobekov, Uran. 2016. "Al-Qaeda, the Turkestan Islamic Party, and the Bishkek Chinese Embassy Bombing." The Diplomat, September 29. https://thediplomat.com/2016/09/al-qaeda-the-turkestan-islamic-party-and-the-bishkek-chinese-embassy-bombing/.

Boix, Carles, and Milan W. Svolik. 2013. "The Foundations of Limited Authoritarian Government: Institutions, Commitment, and Power-Sharing in Dictatorships." *The Journal of Politics* 75 (2): 300–316.

Box-Steffensmeier, Janet M., John R. Freeman, Matthew P. Hitt, and Jon C. W. Pevehouse. 2014. *Time Series Analysis for the Social Sciences*. New York: Cambridge University Press.

Boxun News. 2012. "'One Village, One Police', Xinjiang recruits 8,000 Policemen to Preserve Stability [一村一警 新疆新招8000名民警维护稳定]." January 31. https://news.boxun.com/news/gb/china/2012/01/201201311408.shtml.

Bovingdon, Gardner. 2010. *Uyghurs: Strangers in Their Own Land*. New York: Columbia University Press.

Brandt, Patrick T., and John T. Williams. 2007. *Modeling Multiple Time Series*. Thousand Oaks, CA: Sage Publications.

Branigan, Tania. 2008. "This Is Not a Natural Disaster – This Is Done by Humans." *The Guardian*, May 13. www.theguardian.com/world/2008/may/13/china.naturaldisasters3.

Brownlee, Jason. 2007. *Authoritarianism in an Age of Democratization*. Cambridge: Cambridge University Press.

Brzezinski, Zbigniew. 1997. *The Grand Chessboard*. New York: Basic Books.

Buckley, Chris. 2013. "China Takes Aim at Western Ideas." The New York Times, August 20. www.nytimes.com/2013/08/20/world/asia/chinas-new-leadership-takes-hard-line-in-secret-memo.html.

Buckley, Chris, and Keith Bradsher. 2018. "When Xi Speaks, Chinese Officials Jump. Maybe Too High." *The New York Times*, March 16. www.nytimes.com/2018/03/16/world/asia/xi-jinping-china-power.html.

Buckley, Chris, and Paul Mozur. 2019. "How China Uses High-Tech Surveillance to Subdue Minorities. *The New York Times*, May 22. www.nytimes.com/2019/05/22/world/asia/china-surveillance-xinjiang.html.

Bueno de Mesquita, Ethan. 2008. "The Political Economy of Terrorism: A Selective Overview of Recent Work." *The Political Economist* 10 (1): 1–12.

Bueno de Mesquita, Ethan, and Eric S. Dickson. 2007. "The Propaganda of the Deed: Terrorism, Counterterrorism, and Mobilization." *American Journal of Political Science* 51 (2): 364–381.

Byler, Darren. 2018. "Violent Paternalism: On the Banality of Uyghur Unfreedom." *The Asia-Pacific Journal* 16 (24): 4.

Byman, Daniel. 2013. "Outside Support for Insurgent Movements." *Studies in Conflict & Terrorism* 36 (12): 981–1004.

Callahan, William A. 2004. "National Insecurities: Humiliation, Salvation, and Chinese Nationalism." *Alternatives* 29 (2): 199–218.

Cao, Huhua. 2010. "Urban–Rural Income Disparity and Urbanization: What Is the Role of Spatial Distribution of Ethnic Groups? A Case Study of Xinjiang Uyghur Autonomous Region in Western China." *Regional Studies* 44 (8): 965–982.

Cao, Xun, Haiyan Duan, Chuyu Liu, James A. Piazza, and Yingjie Wei. 2018a. "Digging the 'Ethnic Violence in China' Database: The Effects of Inter-ethnic Inequality and Natural Resources Exploitation in Xinjiang." *China Review* 18 (2): 121–154.

Cao, Xun, Haiyan Duan, Chuyu Liu, and Yingjie Wei. 2018b. "Local Religious Institutions and the Impact of Interethnic Inequality on Conflict." *International Studies Quarterly* 62 (4): 765–781.

Caravelli, John M. 1983. "Soviet and Joint Warsaw Pact Exercises: Functions and Utility." *Armed Forces & Society* 9 (3): 393–426.

Carter, Erin Baggott, and Brett L. Carter. 2022. "When Autocrats Threaten Citizens with Repression: Evidence from China." *British Journal of Political Science* 52 (2): 671–696.

Cave, Danielle, Samantha Hoffman, Alex Joske, Fergus Ryan, and Elise Thomas. 2019. *Mapping China's Tech Giants*. Australian Strategic Policy Institute's International Cyber Policy Centre, April 18. www.aspi.org.au/report/mapping-chinas-tech-giants#.

Chan, Minnie. 2015. "PLA to Announce Overhaul: Five 'Strategic Zones' Will Replace Regional Commands, Most Army HQ to Be Scrapped." *South China Morning Post*, December 20. www.scmp.com/news/china/diplomacy-defence/article/1893468/peoples-liberation-army-be-split-five-combat-regions.

Chang, Felix K. 2016. "China's Encirclement Concerns." Foreign Policy Research Institute, June 24. www.fpri.org/2016/06/chinas-encirclement-concerns/.

Charbonneau, Louis. 2019. "Countries Blast China at UN over Xinjiang Abuses." *Human Rights Watch*, October 30. www.hrw.org/news/2019/10/30/countries-blast-china-un-over-xinjiang-abuses#.

Charles, Deborah. 2008. "Group Threatens Olympics Attack, Claims Bombed Buses." *Reuters*, July 26. www.reuters.com/article/us-olympics-threat/group-threatens-olympics-attack-claims-bombed-buses-idUSN2529568020080725.

Chase, Steven. 2020. "Ottawa Faces Call to Probe Forced-Labour Camps Operating in China's Xinjiang Province." *The Globe and Mail*, July 29, www.theglobeandmail.com/politics/article-ottawa-faces-call-to-probe-forced-labour-camps-operating-in-chinas/.

Chaudhury, Dipanjan Roy. 2019. "Baloch Liberation Army Attacks Chinese Assets for 3rd Time since Aug 2018." *Economic Times*, April 1. https://economictimes.indiatimes.com/news/defence/22-bsf-personnel-test-positive-for-covid-19-in-tripura/articleshow/75584000.cms.

Chaziza, Mordechai. 2018. "China's Counterterrorism Policy in the Middle East." In *Terrorism and Counterterrorism in China: Domestic and Foreign Policy Dimensions*, edited by Michael Clarke, 141–156. New York: Oxford University Press.

Chen, Dingding, and Xuejie Ding. 2014. "How Chinese Think about Terrorism: A Survey of Chinese Attitudes in the Wake of the March Attack on Kunming." *The Diplomat*, April 19. https://thediplomat.com/2014/04/how-chinese-think-about-terrorism/.

Chenoweth, Erica. 2010. "Democratic Competition and Terrorist Activity." *The Journal of Politics* 72 (1): 16–30.

Chenoweth, Erica. 2013. "Terrorism and Democracy." *Annual Review of Political Science* 16 (1): 355–378.

Chenoweth, Erica, and Maria J. Stephan. 2011. *Why Civil Resistance Works: The Strategic Logic of Nonviolent Conflict*. New York: Columbia University Press.

Chin, Josh. 2020. "Wuhan Mayor Says Beijing Rules Partially Responsible for Lack of Transparency." *The Wall Street Journal*, January 27. www.wsj.com/articles/chinas-premier-tours-virus-epicenter-as-anger-bubbles-at-crisis-response-11580109098.

Chin, Josh, and Clément Bürge. 2017. "Twelve Days in Xinjiang: How China's Surveillance State Overwhelms Daily Life." *The Wall Street Journal*, December 19. www.wsj.com/articles/twelve-days-in-xinjiang-how-chinas-surveillance-state-overwhelms-daily-life-1513700355?mg=prod/accounts-wsj.

China.org.cn. 2012. "CPC Leaders Visit 'Road to Revival'." November 30. www.china.org.cn/video/2012-11/30/content_27272086.htm.

China Daily. 2014. "China Eyes More Enabling International Environment for Peaceful Development." November 30. www.chinadaily.com.cn/china/2014-11/30/content_18998580.htm.

China Daily. 2015. "Chinese FM Calls for United Front to Fight Terrorism." November 16. www.chinadaily.com.cn/world/2015xiattendG20APEC/2015-11/16/content_22464090.htm.

China Daily. 2016. "自治区召开'访惠聚'总结表彰动员送行大会 [The Autonomous Region Holds Convention to See Off *Fanghuiju* Working Groups]." February 25. https://china.chinadaily.com.cn/2016-02/25/content_23642621.htm.

China Internet Network Information Center. 2014. *Statistical Report on Internet Development in China*. July 2014. https://cnnic.com.cn/IDR/ReportDownloads/201411/P020141102574314897888.pdf.

Ching, Frank. 2011. "Why China Needed Bin Laden." *The Diplomat*, May 26. https://thediplomat.com/2011/05/why-china-needed-bin-laden/.

Chung, Chien-peng. 2004. "The Shanghai Co-operation Organization: China's Changing Influence in Central Asia." *The China Quarterly* 180: 989–1009.

Ciorciari, John, Philip Potter, Javed Ali, and Ryan Van Wie. 2020. "The High Costs of a Precipitous US Withdrawal from Afghanistan." *The Hill*, January 4.

Clark, Hunter, Maxim Pinkovskiy, and Xavier Sala-i-Martin. 2017. *China's GDP Growth May Be Understated*. National Bureau of Economic Research Working Paper No. w23323.

Clarke, Michael. 2015. "Xinjiang from the 'Outside-In' and the 'Inside-Out': Exploring the Imagined Geopolitics of a Contested region." In *Inside Xinjiang: Space, Place and Power in China's Muslim Far Northwest*, edited by Anna Hayes and Michael Clarke, 225–260. Abingdon: Routledge.

Clarke, P. Colin, and Paul Rexton Kan. 2017. *Uighur Foreign Fighters: An Underexamined Jihadist Challenge*. The Hague: International Centre for Counter-Terrorism.

Clayton, Thomas. 2020. *Al Qaeda and Islamic State Affiliates in Afghanistan*. Congressional Research Service, January 31. https://fas.org/sgp/crs/row/IF10604.pdf.

Clover, Charles. 2017. "Mystery Deepens over Chinese Forces in Afghanistan." *Financial Times*, February 26. www.ft.com/content/0c8a5a2a-f9b7-11e6-9516-2d969e0d3b65.

Cohen, Ariel. 2006. *The Dragon Looks West: China and the Shanghai Cooperation Organization*. Washington, DC: Heritage Foundation.

Collier, Paul, and Anke Hoeffler. 2004. "Greed and Grievance in Civil War." *Oxford Economic Papers* 56 (4): 563–595.

Comolli, Virginia. 2015. *Boko Haram: Nigeria's Islamist Insurgency*. London: C. Hurst & Co.

Computational Event Data System. 2013. *Cameo Event Data Codebook*. August 21. http://eventdata.parusanalytics.com/data.dir/cameo.html.

Counterterrorism Law of the People's Republic of China (Order No. 36 of the President of the PRC). 2015. Chinalawinfo Co. Ltd, Peking University Center for Legal Information. http://en.pkulaw.cn/display.aspx?id=4a6094a588ac744ebdfb&lib=law&SearchKeyword=Counterterrorism&SearchCKeyword=.

CPC News. 2016. "Xi Jinping tiguo de sange 'xianjing dinglv' shisha? [What Are the Three Traps and Dilemmas Mentioned by Xi Jinping]." May 18.

Creemers, Rogier. 2017. "Cyber China: Upgrading Propaganda, Public Opinion Work and Social Management for the Twenty-First Century." *Journal of Contemporary China* 26 (103): 85–100.

Crelinsten, Ronald D. 1989. "Terrorism and the Media: Problems, Solutions, and Counterproblems." *Political Communication* 6 (4): 311–339.

Crenshaw, Martha. 1981. "The Causes of Terrorism." *Comparative Politics* 13 (4): 379–399.

Cronin, A. K. 2009. *How Terrorism Ends: Understanding the Decline and Demise of Terrorist Campaigns*. Princeton: Princeton University Press.

Cui, Liru. 2018. "China's 'Period of Historic Opportunities.'" *China US Focus*, February 1. www.chinausfocus.com/foreign-policy/chinas-period-of-historic-opportunities.

Cunningham, Edward, Tony Saich, and Jesse Turiel. 2020. *Understanding CCP Resilience: Surveying Chinese Public Opinion through Time*. Harvard Kennedy School Center for Democratic Governance and Innovation. https://ash harvard edu/files/ash/files/final_policy_brief_7 6.

Dai, Yaoyao, and Zijie Shao. 2016. "Populism and Authoritarian Survival in China: Conceptualization and Measurement." *CP: Newsletter of the Comparative Politics Organized Section of the American Political Science Association* 26(2): 31–40.

Dalacoura, K. 2006. "Islamist Terrorism and the Middle East Democratic Deficit: Political Exclusion, Repression and the Causes of Extremism." *Democratization* 13 (3): 508–525.

Dalrymple, Michelle L., Irene Lena Hudson, and Rodney Philip Kinvig Ford. 2003. "Finite Mixture, Zero-Inflated Poisson and Hurdle Models with Application to SIDS." *Computational Statistics & Data Analysis* 41 (3–4): 491–504.

Dang, Xiaofei. 2017. "Enhance Cooperation on Anti-terrorism to Safeguard World Peace and Stability: Interview with Cheng Guoping, State Commissioner for Counter-Terrorism and Security Matters of China." *China Today*, May 5. www.chinatoday.com.cn/english/report/2017-05/05/content_740109.htm.

Davenport, Christian. 2007. "State Repression and the Tyrannical Peace." *Journal of Peace Research* 44 (4): 485–504.

Defense Science Board. 1997. "The Defense Science Board 1997 Summer Study Task Force on DoD Response to Transnational Threats." Volume 1, Final Report. Washington, DC: Department of Defense.

De Figueiredo, R., and Barry Weingast. 2000. *Vicious Cycles: Endogenous Political Extremism and Political Violence.* UC Berkeley: Institute of Governmental Studies. https://escholarship.org/uc/item/5j47x3jv.

Deng, Yong, and Fei-Ling Wang. 2005. *China Rising: Power and Motivation in Chinese Foreign Policy.* Lanham: Rowman & Littlefield.

Department of Defense, Office of the Secretary of Defense. 2018. *Annual Report to Congress: Military and Security Developments Involving the People's Republic of China 2018.* May 16. https://media.defense.gov/2018/Aug/16/2001955282/-1/-1/1/2018-CHINA-MILITARY-POWER-REPORT.PDF.

De Tocqueville, Alexis. 1955 [1856]. *The Old Regime and the Revolution,* translated by Stuart Gilbert. New York: Anchor.

De Tocqueville, Alexis. 2010. *The Old Regime and the French Revolution.* New York: Anchor.

Dillon, Michael. 2004. *Xinjiang–China's Muslim Far Northwest.* London and New York: Routledge.

Dillon, Michael. 2018. *Xinjiang in the Twenty-First Century: Islam, Ethnicity and Resistance.* London and New York: Routledge.

D'Orazio, Vito. 2012. "War Games: North Korea's Reaction to US and South Korean Military Exercises." *Journal of East Asian Studies* 12 (2): 275–294.

D'Orazio, Vito. 2013. "Joint Military Exercises: 1970–2010." PhD thesis, Pennsylvannia University. www.vitodorazio.com/uploads/1/3/0/2/13026085/jmes.pdf.

Doyon, Jerome. 2019. "'Counter-Extremism' in Xinjiang: Understanding China's Community-Focused Counterterrorism Tactics." *War on the Rocks,* January 14. https://warontherocks.com/2019/01/counter-extremism-in-xinjiang-understanding-chinas-community-focused-counter-terrorism-tactics/.

Dragu, Tiberiu. 2017. "On Repression and Its Effectiveness." *Journal of Theoretical Politics* 29 (4): 599–622.

Dragu, Tiberiu, and Mattias Polborn. 2014. "The Rule of Law in the Fight against Terrorism." *American Journal of Political Science* 58 (2): 511–525.

Drakos, Konstantinos, and Andreas Gofas. 2006. "In Search of the Average Transnational Terrorist Attack Venue." *Defense and Peace Economics* 17 (2): 73–93.

Dreyer, June Teufel. 1999. "China, the Monocultural Paradigm." *Orbis* 43 (4): 581–597.

Duchâtel, Mathieu. 2016. *Terror Overseas: Understanding China's Evolving Counter-Terror Strategy*. European Council on Foreign Relations, October 26. www.ecfr.eu/publications/summary/terror_overseas_understanding_chinas_evolving_counter_terror_strategy7160.

Duchâtel, Mathieu. 2019. "China's Foreign Fighters Problem." *War on the Rocks*. January 25. warontherocks.com/2019/01/chinas-foreign-fighters-problem/.

Duchâtel, Mathieu, Manuel Lafont-Rapnouil, and Richard Gowan. 2016. *Into Africa: China's Global Security Shift*. The European Council on Foreign Relations. www.ecfr.eu/publications/summary/into_africa_chinas_global_security_shift.

Dupré, Jean-François. 2020. "Making Hong Kong Chinese: State Nationalism and Its Blowbacks in a Recalcitrant City." *Nationalism and Ethnic Politics* 26 (1): 8–26.

DW. 2014. "World Uyghur Congress Claims that the Attack in Shache, Xinjiang Caused Nearly 100 Casualties." July 30. https://p.dw.com/p/1CmB4.

DW. 2018. "Vostok 2018: Russia Lets the War Games with China Begin." September 10. www.dw.com/en/vostok-2018-russia-lets-the-war-games-with-china-begin/a-45435748.

Dzyubenko, Olga. 2016. "Kyrgyzstan Says Uighur Militant Groups behind Attack on China's embassy." *Reuters*, September 6. www.reuters.com/article/us-kyrgyzstan-blast-china/kyrgyzstan-says-uighur-militant-groups-behind-attack-on-chinas-embassy-idUSKCN11C1DK.

Economy, Elizabeth C. 2019. "Yes, Virginia, China Is Exporting Its Model." Council on Foreign Relations, December 11. www.cfr.org/blog/yes-virginia-china-exporting-its-model.

Editorial Board. 2018a. "We Can't Ignore This Brutal Cleansing in China." *The Washington Post*, August 14. www.washingtonpost.com/opinions/global-opinions/we-cant-ignore-this-brutal-cleansing-in-china/2018/08/14/e0b7b0f0-9f19-11e8-83d2-70203b8d7b44_story.html.

Editorial Board. 2018b. "China's Orwellian Tools of High-Tech Repression." *The Washington Post*, September 17. www.washingtonpost.com/opinions/global-opinions/chinas-orwellian-tools-of-high-tech-repression/2018/09/17/b06a9a72-baa1-11e8-9812-a389be6690af_story.html.

Eland, Ivan. 1998. *Does U.S. Intervention Overseas Breed Terrorism? The Historical Record*. Cato Institute, December 17. www.cato.org/publications/foreign-policy-briefing/does-us-intervention-overseas-breed-terrorism-historical-record.

Enders, Walter. 2010. *Applied Econometric Time-Series*. 3rd ed. New York: John Wiley and Sons.

Ericson, Andrew S., and Austin M. Strange. 2015. *Six Years at Sea ... and Counting: Gulf of Aden Anti-piracy and China's Maritime Commons Presence*. Washington, DC: The Jamestown Foundation.

Escribà-Folch, Abel. 2012. "Authoritarian Responses to Foreign Pressure: Spending, Repression, and Sanctions." *Comparative Political Studies* 45 (6): 683–713.

Escribà-Folch, Abel. 2013. "Repression, Political Threats, and Survival under Autocracy." *International Political Science Review* 34 (5): 543–560.

Eubank, William Lee, and Leonard Weinberg. 1994. "Does Democracy Encourage Terrorism?" *Terrorism and Political Violence* 6 (4): 417–435.

Eubank, William Lee, and Leonard Weinberg. 2001. "Terrorism and Democracy: Perpetrators and Victims." *Terrorism and Political Violence* 13 (1): 155–164.

Eyerman, Joe. 1998. "Terrorism and Democratic States: Soft Targets or Accessible Systems." *International Interactions* 24 (2): 151–170.

Famularo, Julia. 2018. "'Fighting the Enemy with Fists and Daggers': The Chinese Communist Party's Counter-Terrorism Policy in the Xinjiang Uighur Autonomous Region." In *Terrorism and Counter-Terrorism in China: Domestic and Foreign Policy Dimensions*, edited by Michael Clarke, 39–74. London: Hurst & Company.

Farnen, Russell F. 1990. "Terrorism and the Mass Media: A Systemic Analysis of a Symbiotic Process." *Studies in Conflict and Terrorism* 13 (2): 99–143.

Feldstein, Steven. 2020. "When It Comes to Digital Authoritarianism, China Is a Challenge – But Not the Only Challenge." *War on the Rocks*, February 12. https://warontherocks.com/2020/02/when-it-comes-to-digital-authoritarianism-china-is-a-challenge-but-not-the-only-challenge/.

Felter, Claire, and Lindsay Maizland. 2020. *What You Need to Know about the Coronavirus Outbreak*. Council on Foreign Relations, February 13. www.cfr.org/backgrounder/what-you-need-know-about-coronavirus-outbreak.

Feng, Emily. 2018. "China Extends Uighur Crackdown beyond Its Borders." *Financial Times*, August 26. www.ft.com/content/179dea50-95f9-11e8-b67b-b8205561c3fe.

Finlan, Alastair. 2003. "Warfare by Other Means: Special Forces, Terrorism and Grand Strategy." *Small Wars and Insurgencies* 14 (1): 92–108.

Fishman, Brian. 2011. "Al-Qaeda and the Rise of China: Jihadi Geopolitics in a Post-Hegemonic World." *The Washington Quarterly* 34 (3): 47–62.

Forbes, Andrew D. W., and L. L. C. Forbes. 1986. *Warlords and Muslims in Chinese Central Asia: A Political History of Republican Sinkiang 1911–1949*. New York: Cambridge University Press.

Foreign Ministry of PRC. 2006. "Carry on Traditional Friendship and Deepen All-Round Cooperation." Address by Hu Jintao President of the People's Republic of China at Islamabad Convention Center. November 24. www.fmprc.gov.cn/mfa_eng/wjb_663304/zzjg_663340/yzs_663350/gjlb_663354/2757_663518/2758_663520/t285917.shtml.

Fu, Qiang. 2015. "The Economy of Hotan Is Thriving [喀什和田经济发展蓬勃向上]." *Xinjiang Daily*. September 15. *Reprinted by CPC News*. http://cpc.people.com.cn/n/2015/0917/c398213-27598576.html.

Fuller, Graham E., and Jonathan N. Lipman. 2004. "Islam in Xinjiang." In *Xinjiang: China's Muslim Borderland*, edited by S. Frederick Starr, 320–352. Armonk, NY: Taylor and Francis.

Gaibulloev, Khusrav, James A. Piazza, and Todd Sandler. 2017. "Regime Types and Terrorism." *International Organization* 71 (3): 491–522.

Gandhi, Jennifer. 2008. *Political Institutions under Dictatorship*. Cambridge: Cambridge University Press.

Gandhi, Jennifer, and Adam Przeworski. 2007. "Authoritarian Institutions and the Survival of Autocrats." *Comparative Political Studies* 40 (11): 1279–1301.

Garside, Juliette, and Emma Graham-Harrison. 2019 "UK Calls for UN Access to Chinese Detention Camps in Xinjiang." *The Guardian*, November 25. www.theguardian.com/world/2019/nov/25/uk-calls-for-un-access-chinese-detention-camps-xinjiang.

Gartner, Scott Sigmund, and Patrick M. Regan. 1996. "Threat and Repression: The Non-linear Relationship between Government and Opposition Violence." *Journal of Peace Research* 33 (3): 273–287.

Geddes, Barbara, Joseph Wright, and Erica Frantz. 2014. "Autocratic Breakdown and Regime Transitions: A New Data Set." *Perspectives on Politics* 12 (2): 313–331.

Gehlbach, Scott, Konstantin Sonin, and Milan W. Svolik. 2016. "Formal Models of Nondemocratic Politics." *Annual Review of Political Science* 19: 565–584.

Geng, Shuag. 2021. "Remarks by Ambassador Geng Shuang at Security Council Briefing on the Situation in Afghanistan." *Permanent Mission of the PRC to the UN*, www.fmprc.gov.cn/ce/ceun/eng/hyyfy/t1899842.htm.

Gerner, Deborah J., Philip A. Schrodt, Omur Yilmaz, and Rajaa Abu-Jabr. 2002. "The Creation of CAMEO (Conflict and Mediation Event Observations): An Event Data Framework for a Post Cold War World." Paper presented at Annual Meeting of the American Political Science Association, August 29–September 1.

Gettleman, Jeffrey, and Brian Knowlton. 2007. "Rebels Kill Workers at Chinese Oil Facility in Ethiopia." *The New York Times*, April 24. www .nytimes.com/2007/04/24/world/africa/24iht-addis.5.5427283.html.

Gibler, Douglas M. 2009. *International Military Alliances, 1648–2008.* Washington, DC: CQ Press.

Gibson, Giles. 2016. "Exclusive: Chinese Security Forces Caught Patrolling Deep inside Eastern Afghanistan." *WION*, October 27. www.wionews .com/south-asia/exclusive-chinese-security-forces-caught-patrolling-deep-inside-eastern-afghanistan-8008.

Gilley, Bruce, and Heike Holbig. 2009. "The Debate on Party Legitimacy in China: A Mixed Quantitative/Qualitative Analysis." *Journal of Contemporary China* 18 (59): 339–358.

Gladney, Dru C. 2004a. "The Chinese Program of Development and Control, 1978–2001." In *Xinjiang: China's Muslim Borderland*, edited by S. Frederick Starr, 101–119. Armonk, NY: Taylor and Francis.

Gladney, Dru C. 2004b. "Responses to Chinese rule: Patterns of cooperation and opposition." In *Xinjiang: China's Muslim Borderland*, edited by S. Frederick Starr, 375–396. Armonk, NY: Taylor and Francis.

Gladney, Dru C. 2004c. *Dislocating China: Reflections on Muslims, Minorities, and Other Subaltern Subjects.* Chicago, IL: University of Chicago Press.

Global Times. 2016. "阿中巴塔成立四国军队反恐合作协调机制：不针对任何其他国家 [Afghanistan, China, Pakistan, and Tajikistan Formed QCCM: Do Not Target Any Third-Party Country]." August 4. http://mil .qianlong.com/2016/0804/806943.shtml.

Goldstein, Joshua S. 1992. "A Conflict-Cooperation Scale for WEIS Events Data." *Journal of Conflict Resolution* 36 (2): 369–385.

Grambsch, Patricia M., and Terry M. Therneau. 1994. "Proportional Hazards Tests and Diagnostics Based on Weighted Residuals." *Biometrika* 81 (3): 515–526. https://doi.org/10.1093/biomet/81.3.515.

Gramer, Robbie. 2017. "The Islamic State Pledged to Attack China Next. Here's Why." *Foreign Policy*, March 1. https://foreignpolicy.com/2017/03/01/the-islamic-state-pledged-to-attack-china-next-heres-why/.

Greitens, Sheena Chestnut. 2017. "Rethinking China's Coercive Capacity: An Examination of PRC Domestic Security Spending, 1992–2012." *The China Quarterly* 232: 1002–1025.

Greitens, Sheena Chestnut, Myunghee Lee, and Emir Yazici. 2020. "Counterterrorism and Preventive Repression: China's Changing Strategy in Xinjiang." *International Security* 44 (3): 9–47.

Gul, Ayaz. 2018. "China Calls for 'Responsible' US Withdrawal from Afghanistan." *VOA*, December 31. www.voanews.com/south-central-asia/china-calls-responsible-us-withdrawal-afghanistan.

Gunaratna, Rohan. 2002. *Inside Al Qaeda: Global Network of Terror*. New York: Columbia University Press.

Gunaratna, Rohan, Arabinda Acharya, and Wang Pengxin. 2010. *Ethnic Identity and National Conflict in China*. New York: Palgrave Macmillan.

Guo, Rongxing. 2015a. *China's Spatial (Dis)integration: Political Economy of the Interethnic Unrest in Xinjiang*. Amsterdam: Chandos Publishing.

Guo, Yuandan. 2015b. "专家解读中国军费：054护卫舰30亿 052驱逐舰40亿." *Global Times*, March 6. http://news.ifeng.com/a/20150306/43283652_0.shtml.

Gurr, Ted Robert. 1970. *Why Men Rebel*. Princeton: Princeton University Press.

Haas, Marcel de. 2016. "War Games of the Shanghai Cooperation Organization and the Collective Security Treaty Organization: Drills on the Move!" *The Journal of Slavic Military Studies* 29 (3): 378–406.

Hancock, Tom. 2018. "China Censorship Moves from Politics to Economics." *Financial Times*, November 13. www.ft.com/content/1daaaf52-e32c-11e8-a6e5-792428919cee.

Hannah, Greg, Lindsay Clutterbuck, and Jennifer Rubin. 2008. *Radicalization or Rehabilitation: Understanding the Challenge of Extremist and Radicalized Prisoners*. Santa Monica, CA: RAND Corporation. www.rand.org/pubs/technical_reports/TR571.html.

Hannum, Emily, and Yu Xie. 1998. "Ethnic Stratification in Northwest China: Occupational Differences between Han Chinese and National Minorities in Xinjiang, 1982-1990." *Demography* 35 (3): 323–333.

Hasmath, Reza. 2011. "Managing China's Muslim Minorities: Migration, Labor and the Rise of Ethnoreligious Consciousness among Uyghurs in Urban Xinjiang." In *Religion and the State: A Comparative Sociology*, edited by Jack Barbalet, Adam Possamai, and Bryan S. Turner, 121–137. London: Anthem Press.

Hass, Ryan. 2020. "Why Now? Understanding Beijing's New Assertiveness in Hong Kong." *Brookings*. www.brookings.edu/blog/order-from-chaos/2020/07/17/why-now-understanding-beijings-new-assertiveness-in-hong-kong/.

Hastings, Justin V. 2011. "Charting the Course of Uighur Unrest." *The China Quarterly* 208: 893–912.

Hayes, Anna. 2020. "Sweden Leads the Way on Uighur Rights." *Fair Observer*, June 16. www.fairobserver.com/region/asia_pacific/anna-hayes-uighur-rights-china-persecution-surveillance-concentration-camps-asylum-news-18221/.

He, Bin. 2018. "中巴经济走廊提供了安全和稳定 [CEPC Provides Security and Stability]." *Guangming Daily*, May 3, p. 12.

Higgins, Andrew. 2018. "300,000 Troops and 900 Tanks: Russia's Biggest Military Drills since Cold War." *New York Times*, August 28. www.nytimes.com/2018/08/28/world/europe/russia-military-drills.html.

Hilton, Isabel. 2012. "China's Economic Reforms Have Let Party Leaders and Their Families Get Rich." *The Guardian*, October 26. www.theguardian.com/commentisfree/2012/oct/26/china-economic-reforms-leaders-rich.

Hincks, J. 2017. "China's Restive Xinjiang Province Changes Family Planning Rules to 'Promote Ethnic Equality.'" *Time*, August 1. http://time.com/4881898/china-xinjiang-uighur-children/.

Hoffman, A. M., C. Shelton, and E. Cleven. 2013. "Press Freedom, Publicity, and the Cross-National Incidence of Transnational Terrorism." *Political Research Quarterly* 66 (4): 896–909.

Hoffman, Bruce. 2006. *Inside Terrorism*. New York: Columbia University Press.

Holbig, Heike, and Bruce Gilley. 2010. "Reclaiming Legitimacy in China." *Politics and Policy* 38 (3): 395–422.

Holdstock, Nick. 2015. *China's Forgotten People: Xinjiang, Terror and the Chinese State*. New York: I.B. Touris and Co.

Holz, Carsten A. 2014. "The Quality of China's GDP Statistics." *China Economic Review* 30: 309–338.

Hong, Huaqing, and Xianzhong He. 2015. "Ideologies of Monoculturalism in Confucius Institute Textbooks: A Corpus-Based Critical Analysis." In *Language, Ideology and Education*, edited by Xiao Lan Curdt-Christiansen and Csilla Weninger, 104–122. London: Routledge.

Hong, Ji Yeon, and Wenhui Yang. 2018. "Oilfields, Mosques and Violence: Is There a Resource Curse in Xinjiang?" *British Journal of Political Science* 50 (1): 45–78.

Horgan, John, and Mary Beth Altier. 2012. "The Future of Terrorist De-radicalization Programs." *Georgetown Journal of International Affairs* 13 (2): 83–90.

Hornby, Lucy, and Tom Mitchell. 2017. "Xi Jinping Confirmed as China's Most Powerful Leader since Mao." *Financial Times*, October 24. www.ft.com/content/5b9f4b96-b86d-11e7-8c12-5661783e5589.

Horowitz, Michael C. 2010. "Nonstate Actors and the Diffusion of Innovations: The Case of Suicide Terrorism." *International Organization* 64 (1): 33–64.

Horowitz, Michael C., and Philip B. K. Potter. 2014. "Allying to Kill: Terrorist Intergroup Cooperation and the Consequences for Lethality." *Journal of Conflict Resolution* 58 (2): 199–225.

Horowitz, Michael C., Evan Perkoski, and Philip B. K. Potter. 2018. "Tactical Diversity in Militant Violence." *International Organization* 72 (1): 139–171.

Hou, Yue, and Kai Quek. 2019. "Violence Exposure and Support for State Use of Force in a Non-democracy." *Journal of Experimental Political Science* 6 (2): 120–130.

Howell, Anthony, and C. Cindy Fan. 2011. "Migration and Inequality in Xinjiang: A Survey of Han and Uyghur Migrants in Urumqi." *Eurasian Geography and Economics* 52 (1): 119–139.

Huang, Haifeng, Serra Boranbay-Akan, and Ling Huang. 2016. "Media, Protest Diffusion, and Authoritarian Resilience." *Political Science Research and Methods* 7 (1): 23–42.

Humphreys, Macartan. 2005. "Natural Resources, Conflict, and Conflict Resolution: Uncovering the Mechanisms." *Journal of Conflict Resolution* 49 (4): 508–537.

Hutchings, Graham. 2001. *Modern China: A Guide to a Century of Change.* Cambridge: Harvard University Press.

Ikenberry, G. John. 2008. "The Rise of China and the Future of the West: Can the Liberal System Survive?" *Foreign Affairs*, January. www.foreignaffairs.com/articles/asia/2008-01-01/rise-china-and-future-west.

Information Office of the State Council. 2019. "Vocational Education and Training in Xinjiang." White Paper. August 16. http://english.scio.gov.cn/2019-08/16/content_75106484.htm.

Iredale, Robyn R., Naran Bilik, Wang Su, Fei Guo, and Caroline Hoy. 2001. *Contemporary Minority Migration, Education, and Ethnicity in China.* Cheltenham, UK: Edward Elgar Publishing.

Ismail, Mohammed Sa'id, and Mohammed Aziz Ismail. 1960. Moslems in the Soviet Union and China. Tehran, Iran: Privately printed pamphlet, published as vol. 1. Translation printed in Washington: JPRS 3936, September 19. https://apps.dtic.mil/dtic/tr/fulltext/u2/a365044.pdf.

Jacobs, Andrew. 2016. "Xinjiang Seethes under Chinese Crackdown." *The New York Times*, January 2. www.nytimes.com/2016/01/03/world/asia/xinjiang-seethes-under-chinese-crackdown.html.

Jacobs, Justin. 2010. "The Many Deaths of a Kazak Unaligned: Osman Batur, Chinese Decolonization, and the Nationalization of a Nomad." *The American Historical Review* 115 (5): 1291–1314.

Jankowiak, William. 2008. "Ethnicity and Chinese Identity: Ethnographic Insight and Political Positioning." In *The Cambridge Companion to Modern Chinese Culture*, edited by Kam Louie, 91–114. Cambridge: Cambridge University Press.

Jedinia, Mehdi, and Sirwan Kajjo. 2018. "Analysts: Uighur Jihadis in Syria Could Pose Threat." *VOA News*, December 15. www.voanews.com/extremism-watch/analysts-uighur-jihadis-syria-could-pose-threat.

Jia, Lianrui. 2019. "What Public and Whose Opinion? A Study of Chinese Online Public Opinion Analysis." *Communication and the Public* 4 (1): 21–34.

Johnson, Chalmers. 2001. "Blowback." *The Nation* 273 (11): 13–15. www.thenation.com/article/archive/blowback/.

Joscelyn, Thomas. 2019a. "Al Qaeda Declares Solidarity with Turkistan Islamic Party in the Face of Chinese Oppression." *Foundation for the Defense of Democracies' Long War Journal*, April 17. www.longwarjournal.org/archives/2019/04/al-qaeda-declares-solidarity-with-turkistan-islamic-party-in-the-face-of-chinese-oppression.php.

Joscelyn, Thomas. 2019b. "Turkistan Islamic Party Musters Large Force for Battles in Syria." *Foundation for the Defense of Democracies' Long War Journal*, June 29. www.fdd.org/analysis/2019/06/29/turkistan-islamic-party-musters-large-force-for-battles-in-syria/.

Kaiman, Jonathan. 2013. "Islamist Group Claims Responsibility for Attack on China's Tiananmen Square." *The Guardian*, November 25. www.theguardian.com/world/2013/nov/25/islamist-china-tiananmen-beijing-attack.

Kan, Shirley A. 2010. *US-China Counterterrorism Cooperation: Issues for US Policy*. Congressional Research Service, July 15. https://fas.org/sgp/crs/terror/RL33001.pdf.

Kang, Dake. 2019. "China Locks Down Xinjiang a Decade after Deadly Ethnic Riots." *Associated Press News*, July 5. www.apnews.com/1e095c203d4a40c0a79d78d1a41634ab.

Kaplan, Jeffrey. 2010. *Terrorist Groups and the New Tribalism: Terrorism's Fifth Wave*. New York and London: Routledge.

Kaufman, Alison. 2010. "The 'Century of Humiliation,' Then and Now: Chinese Perceptions of the International Order." *Pacific Focus* 25 (1): 1–33.

Kaufman, Alison. 2011. "The 'Century of Humiliation' and China's National Narratives." Testimony before the U.S.–China Economic and Security Review Commission Hearing on "China's Narratives regarding National Security Policy." www.uscc.gov/sites/default/files/3.10.11Kaufman.pdf.

Keck, Zachary. 2014. "Al-Qaeda Declares War on China, Too." *The Diplomat*, October 22. https://thediplomat.com/2014/10/al-qaeda-declares-war-on-china-too/.

Keefe, John. 2002. *Anatomy of the Ep-3 Incident, April 2001*. Arlington County, VA: Center for Naval Analyses.

Kendzior, Sarah. 2013. "The Curse of Stability in Central Asia." *Foreign Policy* 19: 66–39.

King, Gary, Jennifer Pan, and Margaret E. Roberts. 2013. "How Censorship in China Allows Government Criticism but Silences Collective Expression." *American Political Science Review* 107 (2): 326–343.

Kuang, X. 2018. "Central State vs. Local Levels of Government: Understanding News Media Censorship in China." *Chinese Political Science Review* 3: 154–171.

Kuhn, Robert Lawrence. 2004. *The Man Who Changed China: The Life and Legacy of Jiang Zemin.* New York: Crown Publishers.

Lacey, Marc. 2001. "Powell to Allow Taiwan's President to Stop Briefly in U.S." *The New York Times,* May 15, A10.

LaFree, Gary, Laura Dugan, and Erin Miller. 2014. *Putting Terrorism in Context: Lessons from the Global Terrorism Database.* Abingdon: Routledge.

Laliberté, André, and Marc Lanteigne, ed. 2007. *The Chinese Party-State in the 21st Century: Adaptation and the Reinvention of Legitimacy.* New York and London: Routledge.

Lam, Willy Wo-Lap. 2001. "China, U.S. Boost Ties against Terrorism." *CNN,* October 19. http://edition.cnn.com/2001/WORLD/asiapcf/east/10/19/willy.lam/index.html.

Lampton, David M. 2001. *The Making of Chinese Foreign and Security Policy in the Era of Reform, 1978–2000.* Stanford, CA: Stanford University Press.

Lau, Lawrence J. 2018. "Why Now? The Rationale behind Xi Jinping's Power Consolidation." *South China Morning Post,* March 7. www.scmp.com/comment/insight-opinion/article/2135962/why-now-rationale-behind-xi-jinpings-power-consolidation.

Lau, Mimi. 2019. "Wanted: Chinese Cadres to Hold Beijing's Line in Xinjiang as Han Chinese Head for the Exits" *South China Morning Post,* December 4. www.scmp.com/news/china/politics/article/3040628/wanted-chinese-cadres-hold-beijings-line-xinjiang-han-head.

Leading Industry Research. 2020. "2007–2019: National and Xinjiang Public Security Expenditures." March 24. www.leadingir.com/datacenter/view/4837.html.

Legal Daily. 2014. "Xinjiang Public Security Agencies Launched 'Zero Point' Operation to Strike Terrorism. 23 Crime Groups and over 200 Suspects Were Overthrown and Arrested [新疆警方"零点行动"严打暴恐 三地打掉23个犯罪团伙抓获200余嫌犯]." May 25. www.legaldaily.com.cn/index_article/content/2014-05/25/content_5546323.htm?node=5955.

Lei, Yu-Hsiang, and Guy Michaels. 2014. "Do Giant Oilfield Discoveries Fuel Internal Armed Conflicts?" *Journal of Development Economics* 110: 139–157.

Leibold, James. 2014. "Xinjiang Work Forum Marks New Policy of 'Ethnic Mingling.'" *China Brief* 14 (12): 3–6.

Leibold, James. 2019a. Planting the Seed: Ethnic Policy in Xi Jinping's New Era of Cultural Nationalism. *China Brief*, 19 (22): 9–14.

Leibold, James. 2019b. "The Spectre of Insecurity: The CCP's Mass Internment Strategy in Xinjiang." *China Leadership Monitor*, March 1. www .prcleader.org/leibold.

Li, Boyang. 2014. "Chinese Narratives of 'National Humiliation' and Japan's Role in the Construction of China's National Identity, 1915 to the early 2000s." https://researcharchive.vuw.ac.nz/xmlui/bitstream/handle/10063/3419/thesis.pdf?sequence=2.

Li, Haiqing. 2017. "Xianjing yici xu shenyong [The Term 'Trap' Needs to Be Used with Caution]." *People's Daily*, December 17.

Li, Jiayao. 2019. "Chinese Navy Sees Broadened Horizon, Enhanced Ability through 10 Years of Escort Missions." *China Military*, January 2. http:// eng.chinamil.com.cn/view/2019-01/02/content_9392807.htm.

Li, Quan. 2005. "Does Democracy Promote or Reduce Transnational Terrorist Incidents?" *Journal of Conflict Resolution* 49 (2): 278–297.

Li, Xiaoxia. 2018. The Change of the Stability Status in Xinjiang and Analysis of Xinjiang's Stability Maintenance Policies [新疆稳定形式变化及维稳政策分析]." www.shehui.pku.edu.cn/upload/editor/file/20180820/201 80820234045_3372.pdf.

Licht, Amanda A., and Susan Hannah Allen. 2018. "Repressing for Reputation: Leadership Transitions, Uncertainty, and the Repression of Domestic Populations." *Journal of Peace Research* 55 (5): 582–595.

Lippman, Thomas W. 1999. "Bush Makes Clinton's China Policy an Issue." *The Washington Post*, August 20, A9.

Liu, Amy H., and Kevin Peters. 2017. "The Hanification of Xinjiang, China: The Economic Effects of the Great Leap West." *Studies in Ethnicity and Nationalism* 17 (2): 265–280.

Liu, Chuyu. 2019. "Local Public Goods Expenditure and Ethnic Conflict: Evidence from China." *Security Studies* 28 (4): 739–772.

Liu, Qingjian. 2014. "中国外交的战略基础：形成，发展与挑战 [The Foundations of China's Diplomatic Strategy: Origins, Development, and Challenges]." *CPCNEWS.CN*, October 14. http://cpc.people.com .cn/n/2014/1014/c68742-25828466.html.

Liu, S. 2011. "Structuration of Information Control in China." *Cultural Sociology* 5 (3): 323–339.

Lorentzen, Peter. 2014. "China's Strategic Censorship." *American Journal of Political Science* 58 (2): 402–414.

Lust-Okar, Ellen. 2005. *Structuring Conflict in the Arab World: Incumbents, Opponents, and Institutions*. Cambridge: Cambridge University Press.

Lyall, Jason. 2009. "Does Indiscriminate Violence Incite Insurgent Attacks? Evidence from Chechnya." *Journal of Conflict Resolution* 53 (3): 331–362.

Made, Jan van der. 2019. "European Countries Demand UN Access to China's Xinjiang Camps after New Leaks." *RFI*. November 26. www .rfi.fr/en/20191126-european-countries-demand-access-china-s-xinjiang-education-camps-after-new-leak.

Maizland, Lindsay. 2020. "China's Repression of Uighurs in Xinjiang." Council on Foreign Relations. www.cfr.org/backgrounder/chinas-repression-uighurs-xinjiang.

Malik, J. Mohan. 2002. "Dragon on Terrorism: Assessing China's Tactical Gains and Strategic Losses after 11 September." *Contemporary Southeast Asia* 24 (2): 252–293.

Mao, Zedong. 1956. "On the Ten Major Relationships." *Selected Works of Mao Tsetung* 5: 284–307.

Marano, S. George. 2019. "US Exit from Afghanistan Would Leave the Way Clear for China to Increase Its Influence in the Region." *South China Morning Post*, December 11. www.scmp.com/comment/opinion/article/3041372/us-exit-afghanistan-would-leave-way-clear-china-increase-its.

Martin, L. John. 1985. "The Media's Role in International Terrorism." *Terrorism* 8 (2): 127–146.

Martina, Michael. 2017. "China Warns of Imminent Attacks by 'Terrorists' in Pakistan." Reuters, December 8. www.reuters.com/article/us-china-silkroad-pakistan/china-warns-of-imminent-attacks-by-terrorists-in-pakistan-idUSKBN1E216N.

Martina, Michael, and Megha Rajagopalan. 2014. "Islamist Group Claims China Stations Bombing: SITE." Reuters, May 14. www.reuters.com/article/cnews-us-china-xinjiang-idCABREA4D07H20140514.

Marty, Franz J. 2017. "The Curious Case of Chinese Troops on Afghan Soil." The Central Asia-Caucasus Institute, February 3. www .cacianalyst.org/publications/analytical-articles/item/13424-the-curious-case-of-chinese-troops-on-afghan-soil.html.

Mattes, Michaela, and Mariana Rodriguez. 2014. "Autocracies and International Cooperation." *International Studies Quarterly* 58 (3): 527–538.

Mattes, Michaela, Brett Ashley Leeds, and Royce Carroll. 2015. "Leadership Turnover and Foreign Policy Change: Societal Interests, Domestic Institutions, and Voting in the United Nations." *International Studies Quarterly* 59 (2): 280–290.

Mattingly, Daniel. 2020. "Xi Jinping May Lose Control of the Coronavirus Story." *Foreign Policy*, February 10. https://foreignpolicy .com/2020/02/10/xi-jinping-may-lose-control-of-the-coronavirus-story/.

Maurer-Fazio, Margaret. 2012. "Ethnic Discrimination in China's Internet Job Board Labor Market." *IZA Journal of Migration* 1 (1): 12.

McDermott, Roger. 2004. *Countering Global Terrorism: Developing the Antiterrorist Capabilities of the Central Asian Militaries*. Carlisle, PA: Strategic Studies Institute, US Army War College.

McMillen, Donald H. 1984. "Xinjiang and Wang Enmao: New Directions in Power, Policy and Integration?" *The China Quarterly* 99: 569–593.

Mei, Shixiong, and Zurong Yang. 2002. "第一次与外军举行联合演习: 2002年中吉反恐演习 [The First Joint Military Exercise with Foreign Forces: 2002 China–Kyrgyzstan Counter-Terrorism Exercise]." Xinhua, August 15. www.xinhuanet.com//2017-08/15/c_1121487737.htm.

Metcalf, Mark. "The National Humiliation Narrative: Dealing with the Present by Fixating on the Past." *Education about Asia* 25: 43–50. www .asianstudies.org/wp-content/uploads/the-national-humiliation-narrative-dealing-with-the-present-by-fixating-on-the-past.pdf.

Millward, James. 2004. *Violent Separatism in Xinjiang: A Critical Assessment*. Washington, DC: East-West Center.

Millward, James. 2009. *Eurasian Crossroads: A History of Xinjiang*. New York: Columbia University Press.

Millward, James A. 2021. *Eurasian Crossroads: A History of Xinjiang*. London: Hurst Publishers.

Ministry of Finance. 2016. "Notice of the Ministry of Finance on Printing and Distributing of the Reform Plan of the Categorization of Government Income and Expenditures." http://xzzf.mof.gov.cn/mofhome/mof/zhengwuxinxi/caizhengwengao/caizhengbuwengao2006/caizhengbuwengao20062/200805/t20080519_23693.html.

Ministry of Foreign Affairs. 2021a. "Wang Yi Meets with U.S. Deputy Secretary of State Wendy Sherman." July 26. www.fmprc.gov.cn/mfa_eng/zxxx_662805/t1895278.shtml.

Ministry of Foreign Affairs. 2021b. "Wang Yi Meets with Head of the Afghan Taliban Political Commission Mullah Abdul Ghani Baradar." July 28. www.mfa.gov.cn/ce/cgfirenze/ita/zxhd/t1895950.htm.

Ministry of National Defense. 2011. "National Defense White Paper 2006." January 6. www.mod.gov.cn/regulatory/2011-01/06/content_4617808_4.htm.

Ministry of National Defense of the People's Republic of China. 2018. "和平使命-2016 上合组织成员国联合军演将在吉尔吉斯斯坦举行 [Peace Mission-2016 SCO Joint Military Exercise Will Be Held in Kyrgyzstan]." www.mod.gov.cn/topnews/2016-09/14/content_4730811.htm.

Minzner, Carl F. 2009. "Riots and Cover-ups: Counterproductive Control of Local Agents in China." *University of Pennsylvania Journal of International Law* 31 (1): 53–124.

Moore, Malcolm. 2009. "Al-Qaeda Vows Revenge on China over Uighur Deaths." *The Telegraph*, July 14. www.telegraph.co.uk/news/worldnews/asia/china/5822791/Al-Qaeda-vows-revenge-on-China-over-Uighur-deaths.html.

Mozur, Paul, and Edward Wong. 2019. "By Taking Aim at Chinese Tech Firms, Trump Signals a Strategy Shift." *New York Times*. www.nytimes.com/2019/10/08/business/china-human-rights-technology-xinjiang.html.

Mulcahy, Elizabeth, Shannon Merrington, and Peter Bell. 2013. "The Radicalisation of Prison Inmates: A Review of the Literature on Recruitment, Religion and Prisoner Vulnerability." *Journal of Human Security* 9 (1): 4–14.

Mumford, Andrew. 2018. "Theory-Testing Uyghur Terrorism in China." *Perspectives on Terrorism* 12 (5): 18–26.

Nacos, Brigitte L. 2002. *Mass-Mediated Terrorism: The Central Role of the Media in Terrorism and Communication*. New York: Rowman & Littlefield Publishers.

Nacos, Brigitte L. 2006. "Terrorism/Counterterrorism and Media in the Age of Global Communication." In *United Nations University Global Seminar Second Shimame-Yamaguchi Session, Terrorism—A Global Challenge*. Unpublished paper. https://archive.unu.edu/gs/files/2006/shimane/Nacos_text_en.pdf.

Nacos, Brigitte L. 2007. *Mass-Mediated Terrorism: The Central Role of the Media in Terrorism and Counterterrorism*. Lanham, MD: Rowman & Littlefield.

Nacos, Brigitte L. 2016. *Mass-Mediated Terrorism: Mainstream and Digital Media in Terrorism and Counterterrorism*. Lanham, MD: Rowman & Littlefield.

Nathan, Andrew J., and Andrew Scobell. 2012. *China's Search for Security*. New York: Columbia University Press.

Nebehay, Stephany. 2018. "UN Calls on China to Free Uighurs from Alleged Reeducation Camps." Reuters, August 30. www.reuters.com/article/us-china-rights-un/u-n-calls-on-china-to-free-uighurs-from-re-education-camps-idUSKCN1LF1D6.

Neuman, Scott, Emily Feng, and Huo Jingnan. 2020. "China to Investigate after Whistleblower Doctor Dies from Coronavirus." *NPR*, February 7. www.npr.org/sections/goatsandsoda/2020/02/07/803680463/china-to-investigate-after-whistleblower-doctor-dies-from-coronavirus.

Noonan, Michael P., Colin P. Clarke, Jacqueline Deal, June Teufel Dreyer, and Barak Mer. 2019. "Roundtable: The Uyghurs, China, and Islamist Terrorism." Foreign Policy Research Institute. www.fpri.org/article/2019/12/roundtable-the-uyghurs-china-and-islamist-terrorism/.

O'Brien, Kevin J. 1996. "Rightful Resistance." *World Politics* 49 (1): 31–55.

O'Brien, Kevin J., and Lianjiang Li. 2006. *Rightful Resistance in Rural China*. Cambridge: Cambridge University Press.

OECD. 2019. "Consumer Confidence Index (CCI) (Indicator)." https://data.oecd.org/leadind/consumer-confidence-index-cci.htm.

Office of the Press Secretary. 2001. "Meeting with the Dalai Lama." May 23. https://georgewbush-whitehouse.archives.gov/news/releases/2001/05/20010523-3.html.

Office of the Press Secretary. 2002. "President Bush Meets with Chinese President Jiang Zemin." February 21. https://georgewbush-whitehouse.archives.gov/news/releases/2002/02/20020221-7.html.

Office for International Military Cooperation of the Central Military Commission. 2017. www.qstheory.cn/dukan/qs/2017-05/15/c_1120953877.htm.

Olesen, Alexa. 2014. "China Sees Islamic State Inching Closer to Home." *Foreign Policy*, August 11. https://foreignpolicy.com/2014/08/11/china-sees-islamic-state-inching-closer-to-home/.

Orfy, Mohammed Moustafa. 2014. *NATO and the Middle East: The Geopolitical Context Post-9/11*. London: Routledge.

Owyang, Michael T., and Hannah Shell. 2017. "China's Economic Data: An Accurate Reflection, or Just Smoke and Mirrors?" *The Regional Economist* 25 (2): 6–12.

Pa, Ka, Weisen Dai, Fan Yang, and Luisetta Muddie. 2015. "Top Xinjiang Editor Expelled from China's Communist Party foe 'Opposing Party Line.'" *Radio Free Asia*, November 2. www.rfa.org/english/news/uyghur/editor-11022015153453.html.

Pan, Guang. 2004. "China's Anti-terror Strategy and China's Role in Global Anti-terror Cooperation." *Asia Europe Journal* 2: 523–532.

Panda, Jagannath P. 2007. "Assessing the Impact of the Sino-Indian Army Exercise on Bilateral Relations." *China Brief* 7 (15). https://jamestown.org/program/assessing-the-impact-of-the-sino-indian-army-exercise-on-bilateral-relations/.

Pannell, Clifton W., and Philipp Schmidt. 2006. "Structural Change and Regional Disparities in Xinjiang, China." *Eurasian Geography and Economics* 47 (3):329–352.

Palmer, Doug. 2020. "CBP Could Take Action against Xinjiang Cotton Products." *Politico*. www.politico.com/newsletters/weekly-trade/2020/09/08/cbp-could-take-action-against-xinjiang-cotton-products-790272.

Party History Research Office of the CPC Central Committee. 2010. *History of the Communist Party of China*, Volume II: 28. Beijing: History of Chinese Communist Party Publishing House.

People.com. 2001. "Zhonggong Dangshi shang de 80 ju kouhao [80 Slogans in the History of CPC]." June 26. www.people.com.cn/GB/shizheng/252/5303/5304/20010626/497648.html.

People.com. 2008. "人民日报连续三天发文探讨中国为什么这么安全[People's Daily Discusses Why China Is So Safe Three Days in a Row]." http://world.people.com.cn/n1/2018/0209/c1002-29814449.html.

People.com. 2012. "Foreign Media Focus on the Recruitment of 8,000 New Police Officers in Xinjiang When 'One Village, One Police' Policy Was Implemented to Preserve Stability [外媒紧盯新疆增加8000警力 维稳实现一村一警]." February 12. http://military.people.com.cn/GB/172467/16988690.html.

People's Daily. 1966. "The Encirclement of China." www.tandfonline.com/doi/abs/10.1080/00396336608440627?journalCode=tsur20.

People's Daily. 1990. "Wending Yadao Yiqie [Stability above Everything Else]." June 6.

People's Daily. 1995. "Recall the Establishment of XUAR." September 28.

People's Daily. 1998. "Jieshao Xinjiang jingji shehui fazhan qingkuang [Introducing the Economic and Social Development in Xinjiang]." March 13, p. 2.

People's Daily. 1999a. Li Peng jieshou zhongguo jizhe lianhe caifang shi tan dongtu wenti [Li Peng Answers Questions about East Turkestan Issue]." April 19, p. 6.

People's Daily. 1999b. "Li Peng weiyuanzhang fangwen xila tuerqi xuliya bajisitan mengjialaguo he taiguo liuguo qingkuang de shumian baogao [A Written Report about Li Peng's Visit to Greece, Turkey, Syria, Pakistan, Bangladesh, and Thailand]." April 30.

People's Daily. 2000. "Zhu Rongji Meets with Turkish Guests." February 16, p. 1.

People's Daily. 2002a. "'Dongtu kongbu shili nantui zuize' ['East Turkistan' Terrorist Forces Cannot Get Away with Impunity]." January 22, p. 3.

People's Daily. 2002b. "Lianheguo anlihui rending 'dongtu' wei kongbu zuzhi [UN Designated East Turkistan Islamic Movement as a Terrorist Organization]." September 13, p. 3.

People's Daily. 2002c. "Waijiaobu fayanren da jizhe wen [Ministry of Foreign Affairs Spokesman Answers Journalists' Questions]." October 6, p. 2.

People's Daily. 2004. "Waijiaobu fayanren da jizhe wen [Ministry of Foreign Affairs Spokesman Answers Journalists' Questions]." October 30, p. 4.

People's Daily. 2018. "One Million of Xinjiang Cadres Become Families with People from All Ethnic Groups [新疆百万干部职工与各族群众结亲认对]." November 7, p. 11.

People's Daily. 2020. "中共中央国务院关于新时代推进西部大开发形成新格局的指导意见 [The CCP Central Committee and the State Council Unveil Guideline on Advancing Western Development in New Era]." May 18, p. 1.

Piazza, James A. 2006. "Rooted in Poverty? Terrorism, Poor Economic Development, and Social Cleavages." *Terrorism and Political Violence* 18 (1): 159–177.

Piazza, James A. 2017. Repression and Terrorism: A Cross-National Empirical Analysis of Types of Repression and Domestic Terrorism. *Terrorism and Political Violence* 29 (1): 102–118.

Piazza, James A. 2018. "Transnational Ethnic Diasporas and the Survival of Terrorist Organizations." *Security Studies* 27 (4): 607–632.

Pils, Eva. 2006. "Asking the Tiger for His Skin: Rights Activism in China." *Fordham International Law Journal* 30 (4): 1209.

Potter, Phillip B. K. 2013. "Terrorism in China." *Strategic Studies Quarterly* 7 (4): 70–92.

Potter, Philip B. K., and Chen Wang. 2022. "Governmental Responses to Terrorism in Autocracies: Evidence from China." *British Journal of Political Science* 52 (1): 358–380.

Polyakova, Alina, and Chris Meserole. 2019. "Exporting Digital Authoritarianism: The Russian and Chinese Models." The Brookings Institution, August. www.brookings.edu/research/exporting-digital-authoritarianism/.

Putz, Catherine. 2019. "Which Countries Are for or against China's Xinjiang Policies?" *The Diplomat*, July 15. https://thediplomat.com/2019/07/which-countries-are-for-or-against-chinas-xinjiang-policies/.

Qian, Qichen. 2005. *Ten Episodes in China's Diplomacy*. New York: HarperCollins.

Qin, Bei, David Strömberg, and Yanhui Wu. 2017. "Why Does China Allow Freer Social Media? Protests versus Surveillance and Propaganda." *Journal of Economic Perspectives* 31 (1): 117–140.

Qu, Pengfei. 2019. "BRI and the Development of Xinjiang Conference Is Held in Hangzhou ['一带一路'与新疆社会发展学术研讨会在杭州召开]." Guangming, January 22. www.gmw.cn/xueshu/2019-01/22/content_32392446.htm.

Quackenbush, Casey. 2017. "Three Things to Know about China's Kindergarten Abuse Scandal." *Time*, November 27. https://time.com/5037556/china-beijing-kindergarten-abuse-scandal/.

Rabasa, Angel, Stacie L. Pettyjohn, Jeremy Ghez, and Christopher Boucek. 2010. *Deradicalizing Islamist Extremists*. Santa Monica, CA: RAND Corporation. www.rand.org/pubs/monographs/MG1053.html.

Rabinovitch, Simon. 2010. "China's GDP Is 'Man-Made', Unreliable: Top Leader." Reuters, December 6. www.reuters.com/article/us-china-economy-wikileaks-idUSTRE6B527D20101206.

Radio Free Asia. 2015. "Death Toll in Xinjiang Coal Mine Attack Climbs to 50." September 30. www.rfa.org/english/news/Uighur/attack-09302015174319.html.

Radio Free Asia. 2018. "Chinese Authorities Jail Four Wealthiest Uighurs in Xinjiang's Kashgar in New Purge." January 5. www.rfa.org/english/news/Uighur/wealthiest-01052018144327.html.

Ramzy, Austin, and Chris Buckley. 2019. "'Absolutely No Mercy': Leaked Files Expose How China Organized Mass Detentions of Muslims." *The New York Times*, November 16. www.nytimes.com/interactive/2019/11/16/world/asia/china-xinjiang-documents.html.

Rapoport, David C. 2004. "The Four Waves of Modern Terrorism." In *Attacking Terrorism: Elements of a Grand Strategy*, edited by Audrey Kurth Cronin and James M. Ludes, 46–73. Washington, DC: Georgetown University Press.

Reed, J.Todd, and Diana Raschke. 2010. *The ETIM: China's Islamic Militants and the Global Terrorist Threat*. Santa Barbara, CA: ABC-CLIO.

Regan, James. 2020. "France Says China's Repression of Xinjiang Is Unacceptable." *Bloomberg*, July 22. www.bloomberg.com/news/articles/2020-07-22/france-says-china-s-repression-of-xinjiang-uighurs-unacceptable.

Resolutions of the CPC Central Committee on Major Issues Regarding the Building of a Harmonious Socialist Society. 2006. www.gov.cn/gongbao/content/2006/content_453176.htm.

Reuter, Ora John, and Graeme B. Robertson. 2015. "Legislatures, Cooptation, and Social Protest in Contemporary Authoritarian Regimes." *The Journal of Politics* 77 (1): 235–248.

Reuters. 2009. "Militant Urges Targeting China over Uighurs." August 1. www.reuters.com/news/picture/militant-urges-targeting-china-over-uigh-idUSTRE5701SS20090801.

Roberts, Sean R. 2020. *The War on the Uyghurs*. Princeton: Princeton University Press.

Roggio, Bill. 2011."Al Qaeda Appoints New Leader of Forces in Pakistan's Tribal Areas." *Foundation for the Defense of Democracies' Long War Journal*, May 9. www.longwarjournal.org/archives/2011/05/al_qaeda_appoints_ne_2.php.

Roggio, Bill. 2012."Turkistan Islamic Party Leader Thought Killed in US Drone Strike." *Foundation for the Defense of Democracies' Long War Journal*, August 25. www.longwarjournal.org/archives/2012/08/turkistan_islamic_pa_1.php.

Roggio, Bill. 2015. "Turkistan Islamic Party Emir Thought Killed in 2010 Reemerged to Lead Group in 2014." *Foundation for the Defense of Democracies' Long War Journal*, June 11. www.longwarjournal.org/archives/2015/06/turkistan-islamic-party-emir-thought-killed-in-2010-reemerged-to-lead-group-in-2014.php.

Rohner, Dominic, and Bruno S. Frey. 2007. "Blood and Ink! The Common-Interest-Game between Terrorists and the Media." *Public Choice* 133 (1–2): 129–145.

Ross, Jeffrey Ian. 1993. "Structural Causes of Oppositional Political Terrorism: Towards a Causal Model." *Journal of Peace Research* 30 (3):317–329.

Ross, Michael. 2006. "A Closer Look at Oil, Diamonds, and Civil War." *Annual Review of Political Science* 9: 265–300.

Rudelson, Justin, and William Jankowiak. 2004. "Acculturation and Resistance: Xinjiang Identities in Flux" In *Xinjiang: China's Muslim Borderland*, edited by S. Frederick Starr, 299–319. Armonk, NY: Taylor and Francis.

Ruser, Nathan, James Leibold, Kelsey Munro, and Tilla Hoja. 2020. "Cultural Erasure." Australian Strategic Policy Institute, September 24,.

Ruwitch, John. 2018. "Timeline – The Rise of Chinese Leader Xi Jinping." Reuters, March 16. www.reuters.com/article/us-china-parliament-xi-timeline/timeline-the-rise-of-chinese-leader-xi-jinping-idUSKCN1GS0ZA.

Sampson, Catherine. 1992. "Bombers Raise Chinese Fears." *The Times*, February 22.

Sánchez-Cuenca, I., and De la Calle, L. 2009. Domestic Terrorism: The Hidden Side of Political Violence. *Annual Review of Political Science* 12: 31–49.

Sandler, Todd. 1995. "On the Relationship between Democracy and Terrorism." *Terrorism and Political Violence* 7 (4): 1–9.

Sandler, Todd, John T. Tschirhart, and Jon Cauley. 1983. "A Theoretical Analysis of Transnational Terrorism." *American Political Science Review* 77 (1): 36–54.

Schiavenza, Matt. 2013. How Humiliation Drove Modern Chinese History. *The Atlantic*, October 26.

Schmid, Alex Peter. 1992. "Terrorism and Democracy." *Terrorism and Political Violence* 4 (4): 14–25.

Schmid, Alex Peter. 2004. "Frameworks for Conceptualising terrorism." *Terrorism and Political Violence* 16 (2): 197–221.

Schmid, Alex Peter, and Janny De Graaf. 1982. *Violence as Communication: Insurgent Terrorism and the Western News Media*. Thousand Oaks, CA: Sage Publications.

Schubert, Gunter. 2008. "One-Party Rule and the Question of Legitimacy in Contemporary China: Preliminary Thoughts on Setting up a New Research Agenda." *Journal of Contemporary China* 17 (54): 191–204.

Schweller, Randall L., and Xiaoyu Pu. 2011. "After Unipolarity: China's Visions of International Order in an Era of US Decline." *International Security* 36 (1): 41–72.

Scobell, Andrew, Ely Ratner, and Michael Beckley. 2014. *China's Strategy toward South and Central Asia: An Empty Fortress*. Santa Monica, CA: Rand Corporation.

Senate Foreign Relations Committee. 2002. "Hearing: Fiscal Year 2003 Foreign Affairs Budget." February 5. https://lawcat.berkeley.edu/record/18525.

Shadmehr, Mehdi. 2015. "Extremism in Revolutionary Movements." *Games and Economic Behavior* 94: 97–121.

Shakil, F. M. 2021. "Why China Fears US Withdrawal from Afghanistan." *Asia Times*. January 12. https://asiatimes.com/2021/01/why-china-fears-us-withdrawal-from-afghanistan/.

Shambaugh, David L. 2000. "China's Military Views the World: Ambivalent Security." *International Security* 24 (3): 52–79.

Shambaugh, David L. 2007. "China's Propaganda System: Institutions, Processes and Efficacy." *The China Journal* 57: 25–58.

Shambaugh, David L. 2008. *China's Communist Party: Atrophy and Adaptation*. Berkeley, CA: University of California Press.

Shambaugh, David. 2013. "Assessing China's New Leadership One Year On." Carnegie Endowment for International Peace. https://carnegieendowment.org/files/David_Shambaugh.pdf.

Shao, L. 2018. "The Dilemma of Criticism: Disentangling the Determinants of Media Censorship in China." *Journal of East Asian Studies* 18 (3): 279–297.

Shen, S. 2007. *China and Antiterrorism*. New York: Nova Science Publishers.

Shi, Xiaobin. 2017. "Statement by Mr. Shi Xiaobin of the Chinese Delegation at the 72nd session of the UN General Assembly under Agenda Item 109: Measures to Eliminate International Terrorism." Permanent Mission of the PRC to the UN. http://webcache.googleusercontent.com/search?q=cache:78F3xhoBmWMJ:chnun.chinamission.org.cn/eng/hyyfy/t1499504.htm+&cd=1&hl=en&ct=clnk&gl=us.

Shi, Yinglun. 2018. "Interview: SCO Summit to Enhance Anti-terrorism Cooperation, Boost Regional Connectivity – Afghan President." Xinhua, June 8. www.xinhuanet.com/english/2018-06/08/c_137240396.htm.

Shichor, Yitzhak. 2004. "The Great Wall of Steel: Military and Strategy in Xinjiang." In *Xinjiang: China's Muslim Borderland*, edited by S. Frederick Starr, 120–160. Abington: Routledge.

Shih, Gerry. 2019. "In Central Asia's Forbidding Highlands, a Quiet Newcomer: Chinese Troops." *The Washington Post*, February 18. www.washingtonpost.com/world/asia_pacific/in-central-asias-forbidding-highlands-a-quiet-newcomer-chinese-troops/2019/02/18/78d4a8d0-1e62-11e9-a759-2b8541bbbe20_story.html?noredirect=on&utm_term=.f851f1f72570.

Shirk, Susan L., ed. 2011. *Changing Media, Changing China*. Oxford: Oxford University Press.

Simpson, Peter. 2012. "China's Vice President Orders More Thought Control over Students." *The Telegraph*, January 5. www.telegraph.co.uk/news/worldnews/asia/china/8995123/Chinas-vice-president-orders-more-thought-control-over-students.html.

Sims, Christopher A. 1980. "Macroeconomics and Reality." *Econometrica: Journal of the Econometric Society* 48 (1): 1–48.

Sina. 2009. "SWAT Forces from Thirty-One Cities Dispatched to Xinjiang to Maintain Stability after 7.5 Event [7-5事件后全国31个城市特警乘专机赴疆维稳]." August 17. http://news.sina.com.cn/c/2009-08-17/090718450526.shtml.

Siqueira, Kevin, and Todd Sandler. 2006. "Terrorists versus the Government: Strategic Interaction, Support, and Sponsorship." *Journal of Conflict Resolution* 50 (6): 878–898.

SITE Intelligence Group. 2013. "TIP Leader Speaks on Suicide Attack at Tiananmen Square." November 22. https://news.siteintelgroup.com/Jihadist-News/tip-leader-speaks-on-suicide-attack-at-tiananmen-square.html.

Small, Andrew. 2010 "China's Caution on Afghanistan–Pakistan." *The Washington Quarterly* 33 (3): 81–97.

Small, Andrew. 2018. "China and Counter-Terrorism: Beyond Pakistan?" In *Terrorism and Counter-Terrorism in China: Domestic and Foreign Policy Dimensions*, edited by Michael Clarke, 129–140. New York: Oxford University Press.

SmithFinley, Joanne. 2019. "The Wang Lixiong Prophecy: 'Palestinization' in Xinjiang and the Consequences of Chinese State Securitization of Religion." *Central Asian Survey* 38 (1): 81–101.

Sohu News. 2007. "PAP Searched for East Turkestan Terrorists with Helicopters [武警乘直升飞机搜索'东突'分子]." http://news.sohu.com/20070118/n247680609.shtml.

Sohu News. 2014. "中外联合军演花销巨大，谁来出钱? [Joint Military Exercises Are Expensive, Who Pays?]." August 24. https://m.sohu.com/n/556320341/

Sohu News. 2017. "Serve the Frontline of Stability-Maintenance, Keda Systems Are Installed in over 3000 Convenience Police Stations in Xinjiang [服务维稳第一线，科达驻守新疆3000多个便民警务站]." February 17. www.sohu.com/a/126497275_219099.

Sohu News. 2019. "Another Heavy Punch to Promote Ethnic Mingling in Xinjiang, Big Change to the Preferential Policy That Awards Bonus Points in the National College Entrance Exams! [新疆加强民族交融再出重拳，高考加分政策重大改革!]." May 12. www.sohu.com/a/313397034_679976.

"Special Operations Forces and Counter-Terrorism." 2006. *Strategic Comments* 12(7):1–2.www.tandfonline.com/doi/abs/10.1080/1356788061272.

Speckhard, Anne, and Ardian Shajkovci. 2018. "Prison: Militant Jihadist Recruiting Grounds or Refuge for Rehabilitation?" *Homeland Security Today*, December 11. www.hstoday.us/subject-matter-areas/terrorism-study/prison-militant-jihadist-recruiting-grounds-or-refuge-for-rehabilitation/.

Starr, S. Frederick, ed. 2004. *Xinjiang: China's Muslim Borderland.* Armonk, NY: Taylor and Francis.

(START) National Consortium for the Study of Terrorism and Responses to Terrorism. 2018. Global Terrorism Database (GTD). www.start.umd.edu/gtd/.

START (National Consortium for the Study of Terrorism and Responses to Terrorism). 2021. *Global Terrorism Database Codebook: Methodology, Inclusion Criteria, and Variables.* University of Maryland, August. www.start.umd.edu/gtd/downloads/Codebook.pdf.

Stern, Rachel E., and Jonathan Hassid. 2012. "Amplifying Silence: Uncertainty and Control Parables in Contemporary China." *Comparative Political Studies* 45 (10): 1230–1254.

Stewart, Elliot. 2021. "The Islamic State Stopped Talking about China" *War on the Rocks.* https://warontherocks.com/2021/01/the-islamic-state-stopped-talking-about-uighurs/.

Stimson Center. 2018. *Counterterrorism Spending: Protecting America While Promoting Efficiencies and Accountability.* www.stimson.org/wp-content/files/file-attachments/CT_Spending_Report_0.pdf.

Stockmann, Daniela, and Mary E. Gallagher. 2011. "Remote Control: How the Media Sustain Authoritarian Rule in China." *Comparative Political Studies* 44 (4): 436–467.

Stojanovic, Dusan. 2019. "Chinese Snooping Tech Spreads to Nations Vulnerable to Abuse." *Associated Press News*, October 17. https://apnews.com/9fd1c38594444d44acfe25ef5f7d6ba0.

Storey, Henry. 2019. "Why Nobody Is Taking Action on Xinjiang and Why It Matters." *Australian Institute of International Affairs* (blog), December 30. www.internationalaffairs.org.au/australianoutlook/taking-action-xinjiang-matters/.

Svolik, Milan W. 2012. *The Politics of Authoritarian Rule.* Cambridge: Cambridge University Press.

Svolik, Milan W. 2013. "Contracting on Violence: The Moral Hazard in Authoritarian Repression and Military Intervention in Politics." *Journal of Conflict Resolution* 57 (5): 765–794.

Swanson, Ana, and Edward Wong. 2020. "U.S. Adds Sanctions over Internment of Muslims in China." *New York Times.* www.nytimes.com/2020/07/31/us/politics/sanctions-china-xinjiang-uighurs.html.

Swanstrom, Niklas. 2005. "China and Central Asia: A New Great Game or Traditional Vassal Relations?" *Journal of Contemporary China* 14 (45): 569–584.

Tang, Jiaxuan. 2011. *Heavy Storm and Gentle Breeze: A Memoir of China's Diplomacy*. New York: HarperCollins.

Tanner, Murray Scot, and James Bellacqua. 2016. "China's Response to Terrorism." CNA Report. CNA Analysis and Solutions. www.uscc.gov/sites/default/files/Research/Chinas%20Response%20to%20Terrorism_CNA061616.pdf.

Taubman, Philip. 1981. "U.S. and Peking Join in Tracking Missiles in Soviet." *New York Times*, June 18, A1.

Thatcher, Margaret. 1985. "Speech to American Bar Association." www.margaretthatcher.org/document/106096.

The Economist. 2009. "Riots in Xinjiang: Beijing's nightmare." July 9. www.economist.com/leaders/2009/07/09/beijings-nightmare.

The Economist. 2018. "Russia and China Hold the Biggest Military Exercises for Decades." September 6. www.economist.com/europe/2018/09/06/russia-and-china-hold-the-biggest-military-exercises-for-decades.

The Guardian. 2014. "Chinese Authorities Offer Cash to Promote Interethnic Marriages." September 2. www.theguardian.com/world/2014/sep/02/chinese-authorties-cash-inter-ethnic-marriages-uighur-minority.

The Ministry of Public Security of the PRC. 2012. "The Third List of Identified Terrorists." April 6. www.gov.cn/gzdt/2012-04/06/content_2107385.htm.

The Montreal Gazette. 1950. "Chinese Moslem Head Says War Will Go On." January 10. https://news.google.com/newspapers?id=bDIrAAAAIBAJ&sjid=SpkFAAAAIBAJ&pg=4393,1365448&dq=ma+pu-fang&hl=en.

The State Council Information Office. 2011. "China's National Defense in 2010." March 11. www.scio.gov.cn/zxbd/nd/2011/Document/883530/883530.htm.

The State Council Information Office. 2019. "Vocational Education and Training in Xinjiang." http://english.www.gov.cn/archive/whitepaper/201908/17/content_WS5d57573cc6d0c6695ff7ed6c.html.

Thomas, Neil. 2019. "How Beijing Embraces Public Opinion to Govern and Control." Paulson Institute. https://macropolo.org/china-public-opinion-authoritarian-resilience/?rp=m.

Thum, Rian. 2018. "The Uyghurs in Modern China." In *Oxford Research Encyclopedia of Asian History*. https://oxfordre.com/asianhistory/view/10.1093/acrefore/9780190277727.001.0001/acrefore-9780190277727-e-160.

Tiezzi, Shannon. 2019. "Rival Camps Clash over Xinjiang at UN Committee Session." *The Diplomat*, October 31. https://thediplomat.com/2019/10/rival-camps-clash-over-xinjiang-at-un-committee-session/.

Tilly, Charles. 2004. "Terror, terrorism, terrorists." *Sociological Theory* 22 (1): 5–13.

Tohti, Ilham. 2015. "Present-Day Ethnic Problems in Xinjiang Uighur Autonomous Region: Overview and Recommendations (4) – Ethnic Alienation and Segregation." translated by Cindy Carter. *China Change*, May 4. https://chinachange.org/2015/05/04/present-day-ethnic-problems-in-xinjiang-uighur-autonomous-region-overview-and-recommendations-4-ethnic-alienation-and-segregation/.

Trédaniel, Marie, and Pak K. Lee. 2017. "Explaining the Chinese Framing of the 'Terrorist' Violence in Xinjiang: Insights from Securitization Theory." *Nationalities Papers* 46 (1): 177–195.

Truex, Rory. 2019. "Focal Points, Dissident Calendars, and Preemptive Repression." *Journal of Conflict Resolution* 63 (4): 1032–1052.

Tschantret, Joshua. 2018. "Repression, Opportunity, and Innovation: The Evolution of Terrorism in Xinjiang, China." *Terrorism and Political Violence* 30 (4): 569–588.

Turkel, Nury. 2020. "The U.S. Must Use the New Uyghur Human Rights Policy Act to Sanction Chinese Officials for Religious Persecution." *Time*. https://time.com/5847184/uyghur-human-rights-policy-act-china/.

United Nations Security Council. 2011."Eastern Turkistan Islamic Movement." April 7. www.un.org/securitycouncil/sanctions/1267/aq_sanctions_list/summaries/entity/eastern-turkistan-islamic-movement.

United Nations Security Council. 2020. "Letter from the Chair of the Security Council Committee." January 20. https://undocs.org/S/2020/53.

Uyghur Human Rights Project. 2017. "Simulated Autonomy: Uyghur Underrepresentation in Political Office." https://uhrp.org/docs/political-representation-repor.pdf.

Vagneur-Jones, Antoine. 2017. "War and Opportunity: The Turkistan Islamic Party and the Syrian conflict." *Foundation pour la Recherche Strategique*, March 2. www.frstrategie.org/en/publications/notes/war-and-opportunity-turkistan-islamic-party-syrian-conflict-2017.

Verma, Pranshu, and Edward Wong. 2020. "U.S. Imposes Sanctions on Chinese Officials over Mass Detention of Muslims." *New York Times*. www.nytimes.com/2020/07/09/world/asia/trump-china-sanctions-uighurs.html.

Voice of America. 2021. "观察人士：美军撤离阿富汗，中国的担忧与日俱增 [Observers: US Withdraw from Afghanistan, China's Worries Grows]." www.voachinese.com/a/china-Afghanistan-08102021/5997945.html.

Wallace, Kelly. 2001. "Bush Pledges Whatever It Takes to Defend Taiwan." CNN, April 25. www.cnn.com/2001/ALLPOLITICS/04/24/bush.taiwan.abc/index.html.

Wan, William. 2013. "Chinese Police Say Tiananmen Square Crash Was 'Premeditated, Violent, Terrorist Attack.'" *The Washington Post*, October 30. www.washingtonpost.com/world/asia_pacific/chinese-police-say-tiananmen-square-crash-was-premeditated-violent-terrorist-attack/2013/10/30/459e3e7e-4152-11e3-8b74-d89d714ca4dd_story.html.

Wang, Adrian, and Teddy Ng. 2014. "Urumqi Bombing Was Suicide Attack by Uighur Extremists." *South China Morning Post*, May 1. www.scmp.com/news/china/article/1502056/two-religious-extremists-carried-out-suicide-attack-urumqi-xinjiang.

Wang, David D. 1998. "East Turkestan Movement in Xinjing." *Journal of Chinese Political Science* 4 (1): 1–18.

Wang, Yongqing 王永庆. 2012. *Li Shide huisheng: Gercia huiyi lu* 历史的回声：格尔夏回忆录 [The Echo of History: A Memoir of Gercia]. Xinjiang: Xinjiang shengchan jianshe bingtuan chubanshe.

Wang, Yuhua. 2019. "The Political Legacy of Violence during China's Cultural Revolution." *British Journal of Political Science* 51 (2): 463–487.

Wang, Yuhua, and Carl Minzner. 2015. "The Rise of the Chinese Security State." *The China Quarterly* 222: 339–359.

Wang, Zheng. 2008. "National Humiliation, History Education, and the Politics of Historical Memory: Patriotic Education Campaign in China." *International Studies Quarterly* 52 (4): 783–806.

Wang, Zheng. 2014. *Never Forget National Humiliation: Historical Memory in Chinese Politics and Foreign Relations*. New York: Columbia University Press.

Wayne, Martin I. 2007. *China's War on Terrorism: Counter-Insurgency, Politics and Internal Security*. New York: Routledge.

Wayne, Martin I. 2008. *China's War on Terrorism: Counter-Insurgency, Politics, and Internal Security*. New York: Routledge.

Weber, I., and L. Jia. 2007. "Internet and Self-Regulation in China: The Cultural Logic of Controlled Commodification." *Media, Culture & Society* 29 (5): 772–789.

Weeks, Jessica L. P. 2014. *Dictators at War and Peace*. Ithaca, NY: Cornell University Press.

Weinberg, Leonard, Ami Pedahzur, and Sivan Hirsch-Hoefler. 2004. "The Challenges of Conceptualizing Terrorism." *Terrorism and Political Violence* 16 (4): 777–794.

Weiss, Caleb. 2020 "Jihadists Discuss Coronavirus, Offer Advice." *Foundation for the Defense of Democracies' Long War Journal*, March 13. www.longwarjournal.org/archives/2020/03/jihadists-discuss-coronavirus-offer-advice.php.

Weiss, Jessica Chen. 2014. *Powerful Patriots: Nationalist Protest in China's Foreign Relations*. Oxford: Oxford University Press.

Weitz, Richard. 2015. *Parsing Chinese-Russian Military Exercises*. Carlisle, PA: Strategic Studies Institute, US Army War College.

Wilkinson, Paul. 1997. "The Media and Terrorism: A Reassessment." *Terrorism and Political Violence* 9 (2): 51–64.

Wilkinson, Paul. 2001. *Terrorism versus Democracy: The Liberal State Response*. London: Frank Cass.

Wilson, Matthew C., and James A. Piazza. 2013. "Autocracies and Terrorism: Conditioning Effects of Authoritarian Regime Type on Terrorist Attacks." *American Journal of Political Science* 57 (4): 941–955.

Wines, Michael. 2011."Militant Band Claims Role in Western China Attacks." *The New York Times*, September 8. www.nytimes.com/2011/09/09/world/asia/09china.html.

Wines, Michael, and Jonathan Ansfield. 2010. "China Says It Is Slowing Down Military Spending." *The New York Times*, March 4. www.nytimes.com/2010/03/05/world/asia/05china.html.

Withnall, Adam. 2018. "China Sends State Spies to Live in Uighur Muslim Homes and Attend Private Family Weddings and Funerals." *The Independent*, November 30. www.independent.co.uk/news/world/asia/china-uighurs-muslim-xinjiang-weddings-minority-communist-party-a8661006.html.

Womack, Brantly. 2005. "Democracy and the Governing Party (执政党): A Theoretical Perspective." *Journal of Chinese Political Science* 10 (1): 23–42.

Wong, Edward. 2009. "Clashes in China Shed Light on Ethnic Divide." *The New York Times*, July 7. www.nytimes.com/2009/07/08/world/asia/08china.htmlE.

Wood, Reed M. 2008. "'A Hand upon the Throat of the Nation': Economic Sanctions and State Repression, 1976–2001." *International Studies Quarterly* 52 (3): 489–513.

World Uyghur Congress. 2008. "Demonstration for the Rights of the Uyghurs in China." https://webcache.googleusercontent.com/search?q=cache:WFes0p5CsFsJ:https://uhrp.org/news/demonstration-rights-uighurs-china+&cd=2&hl=en&ct=clnk&gl=us.

Wu, Xiaogang, and Guangye He. 2018. "Ethnic Autonomy and Ethnic Inequality: An Empirical Assessment of Ethnic Policy in Urban China." *China Review* 18 (2): 185–216.

Wu, Xiaogang, and Xi Song. 2014. "Ethnic Stratification amid China's Economic Transition: Evidence from the Xinjiang Uighur Autonomous Region." *Social Science Research* 44: 158–172.

Wuthnow, Joel. 2019. *China's Other Army: The People's Armed Police in an Era of Reform*. Washington, DC: National Defense University Press.

Xi, Jinping. 2014. "Safeguard National Security and Social Stability." *Qiushi.* April 15. http://webcache.googleusercontent.com/search?q=cache: Bsuu0Tl6ALEJ:en.qstheory.cn/2020-12/07/c_568712.htm+&cd=1&hl= en&ct=clnk&gl=us.

Xinhua News Agency. 2019. "Commentary: Xinjiang-Related Bill again Reveals U.S. True Nature of Hegemony." December 5. www.xinhuanet .com/english/2019-12/05/c_138607715.htm.

Xinhua News Agency. 2011. "China-Pakistan Successfully Held Counter-Terrorism Joint Military Exercises in Pakistan." November 24. www .gov.cn/jrzg/2011-11/24/content_2002920.htm.

Xinhua News Agency. 2014. "习近平在第二次中央新疆工作座谈会上发表重要讲话 [Xi Jinping Delivers an Important Speech at the Second Xinjiang Work Forum]." May 29. http://webcache.googleusercontent .com/search?q=cache:OJwoYSdeyFcJ:www.xinhuanet.com/photo/2014- 05/29/c_126564529.htm+&cd=1&hl=en&ct=clnk&gl=us.

Xinhua News Agency. 2017. "Ministry of Defense: The Fundamental Function and Responsibility of the PAP Is Not Changed." December 28. www .xinhuanet.com/2017-12/28/c_1122181068.htm.

Xinhua News Agency. 2019. "Commentary: Xinjiang-Related Bill again Reveals U.S. True Nature of Hegemony." December 5. www.xinhuanet .com/english/2019-12/05/c_138607715.htm.

Xu, Beina, and Eleanor Albert. 2017. "Media Censorship in China." Council on Foreign Relations, February 17. www.cfr.org/backgrounder/ media-censorship-china.

Xu, Beina, Holly Fletcher, and Jayshree Bajoria. 2014. "The East Turkestan Islamic Movement (ETIM)." Council on Foreign Relations, September 4. www.files.ethz.ch/isn/183551/The%20East%20Turkestan%20 Islamic%20Movement%20(ETIM)%20-%20Council%20on%20Foreign%20Relations.pdf.

Xu, Xu. 2021. "To Repress or To Co-opt? Authoritarian Control in the Age of Digital Surveillance." *American Journal of Political Science* 65 (2): 309–325.

XUAR Department of Justice. 2017. "Key Points in the Work of XUAR Grassroots Justice and Administration." Yuli Government Information Open Platform. www.yuli.gov.cn/Government/PublicInfoShow .aspx?ID=27973

Xue, Ruixin. 2015. "新疆拟立法反恐, 将依法赋予军队反恐权力 [Xinjiang Is Drafting Laws to Back Counterterrorism, Which Will Legally Allow the Military to Conduct Counterterrorism Activities]." *China National Defense News*, February 4. http://webcache.googleusercontent.com/ search?q=cache:lDyNpQUHn_4J:www.www.81.cn/tzjy/2015-02/04/content_6340392.htm+&cd=1&hl=en&ct=clnk&gl=us.

Yan, Xuetong. 2014. "From Keeping a Low Profile to Striving for Achievement." *The Chinese Journal of International Politics* 7 (2): 153–184.

Yang, Yuan. 2019. "Xinjiang Security Crackdown Sparks Han Chinese Exodus" *Financial Times*, December 21. www.ft.com/content/fa6bd0b0-1d87-11ea-9186-7348c2f183af.

Yang, Zi. 2016. "The Chinese People's Armed Police in a Time of Armed Forces Restructuring." *China Brief* 16 (6): 9–13. https://jamestown.org/program/the-chinese-peoples-armed-police-in-a-time-of-armed-forces-restructuring/.

Yang, Zi. 2017. "Xi Jinping and China's Traditionalist Restoration." *China Brief* 17 (9): 9–13. https://jamestown.org/program/xi-jinping-chinas-traditionalist-restoration/.

Yu, H. 2006. "From Active Audience to Media Citizenship: The Case of Post-Mao China." *Social Semiotics* 16 (2): 303–326.

Yu, Zeyuan. 2016. "The Debut of the Former Xinjiang Party Secretary Indicates No Rejection of Zhang Chunxian's Approach to Xinjiang [卸任新疆党委书记首度亮相显示 张春贤治疆策略未遭否定]." *Lianhe Zaobao*. October 17. www.zaobao.com.sg/news/china/story20161017-678651.

Yuan, Yang. 2018. "Artificial Intelligence Takes Jobs from Chinese Web Censors." *Financial Times*, May 21. www.ft.com/content/9728b178-59b4-11e8-bdb7-f6677d2e1ce8.

Zeileis, Achim, Christian Kleiber, and Simon Jackman. 2008. "Regression Models for Count Data in R." *Journal of Statistical Software* 27 (8): 1–25.

Zenz, Adrian. 2018. "Corralling the People's Armed Police: Centralizing Control to Reflect Centralized Budgets." *China Brief* 18 (7). https://jamestown.org/program/corralling-the-peoples-armed-police-centralizing-control-to-reflect-centralized-budgets/.

Zenz, Adrian, and James Leibold. 2017. "Xinjiang's Rapidly Evolving Security State." *China Brief* 17 (4): 21–27. https://jamestown.org/program/xinjiangs-rapidly-evolving-security-state/.

Zhang, Chunxian. 2016. "Keep Deepening the *fanghuiju* Work: Contribute to Building a Beautiful Xinjiang and Achieving the National Dream." *Xinjiang Today*. Issue 2. http://webcache.googleusercontent.com/search?q=cache:l0lUkhSN9foJ:www.xjdx.gov.cn/view.php%3Fid%3D5823+&cd=1&hl=en&ct=clnk&gl=us.

Zhang, Jiadong. 2014. "反恐也需要'内病外治' [Counterterrorism Needs External Therapy for the Internal Disease]." *People's Daily*, May 12.

Zhang, Wei. 2016. "走出西方国家反恐的误区 [Avoid the Western Misunderstanding of Counter-Terrorism]." *People's Daily*, April 11, p. 9.

Zhang, Yuxi. 2003. "Anti-Separatism Struggle and Its Historical Lessons since the Liberation of Xinjiang." English translation and web publishing by Uyghur American Association.

Zhao, Kejin. 2015. "一带一路应强化安全为基 [BRI Needs Strengthened Security Measures]." Carnegie-Tsinghua Center for Global Policy, June 15. https://carnegietsinghua.org/2015/06/15/zh-pub-60676.

Zhao, Tong. 2010. "Social Cohesion and Islamic Radicalization: Implications from the Uighur Insurgency." *Journal of Strategic Security* 3 (3): 39–52.

Zhao, Yuezhi. 2009. "Rethinking Chinese Media Studies: History, Political Economy and Culture." In *Internationalizing Media Studies*, edited by Daya Kishan Thussu, 189–209. London: Routledge.

Zheng, Yanjiang. 2016. "*Fanghuiju*, a New Exploration in Grassroot Governance in Xinjiang." *iFeng News*, August 29. http://webcache .googleusercontent.com/search?q=cache:NdmzJUAmlwAJ:news.ifeng .com/a/20160829/49854900_0.shtml+&cd=1&hl=en&ct=clnk&gl=us.

Zhong, Yuhao. 2016. "Why Do These PAP Provincial Heads Enjoy Army GradeBenefits?[同是省一级武警总队,为何这几个军政主官是正军职?]." *The Paper*, August 3. www.thepaper.cn/newsDetail_forward_1508045.

Zhou, Enlai. 1957. "Some Questions regarding China's Ethnic Policies." *Beijing Review*, March 3.

Zhou, Minglang. 2010. "The Fate of the Soviet Model of Multinational State-Building in the People's Republic of China." In *China Learns from the Soviet Union, 1949–Present,*edited by Thomas P. Bernstein and Hua-Yu Li, 477–503. Lanham, MD: Lexington Books.

Zhou, Zunyou. 2019. "Chinese Strategy for De-radicalization." *Terrorism and Political Violence* 31 (6): 1187–1209.

Zhu, Yuchao. 2011. "'Performance Legitimacy' and China's Political Adaptation Strategy." *Journal of Chinese Political Science* 16 (2): 123–140.

Zi, Yang. 2018. "*Securing China's Belt and Road Initiative*." United States Institute of Peace, November 26.

Index

Lightning Source UK Ltd.
Milton Keynes UK
UKHW010633071222
413514UK00002B/24

9 781009 114905